Perfect Days in...

CA▮▮▮A

Travel with **Insider** Tips

Contents

 TOP 10   4

That California Feeling   6

For chapters: See inside front cover

TOP 10

Not to be missed!
Our TOP 10 hits – from the absolute No. 1 to No. 10 –
help you plan your tour of the most important sights.

⭐1 YOSEMITE N.P. ➤ 80

Nature doesn't get much more spectacular than this. Revel in the steep cliffs, mighty waterfalls, lush valleys and groves of giant sequoias (left).

⭐2 HOLLYWOOD ➤ 132

Even though most of the studios have now moved north to Burbank, the giant "Hollywood" sign, the majestic cinemas and the Oscars ceremony keep the legend of this place much alive.

⭐3 DISNEYLAND® PARK ➤ 136

Visitors heading through the gates at Disneyland® Park in Anaheim leave the real world behind them to go on a magical adventure with Mickey and all his friends.

⭐4 CHINATOWN & NORTH BEACH ➤ 48

Around 100,000 people live in San Francisco's Chinatown, the largest and oldest Chinese neighborhood in North America. It's also one of the city's greatest tourist attractions.

⭐5 DEATH VALLEY NATIONAL PARK ➤ 166

Death Valley, a protected National Park, is filled with salt flats, colorful rock formations and sandy deserts. You'll even find lodgings at the Furnace Creek Resort.

⭐6 WINE COUNTRY ➤ 84

Many fantastic vintages are produced in California's Wine Country, where a number of vineyards open their doors for wine tastings, tours and special events.

⭐7 BIG SUR ➤ 108

Highway No. 1 begins south of Monterrey and meanders for nearly 125 miles (200km) along a spectacular route down to Morro Bay.

⭐8 SANTA BARBARA ➤ 109

Built in a Mediterranean style, this luxury residential area from the late 1920s draws in lots of visitors with its sleek ambience. Stroll through its classy shopping malls and along its bewitching beaches.

⭐9 THE GETTY CENTER ➤ 138

The white buildings of this complex in the southern foothills of the Santa Monica Mountains house around 50,000 works of art ranging from Rembrandt and Monet to contemporary photography.

⭐10 SAN DIEGO ZOO ➤ 169

This world-famous zoo with over 4,000 animals occupies more than a quarter of Balboa Park on the northern edge of downtown San Diego. The zoo's Safari Park sits on a second site in Escondido.

THAT
CALIFORNIA

Find out what makes The Golden State tick and experience its unique flair – just like the Californians themselves.

CLIMB ABOARD SAN FRANCISCO'S CABLE CARS

Pulled along by steel ropes, these old-time cable cars have been rattling unhurriedly through the streets of San Francisco since 1873. Despite once being the city's principal mode of transport, only three routes still run along the remaining 11mi (17km) of track today. The cars are a real hit with both locals and tourists alike.

BEACH VOLLEYBALL ON SANTA BARBARA'S SANDS

California's long, sandy shorelines are considered the birthplace of beach volleyball. You'll usually see a sizzling game underway on Santa Barbara's city beaches – Goleta Beach by the university is a particular hotspot.

A PROMENADE AMONG THE PALMS

Head a few miles from downtown Palm Springs and you'll reach a hiking route that leads you under the shade of several hundred trees in Palm Canyon's peacefully impressive grove of Washingtonia palms. As with large parts of Palm Springs itself, the land here belongs to the reservation of the Agua Caliente Indians.

A TALE OF TWO MANSIONS

Two Americans made their dreams come true with two extraordinary buildings in San Simeon and Cambria just south of Big Sur. Media mogul William Randolph Hearst built the unique "Hearst Castle" on a hilltop, while trash collector Arthur Beal (a.k.a. "Captain Nitt Witt") spent over 50 years assembling "Nitt Witt Ridge" – his own dream home – out of junk and items he found. Although it doesn't officially exist, Beal's hillside creation is a listed Historical Landmark today.

INLINE SKATING AT VENICE BEACH

The ultimate place to see and be seen, Venice Beach is a Boulevard of the Vanities where the stylish and outlandishly dressed can strut their stuff with little wheels on their

FEELING

Traveling in Style: A trip aboard a San Francisco Cable Car

That California Feeling

feet. The best are sure to gain the recognition and approval of the crowds and the clients sitting at the many nearby cafés.

CALIFORNIA STATE RAILROAD MUSEUM

The railroad helped the USA conquer the West and made several tycoons extremely rich in the process. This museum in Sacramento tells the history of the railroad's construction, its magnates, and the many legendary wagons and locomotives of its Golden Age.

THE ELLIS ISLAND OF THE WEST

Angel Island in San Francisco Bay has a long and varied past: it's been a hunting ground of the Miwok Indians, a post-WW2 internment camp, and the point of arrival for legions of immigrants. The island's restored Immigration Station tells the story of around 175,000 Chinese migrants who were held there for up to two years before being allowed to enter the country.

GIANT SEQUOIAS, MUIR WOODS NATIONAL MONUMENT

This small forest of 330ft (100m)-tall giant sequoias just north of the Golden Gate bridge is dedicated to John Muir, a Scottish immigrant who broke with contemporary indifference and spent his life preserving these natural wonders over a century ago. The Sierra Club, the society he founded, is one of the most influential environmental organizations in North America today.

The giant trees of the Muir Woods National Monument near San Francisco

The Magazine

The Magazine

The Californian Wa

California clichés come fast, furious and familiar – think sun-bleached blondes, celebrity meltdowns, swimming pools and the Summer of Love – and TV, movies and the hungry public often embrace these stereotypes.

So how to separate fact from fiction? Well, it's true that in the 20th century, California became known for fast cars, movie stars, face-lifts, trendsetting fashions, and wacky cults. In the process, "California" and "airhead" became synonymous. "You lose 10 points off your IQ every year you stay there," went a line in one of Woody Allen's early movies.

But beneath its frivolous exterior, California has for the last 150 years been about serious business – mining, agriculture, railroad building, movie-making, oil refining, defense contracting and technological innovation. With all its residents have accomplished – the state's economy, the world's eighth largest, generates 13 percent of America's gross national product – it's a wonder there's time to hit those beaches at all.

"The Californians are an idle, thriftless people, and can make nothing for themselves," griped Richard Henry Dana, Jr. in *Two Years before the Mast*, published in 1840. Had Dana arrived a century earlier, before the Spanish began colonizing in earnest, he might have marveled at the self-sufficiency of the Native American population. And had he dropped by a decade or so after he did, when the Gold Rush was in full swing, he might have seen how an international influx of talent had inspired no end of entrepreneurial spirit. Three different Californias, all in the space of a century.

> "...beneath its frivolous exterior, California is serious about business"

Creative and Diverse

In the 21st century, California remains huge and diverse – it is the first state in the continental US to have a non-Caucasian population of more than 50 percent – and it welcomes and encourages risk-taking. People have come here to "start over" since the first Asiatic explorers arrived around 20,000bc, and they've done it side by side with pioneers of many cultures. There's often been friction, but the general impetus has been toward coexistence.

Creative minds like George Lucas and Steven Spielberg, innovative companies like Pixar and Apple and a progressive population that often leads the way on social reform. The truth is, California doesn't have time for clichés – it's too busy starring in the next big thing.

The Golden Gate Bridge with San Francisco's skyline in the distance

MOTION
PICTURE PERFECT

Early 20th-century filmmakers were quick to discover the benefits of making movies in California. Plentiful sunshine and striking scenery made Los Angeles a natural for film production, while land was still relatively inexpensive.

Hollywood itself was a quiet farming community until 1910, when New York-based director D.W. Griffith ventured out West to begin filming the first movie ever shot in Hollywood, *In Old California*. Griffith, otherwise known as "the man who invented Hollywood," would go on to shoot *The Birth of a Nation*, a mighty epic that had some unfortunate racist undertones. Word of California's appeal quickly filtered its way back East. Soon filmmakers were converting barns into movie studios and Hollywood was born. Los Angeles also had the added benefit of being on the opposite side of the continental United States from Thomas A. Edison. Many early filmmakers used film equipment that violated the movie-camera patents held by the East Coast inventor, so they could easily slip south of the border if Edison's agents ever came to town.

> "More than 150 movies have been filmed in Red Rock Canyon"

A Natural Movie Set

Ever since, California's landscape has served as the background in a broad spectrum of film. In 1923, the great director Cecil B. DeMille came to the Guadalupe-Nipomo Dunes on California's Central Coast and built a colossal movie set recreating ancient Egypt for the silent movie version of *The Ten Commandments*. Many of California's ranches have played host to Westerns and a variety of other locales. For example, the 2,700-acre (1,090ha) Paramount Ranch, located in the Santa Monica Mountains and purchased by the studio in 1927, doubled as ancient China, colonial Massachusetts, and, ironically, San Francisco. National parks around the state have also

played host to many movie sets. More than 150 movies, including the 1993 blockbuster *Jurassic Park*, have been filmed in Red Rock Canyon State Park, famous for its rock formations and desert cliffs.

Nexus of Filmmaking

While motion picture production still occurs in Hollywood, most major studios, aside from Paramount, are now located elsewhere in LA. The majority of production takes place within a 30-mile (48km) radius of Hollywood, where on any given day as many as 150 movies, TV shows, commercials and music videos are shot. LA has been losing ground in recent years to other regions, including New Mexico and Canada, but it remains the nexus of filmmaking in North America. The movies produced here are responsible for more than half of all tickets sold worldwide.

Movies are now shot all over the state, even in the north, though sometimes the natural setting doesn't satisfy set directors (make-up was applied to Humboldt County's redwoods to make them look more "realistic" in *The Big Trees*). Pixar, maker of films like *Toy Story* (1995) and *WALL-E* (2008), is based out of Emeryville, near Oakland. Now owned by Disney, this animation studio owes its Bay Area roots partly to Apple CEO Steve Jobs, who established an independent studio in 1986 when he bought the computer graphics division of Lucasfilm. from George Lucas.

BIG BUSINESS

An estimated 260,000 Southern Californians work in the entertainment industry, with another 50,000 employed in related fields. The industry directly contributes $30 to $35 billion annually to the state's economy.

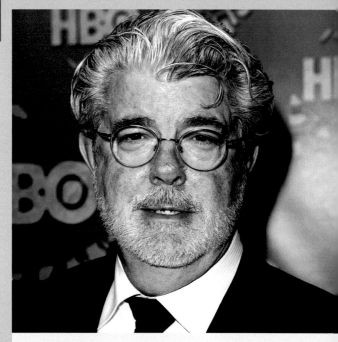

TRANSFORMING AN INDUSTRY

Producer, director, Hollywood icon and maverick, is best known for his involvement with the *Star Wars* and *Indiana Jones* film franchises. Yet despite his success in the creation of these Hollywood blockbusters, Lucas spent much of his career defying the limits of Hollywood, even as he transformed it. While he studied film at the famed University of Southern California School of Cinematic Arts, Lucas returned to Northern California to make movies. He scored early success with *American Graffiti*, a nostalgic homage to his love of cars and motor racing, which he enjoyed growing up in Central California. Still, Lucas had great difficulty attracting production interest from Hollywood for his next big idea, an epic film about a space opera called *Star Wars*. In order to make the film, Lucas agreed to waive his fee as director in exchange for the merchandizing rights to the film. The colossal success of *Star Wars* made Lucas a fortune and allowed him from then on to remain independent of Hollywood.

George Lucas also transformed the film industry by refusing to accept the technological limitations of filmmaking, launching the visual effects company Industrial Light and Magic to deliver the groundbreaking special effects he needed for *Star Wars*, along with Skywalker Sound and THX. The companies are located at his 2,700-acre (1,093ha) state-of-the art production center and "think tank," Skywalker Ranch in Marin County. Lucas's presence is a key reason the San Francisco Bay Area has developed into the nation's third largest center – after LA and New York – for film and TV production.

SUSPENSE IN THE SCENERY

London-born Alfred Hitchcock said his mission in life was "to simply scare
the hell out of people," and he often subverted California's sunny image
to accomplish this. Many of Hitch's productions were shot on back lots in
Southern California. The tram tour at Universal Studios (▶ 144) passes by
the Bates Motel in *Psycho*. He made two of his creepiest films in Sonoma
County. In *Shadow of a Doubt*, Teresa Wright plays a young girl in staid Santa
Rosa shocked to realize that her uncle, played by Joseph Cotten, is a murderer.
In *The Birds*, peaceful, small-town Bodega Bay (Hitch also mixed in shots from
nearby Bodega, Bloomfield and Valley Ford) turns into a living hell when birds
begin attacking the citizens. Hitchcock's masterpiece, the suspenseful *Vertigo*,
is a veritable postcard of late-1950s San Francisco. You can even stay in the
Empire Hotel, located in the heart of San Francisco, where James Stewart
eventually finds Kim Novak. Just don't look for it by that name: it was renamed
The Hotel Vertigo in honor of its legendary Hollywood connection.

WHAT'S THE RUSH?

HOW GOLD CHANGED THE FACE OF CALIFORNIA

"This is a curious rock, I am afraid that it will give us trouble," said James Marshall, who, on January 24 1848, discovered a piece of quartz he thought contained gold. He was right and within months, the stampede to the Sierra foothills east of Sacramento had begun in earnest.

Gold fever struck first among the state's residents, who realized they had a few months' lead on the rest of the world. Sailors jumped ship; farmhands and even farm owners abandoned their crops. "Every seaport as far south as San Diego, and every town, and nearly every rancho – suddenly was drained of human beings," reported the *California Star* in 1848.

When President James Polk confirmed in a December 1848 speech that the rumors of gold discoveries in California were true, Easterners began heading west via two grueling routes. One involved crossing up to 3,000mi (4,825km) of plains, mountains and desert. The other option was by sea to Panama, by land across the Isthmus of Panama (there was no canal back then) and by sea again to San Francisco.

Forty-Niners Influx

Fewer than 1,000 people lived in San Francisco in 1847. More than 30,000 lived there by the end of 1849 – the term "Forty-Niners" refers to that year's influx of "argonauts" – and towns sprang up all over Northern California. Most miners were lucky to strike gold even after months of hard labor. Law enforcement was nearly nonexistent and thieves were everywhere. When justice was meted out, though, it tended to be swift and hangings by vigilantes were commonplace.

Most Easterners and foreign-born prospectors planned to return home after they made their fortunes, so they didn't bring their wives and children. Women were so scarce that one miner was said to have charged for the privilege of seeing his bride. Even at $5 per look, he had many takers. Prostitutes headed West as well; many made more money than the miners did, though disease and poor living conditions took their toll.

Gold's Legacy

The Gold Rush changed California forever, and not all for the better. Downsides included mining techniques that devastated the environment and the theft of land from Native American peoples. The freer atmosphere of the camps and cities such as San Francisco gave rise to an independent spirit, however. Historians have noted that California became a place where it was permissible to fail, as indeed many miners did. This pioneering attitude encouraged the entrepreneurial spirit that transformed the Golden State from an economic backwater into a powerhouse.

James Marshall's discovery of gold (left) brought thousands of prospectors (right)

Farm to Table

French gastronome Jean Anthelme Brillat-Savarin famously said, "Tell me what you eat, I'll tell you who you are." For much of the 20th century, he may not have been happy with the answer in America. For decades, packaged and processed foods were the norm for American families, but in the late 1970s, chefs in California started something of a seismic shift.

That was when the concept of California cuisine began to take hold: eating food that is fresh and locally grown, or "farm to table." The term "local" doesn't have a strict definition, but the idea is that you (and the restaurants you frequent) buy, serve and eat food that is raised and grown by local farmers. And the proximity to the coast means that Californians can enjoy "ocean to table" food as well.

Local Meets International

This movement gained traction in famous kitchens – think celebrity chefs like Wolfgang Puck at Ma Maison (and later Spago) and Jeremiah Tower and Alice Waters at Berkeley's Chez Panisse (▶ 70) – and has found support at the highest levels. Former First Lady Michelle Obama embraced the idea on the opposite coast: In 2009 she planted a produce and herb garden in the grounds of the White House.

The chefs involved were credited with inventing California cuisine, which marked another shift away from creamy, butter-laden French fare that

The Okura Sushi Bar in Palm Springs (top); chefs like Alice Waters pioneered the idea of local food (bottom); grape harvest in Napa (opposite)

MOVABLE FEASTS

Food on the go has become en vogue in California, but it's the food that's on the go, not the eater. Take the humble taco truck, which has recently enjoyed a foodie makeover. In Los Angeles, check online to find the real-time location of the **LA KunFusion Truck** (www.kunfusiontruck.com), which blends flavors from Korea, China, Japan and Latin America, and the **Border Grill taco truck** (www.bordergrill.com) from chefs Mary Sue Milliken and Susan Feniger. San Francisco's famous **Tamale Lady** used to sell her homemade tamales at bars in the Mission, but opened her own restaurant in 2014 on the corner of 16th and Mission when the city put a stop to her itinerant ways.

was no longer the be-all and end-all of fine dining in America. Aided by California's multicultural population and its proximity to Asia and Mexico, mainstream restaurants began to incorporate flavors and ingredients from all over the world, including North America, Asia, Latin America and the Mediterranean.

Washing it Down

As interest in food and cooking has increased, so has the American interest in wine. That's good news for California as its climate, soil and topography, make the state an ideal region for growing and producing wine. Head to the Napa and Sonoma valleys, or any of the hundred-strong wineries along the Central Coast, and you will find that wine is more than a pastime – it's big business.

According to the Wine Institute, only France, Italy and Spain produce more wine than California, and the state produces 90 percent of all U.S. wine. In may be surprising, then, that Californians don't have the highest per capita wine con-

> "eating food that is fresh and locally grown"

sumption in the United States (that honor goes to the District of Columbia). Given the fact that a small glass of wine has between 100 and 125 calories, it could be that the healthy California lifestyle is to blame. Perhaps Brillat-Savarin and his brethren still have more to teach.

PHANTOM RELICS

California reinvents itself so often that its past sometimes gets lost in the shuffle, but there are some bona fide ghost towns along with re-created villages with tales to tell.

Indian Village of the Ahwahnee

The Southern Miwok people, who lived in the Yosemite Valley for 4,000 years, fiercely resisted the encroachment of miners during the early 1850s before finally succumbing. Within a century, the Miwok way of life had vanished, but a re-created village at Yosemite National Park reveals some of their heritage, including a ceremonial roundhouse and sweathouse.

✉ Behind Yosemite Valley Visitor Center ☎ 209/372-0200; www.nps.gov/yose/index.htm

Mission La Purisima Concepcíon

Mission La Purísima, which Franciscan friars founded in 1787, stands on a solitary site about 60mi (97km) north of Santa Barbara. Exhibits show how daily life unfolded for the settlers and indigenous peoples.

✉ 2295 Purisima Road, off Highway 246 (head west from US 101 or east from Highway 1)
☎ 805/733-3713; www.lapurisimamission.org ⏰ Daily 9–5 💰 Donation

Fort Ross State Historic Park

Russia's brief foray into California culminated in the establishment of Fort Ross in 1812. Perched high on a bluff with clear Pacific views, the fort served mainly as a base for fur trappers. By 1821, the Russians had nearly rendered the sea otter extinct. John Sutter, at whose Sierra Nevada mill gold was discovered in 1848, bought the fort in the early 1840s and moved most of its contents to Sacramento.

✉ 19005 Coast Highway 1, Jenner ☎ 707/847-3286; www.parks.ca.gov ⏰ Sat, Sun 10–4:30 💰 $8

Fort Ross (left); Bodie Ghost Town (right)

Malakoff Diggins State Historic Park

Ecology wasn't the strong suit of gold-mining companies. Their most destructive technique, hydraulic mining, consisted of blasting hill-sides with water to dislodge gold and other ore. At Malakoff Diggins, the scars remain visible, yet there's a haunting quality to nature's reclamation of the landscape. Restored buildings in nearby North Bloomfield include the drugstore, general store and town hall.

✉ From Nevada City take Tyler-Foote Crossing Road north to Lake City Road east
☎ 530/265-2740; www.parks.ca.gov ⏱ Times vary 💲 $8

Bodie Ghost Town State Historic Park

In the late 1800s, Bodie at 8,375ft (2,552m) in the Sierra Nevada was one of the wildest mining camps in the West, famous for its wicked citizens, worse weather and bad whiskey. A museum documents the town's history, and you can peek into miners' cabins, a schoolhouse, stores, mine shafts and a church. Guided tours take place daily during the summer.

✉ Highway 270 (last 3mi/5km to town unpaved), east of US 395 ☎ 760/647-6445; www.parks.ca.gov
⏱ Park: mid-May–Oct daily 9–6; shorter hours in winter. Museum: mid-May–Oct daily 9–5 💲 $5

Colonel Allen Allensworth State Historic Park

Many Americans trekked west to seek fortune or freedom, among them people of African descent. In 1908, along with four others, Colonel Allen Allensworth formed the town that bears his name. Allensworth, a Civil War Navy veteran and US Army chaplain hoped to promote economic self-determination for African Americans. During its early years, the town grew, but the Great Depression and other events prompted its decline. The town is now being restored.

✉ Highway 43 (45mi/72km north of Bakersfield) ☎ 661/849-3433; www.parks.ca.gov
⏱ Thu–Sun 10–4

Artistic
LICENSE

California's expansive landscape and its residents' willingness to embrace the unconventional have nourished artists, poets, architects, photographers and writers.

Ansel Adams (1902–84)

The famous photographer broke his nose as a lad of four during San Francisco's 1906 earthquake, an occurrence that may or may not have inspired him to examine nature up close. Adams, Edward Weston and Imogen Cunningham were among the Group f/64 photographers of Northern California known for their starkly realistic prints.

■ Many museums display his images, but plan a trip to Yosemite (▶ 80–83) to see the terrain that inspired Adams's most famous photographs.

Raymond Chandler (1888–1959)

Dames, thugs, losers and the corrupt wealthy mix it up in the deliciously jaundiced detective novels of Raymond Chandler, which evoke Southern California's seamy underside of the mid-20th century.

■ *The Big Sleep* and *Farewell, My Lovely* are two good introductions to the writer's work. "Bay City" in the latter book is Santa Monica (▶ 146).

Richard Diebenkorn (1922–93)

Jazz, classical music, Matisse, W.B. Yeats, abstract expressionism and the clarity of California sunlight were among the many influences on Californian painter Diebenkorn.

■ Paintings are on view at SFMOMA (▶ 52) and the L.A. County Museum of Art (▶ 147).

Jack Kerouac (1922–69)

San Francisco figures prominently in Kerouac's ground-breaking novel, *On the Road*. The author hung out in the 1950s in North Beach (▶ 49) and elsewhere with beat-era cronies such as Allen Ginsberg, Neal Cassady, Gregory Corso, Bob Kaufman and Gary Snyder.

■ Have a drink at Vesuvio (▶ 73).

Ansel Adams is famous for his evocative black-and-white landscape photography

Julia Morgan (1872–1957)

The first female architecture student at École des Beaux Arts in Paris and the first licensed female architect in California, Morgan received many commissions to build homes in San Francisco after the 1906 earthquake. In 40 years of work she designed more than 700 buildings, most of them in California.

- Visit Hearst Castle (▶ 116), the private "ranch" she designed for William Randolph Hearst in San Simeon.
- Stop by San Francisco's Chinese Historical Society of America Museum (formerly a YWCA) at 965 Clay Street (▶ 49).

John Steinbeck (1902–68)

The Golden State was the setting for much of Steinbeck's fiction. According to his sister, California was consistently in her brother's "mind – and imagination." Steinbeck's *The Grapes of Wrath* describes life for Central Valley migrant workers. Steinbeck set *Cannery Row* in Monterey's sardine-processing plants.

- Visit the National Steinbeck Center in Salinas, 17mi (10.5mi) from Monterey.

Frank Lloyd Wright (1869–1959)

Although architect Frank Lloyd Wright is associated mostly with the Midwest, he left his imprint on at least 35 states in the U.S. and in countries all over the world. In California alone he designed dozens of buildings, and more than 30 of them are still standing today.

- Visit Hollyhock House in Hollywood's Barnsdall Park. Built in the 1920s for oil heiress Aline Barnsdall, it's now an art gallery.
- In Palo Alto, visit Honeycomb House, so called because of its hexagonal grid layout (it's also known as Hanna House).

The Magazine

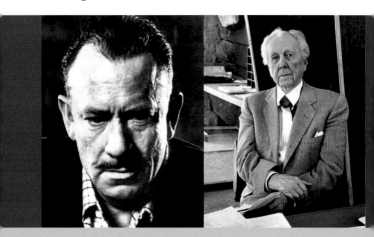

Author John Steinbeck (left) and architect Frank Lloyd Wright (right)

Michael Connelly (b.1956)

Thought by many to be the best writer of crime fiction in the country, and a worthy heir to Raymond Chandler, Connelly has made good use of his years as a police-beat reporter for the *L.A. Times*. Although he now lives in Florida, he researches his mostly L.A.-based novels meticulously.

■ *Angels Flight* is the title of one of Connelly's books and also a little piece of L.A. history. It is a funicular railway that goes between downtown and Bunker Hill.

■ Connelly's detective Hieronymus "Harry" Bosch has a home in the Hollywood Hills with a great view. Visitors can drive the narrow streets and savor L.A.'s sprawl from on high.

Joan Didion (b.1934)

The contradictory nature of the California dream often surfaces in Didion's essays and fiction, most poignantly in *Play It as It Lays*, a novel about disaffected Angelenos. Her late husband was writer John Gregory Dunne.

■ Read *Play It as It Lays* for a window into the life of a despondent B-list actress in Hollywood.

Frank Gehry (b.1929)

Winner of the prestigious Pritzker prize, architect Gehry was born Ephraim Owen Goldberg in Toronto to Polish Jewish parents. The L.A. resident continues to get big commissions, notably the Guggenheim in Bilbao, Spain, and the Dancing House in Prague.

■ Visit the Walt Disney Concert Hall (▶ 147) and Loyola Law School (between 9th Street and Olympic Boulevard) in Los Angeles.

■ Walk by 340 Main Street in Venice (▶ 147), which also features a Claes Oldenberg sculpture.

Architect Frank Gehry (left) and bestselling novelist Amy Tan (right)

Walter Mosley (b.1952)

In *Devil, Black Betty* and other books, Mosley, who was born in South Central Los Angeles, delivers a trenchant slice of late-1940s African-American life in Los Angeles.

Richard Rodriguez (b.1944)

One of contemporary California's most provocative commentators was born in San Francisco and raised in Sacramento. The child of Mexican immigrants, Rodriguez describes himself as the "comic victim of two cultures," namely Latin and Anglo American.

■ Read *Days of Obligation: An Argument with My Mexican Father*, in which he outlines what he's learned from these two cultures.

Amy Tan (b.1952)

The recollections of her mother and her mother's friends informed the Oakland-born author's novel *The Joy Luck Club*, about Chinese immigrants and Chinese Americans in the San Francisco Bay Area.

■ Wander around San Francisco's Chinatown (➤ 48) for a snapshot of the Chinese immigrant life Tan writes about.

Wayne Thiebaud (b.1920)

Artist Thiebaud moved to Long Beach, California, as a baby and he started out professionally as a commercial artist. He is most famous for his paintings of "Americana" objects such as pies, cakes and gumball machines, which were done in the 1950s and 1960s.

■ Visit the Crocker Art Museum in Sacramento or San Francisco's M.H. de Young Museum (➤ 54).

■ Eat an artist-themed dessert (Thiebaud, Mondrian) at the SFMOMA's (➤ 52) rooftop café.

Whole Lotta Shakin' Goin' On

SHATTERING FACTS ABOUT CALIFORNIA'S GEOLOGY

In California years can go by with only desultory trembling, but then along comes a whopper like Southern California's Northridge earthquake of 1994 (6.7 on the Richter Scale) or Northern California's Loma Prieta quake of 1989 (7.1). Streets buckle and undulate like waves, while buildings and freeways collapse; terra firma is a relative term.

What Causes a Quake?

The continents sit on top of plates on the Earth's crust. When one continent's plate shifts against another's – this happens along what are called faults – an eruption occurs. The shock of this eruption is felt on the Earth's surface, causing land, buildings, trees and other objects to shift.

Focusing on the Epicenter

Scientists call the underground point where an earthquake occurs – where those plates shift – the focus. The place where the quake erupts at the earth's surface is called the epicenter. The deeper the focus, the more treacherous the earthquake.

The Richter Scale

A Southern Californian named Charles Richter invented the scale that bears his name in 1935 as a way of calculating the magnitude, or size, of earthquakes. The scale, which uses data supplied by seismographs, is logarithmic, which means that a magnitude 7.0 earthquake is about 31 times more powerful – in terms of earth-shaking energy – than a 6.0 one, and over 900 times more powerful than a 5.0 quake.

How Big was SF's Big One?

The San Francisco earthquake of 1906 would have measured 8.3 on the Richter scale. The quake caused a 250-mile (400km) section of the San Andreas Fault to shift 21 feet (6.5m) in mere seconds. Seven hundred people died and the damage came to more than $400 million in 1906 dollars – equivalent to about $7.6 billion today. A large proportion of the destruction didn't originate from the earthquake itself but was caused by fires started from burst gas pipes.

It Ain't Over Till it's Over

A quake in Long Beach claimed 115 lives back in 1933. In 1994, fifty-seven people died in the Northridge earthquake that rocked the Los Angeles area; astonishingly, nearly 3,000 aftershocks were recorded during the three weeks following the initial tremor. The most recent large quake reached 6.1 on the Richter Scale around Napa Valley in 2014. Luckily, no one was killed. And no, seismologists can't predict when the next big one will occur.

Experiencing that Trembling Feeling?

In case of an earthquake: Get under a door frame, sturdy table or other piece of furniture. Use your arms to protect your head and stay away from glass, windows and light fixtures. Don't run outside – falling objects could hit you.

The 1906 earthquake caused vast cracks in the pavements and devastated the city

CALIFORNIA
Dreaming…and Singing

Surf rock, psychedelic rock, punk rock, alternative rock, indie rock, hip-hop: California has proved its versatility by playing an important role across the musical spectrum.

In addition to the numerous bands and performers with California roots, many have penned songs about the Golden State and its cities. With songs like "Surfin' USA," "Surfer Girl," and "California Girls," how could the Beach Boys feel like anything other than the quintessential Southern California band? And the Beach Boys were exactly that. Though in later years they stared down drugs, depression and band infighting, the early days, which started in 1965, were all about the free-wheeling spirit of surfing and young love.

> "the Beach Boys were the quintessential Southern California band"

Three other California bands launched that same year, however, and with decidedly different sensibilities. When two UCLA film school alums – Jim Morrison and Ray Manzarek – got reacquainted at a Southern California beach, they decided to form the Doors. By 1966 they had a regular gig at Whiskey A-Go-Go on Sunset Boulevard and soon rocketed to fame. While they lacked the longevity of the Beach Boys, in part because of Morrison's death in 1971, The Doors continue to be the subject of films and intrigue.

The Jerry Garcia Amphitheater in San Francisco hosts legendary rock concerts

MUSIC FESTIVALS AND CONCERTS

California promotes music at festivals and concert series throughout the year. Just to name a few, the **Coachella Music & Arts Festival** near Palm Springs attracts tens of thousands of fans, while the **Monterey Jazz Festival** has been doing the same thing for more than 50 years. Classical music is always in the consciousness, too, with high-profile conductors at the **San Francisco Symphony** (the respected Michael Tilson Thomas) and the **LA Philharmonic** (the young Venezuelan upstart, Gustavo Dudamel).

Four hundred miles (248km) north in Northern California, the 1960s counterculture movement was taking a different turn with psychedelic rock bands like Jefferson Airplane and the Grateful Dead. Part of San Francisco's "Summer of Love" in 1967, Jefferson Airplane also performed at the legendary Woodstock festival in 1969. Two of the band's songs cracked *Rolling Stone* magazine's "500 Greatest Songs of all Time" list ("Somebody to Love" and "White Rabbit"). Meanwhile, Jerry Garcia's Grateful Dead attracted a devoted following of Deadheads for 30 years. While some bands made the scene earlier and others sold more records, no group typified the California hippie ethic more than the Grateful Dead.

Alternative Rock

Alternative rock also has strong roots in California. In the 1980s, Jane's Addiction hit the scene in Los Angeles, and in the 1990s, San Diego-based band Stone Temple Pilots developed a fan base for its combination of hard rock and alternative rock. In Berkeley, the band Green Day got credit in the 1990s for helping to reignite the punk scene in the United States. And 10 years after its breakout album, the band made a Grammy Award-winning album in 2004 called "American Idiot," and a Broadway musical of the same name in 2010, showing that California continues to put its stamp on the music scene.

GARCIA

OUTDOOR Activities

California is an ideal destination for active travelers. The Golden State terrain offers the full array of outdoor adventures and activities, while the mild weather translates to almost year-round participation.

Bicycling

From mountain biking to street riding, there's no dearth of cycling possibilities in California. In San Diego, there's a relatively flat, 25-mile (15.5km) ride around San Diego Bay, and also an easier, 14-mile (9km)ride around Mission Bay, which has terrific views of the bay and the ocean. In Los Angeles, there are scenic beach paths in Huntington Beach, Long Beach and Manhattan Beach. In Northern California, many bikers ride across the Golden Gate Bridge and then continue in Marin County. Napa Valley also has leisurely bike tours in and around the Wine Country.

Golf

If golfing hasn't been declared a religion quite yet, then California didn't get the message. The state boasts well over 1,000 golf courses, many of them in Southern California cities like Palm Desert, San Diego and La Quinta. Further north, there are the famous Cypress Point Club and Pebble Beach Golf Links courses located near Monterey. These courses are celebrated as some of the best in North America, so reserve early.

Hiking

California's diverse landscape means great hiking country. The National Park Service operates nine National Parks in the state, with abundant trails that are well-maintained (despite budget cuts) and occupy much of the prime real estate for viewing the state's natural and historical wonders.

Horseback Riding

Horse stables all over the state are open to the public for a day-long visit or more extended excursions. Consider a ride along the pristine coastline and then up into the magnificent redwood forests of Mendocino County. Los Angeles also offers some amazing opportunities for riding, including sunrise and sunset rides on trails in the Santa Monica Mountains.

Left to right: Cypress Point Golf Club; mountaineers in Yosemite N.P.; mountain biking in Monterey; surfing at Hermosa Beach; horse riding on the shore; skiing near Lake Tahoe

Skiing and Snowboarding

In the winter, you can race downhill throughout California in some of North America's finest ski resorts. Most of these recreation areas cater to both skiers and snowboarders, although some go the extra mile to court snowboarders with expansive snow parks and half pipes. Southern California has large resorts like Mammoth, Bear Mountain and Snow Summit. In Northern California, Lake Tahoe is the home to 18 resorts and excellent skiing. Sugar Bowl, Squaw Valley USA (home of the 1960 Winter Olympics) and other resorts also have cross-country skiing and skating.

Water Sports

Hundreds of miles of coastline mean you can "hang ten" at one of the many surfing beaches in Southern California or brave the cooler waters of Northern California. San Diego, Los Angeles and the Bay Area all have excellent harbors and plenty of sailing and windsurfing, too. The Sacramento Delta provides excellent wakeboarding and jet skiing, while Lake Tahoe's American River offers rafting tours in the summer. In Monterey consider humpback whale watching or scuba diving.

WATCH IT LIVE

California has five Major League Baseball teams: the **San Diego Padres** (tel: 619/795-5000), the **Los Angeles Angels** of Anaheim (tel: 888/796-4256) and the **Los Angeles Dodgers** (tel: 866/363-4377) are in Southern California. The **San Francisco Giants** (tel: 415/972-2000) and the East Bay's **Oakland A's** (tel: 510/568-5600) in Northern California.

The National Football League is represented by the **San Diego Chargers** (tel: 877/242-7437), the **Oakland Raiders** (tel: 510/864-5020) and the **San Francisco 49ers** (tel: 415/464-9377). 49ers tickets are difficult to obtain – call Ticketmaster (tel: 800/745-3000), or check the classified ads in the *San Francisco Chronicle*. Surprisingly, Los Angeles no longer has an NFL team.

Four National Basketball Association teams are in California: the **Golden State Warriors** (tel: 510/986-2200) play in Oakland; the **Sacramento Kings** (tel: 888/915-4647) at Arco Arena; the **Los Angeles Lakers** (tel: 310/426-6000) and the **Los Angeles Clippers** (tel: 888/895-8662) at Staples Center.

ARTS & EVENTS

While California is still a relative newcomer by the world's standards, it does have its annual traditions, ranging from cultural to wacky to sweaty. Here are some of the highlights.

January

Tournament of Roses Parade: Featuring floral floats and spirited marching bands in Los Angeles.
www.tournamentofroses.com

February

Chinese New Year Festival and Parade: San Francisco hosts the largest celebration of Asian culture outside of Asia.
www.chineseparade.com

March

L.A. Marathon: An annual 26.2-mile race through Los Angeles.
www.lamarathon.com

April

Toyota Grand Prix of Long Beach: Three days of America's premier street race.
www.gplb.com

Cherry Blossom Festival: A celebration of Japanese culture in San Francisco with a parade, tea ceremonies, etc.
www.sfcherryblossom.org

Coachella Valley Music and Arts Festival: A three-day music and arts festival near Palm Springs.
www.coachella.com

May

Bay to Breakers: An only-in-San Francisco foot race filled with thousands of costumed (sometimes naked) revelers and runners.
www.baytobreakers.com

June

Los Angeles Film Festival: Showcasing American and international filmmaking.
www.lafilmfest.com

Old Globe's Shakespeare Festival: The Bard is performed in San Diego's Balboa Park.
www.theoldglobe.org

July

Gilroy Garlic Festival: A three-day food fair south of San Jose.
www.gilroygarlicfestival.com

August

Italian Family Festa: an event with over 35,000 guests, live music, wine and hearty food in San Jose's Guadalupe River Park.
www.italianfamilyfestasj.org

September

Monterey Jazz Festival: Started in 1958, this is the longest-running jazz festival in the world.
www.montereyjazzfestival.org

October

West Hollywood Halloween Carnaval: 500,000 participants in spooky costumes on Santa Monica Blvd (31 Oct).
www.weho.org/halloween

November

Macy's Union Square Tree Lighting Ceremony: A San Francisco tradition the day after Thanksgiving.

Finding Your Feet

Finding Your Feet

First Two Hours

San Francisco International Airport (SFO), Los Angeles International Airport (LAX) and San Diego International Airport (SAN) are California's main gateways. Most major US and international airlines fly into LAX and SFO, and many serve SAN.

Best Bets for Airport Transfers

- **Taxis** are the foolproof method for getting from all three airports to the city center. In each city, the rate is for the ride, not per passenger.
- **Shared-ride van services** load up with passengers heading to addresses more or less in the same part of town.
- **Public transportation** is not a great option in Los Angeles – it might take you more than two hours to get to your destination. BART trains take a half hour to reach San Francisco. In San Diego public buses or cabs can be convenient if you're staying downtown.

> **Ground Transportation Fees (excluding tip)**
> $ under $12 $$ $12–$20 $$$ $21–$30 $$$$ over $30
> Public transportation from the airports costs less than $5.

San Francisco and The Bay Area

- **San Francisco International Airport** (tel: 650/821-8211; www.flysfo.com) is about 15mi (24km) from downtown.
- Lines for **taxis** ($$$$) form on the lower (arrivals) level.
- **SuperShuttle** (tel: 800/258-3526) provides a shared-ride van service ($$$). Look for signs (yellow letters on a dark-blue background) on the upper-level traffic islands outside each terminal.
- **Bayporter Express** (tel: 415/467-1800) serves Oakland and other East Bay destinations ($$$$), also from the upper level.
- **SamTrans** (tel: 800/660-4287) buses ($) serve San Mateo County, where the airport is located, and parts of San Francisco and Palo Alto.
- **BART** (Bay Area Rapid Transit; tel: 650/992-2278) trains are the best public transport option to downtown San Francisco. The trains also travel to the East Bay and parts of northern San Mateo County. From any terminal, walk or take the AirTrain shuttle to the BART station in the International Terminal. Purchase a ticket ($) from machines in the station.
- **If you're driving,** follow US 101 north to the 4th Street exit.
- **Other Bay Area airports:** Oakland International (OAK; tel: 510/563-3300) San Jose International (SJC; tel: 408/277-4759).

Los Angeles Area

- **Los Angeles International Airport** (tel: 310/646-5252; www.lawa.org) is 18mi (29km) from downtown and about 12mi (19km) from Beverly Hills and West Hollywood.
- All **ground transportation** can be found on the lower (arrivals) level of all terminals.
- **Taxi fares** vary, depending on where you're going ($$$$ for downtown).
- **SuperShuttle** (tel: 310/782-6600 or 800/258-3826) and **Express by ExecuCar** (tel: 800/427-7483) are among the shared-ride vans ($$) offering door-to-door service.

- **Metropolitan Transportation Authority (MTA)** (tel: 323/466-3876) buses ($) leave the airport for many destinations. Some routes (such as West Hollywood) are direct; others involve transfers. For information, visit the transportation desk near baggage claim.
- **MTA Railline** (tel: 213/626-4455 or 800/266-6883) light-rail trains are convenient if you're going downtown ($). Board the shuttle bus to the Metro Green Line's Aviation Station. Stay on the train until the Imperial/Wilmington Station and transfer to the Blue Line heading north.
- **If you're driving,** take Century Boulevard east out of the airport to I-405 (the San Diego Freeway, known locally as the 405) heading north. Then take I-10 (Santa Monica Freeway), heading west for Santa Monica or east for downtown.
- For **West Hollywood or Beverly Hills,** get on the 405 but look immediately for the La Cienega Boulevard sign. Head north on La Cienega. (Just before the 405, you'll cross La Cienega, but you'll save time if you access it via the freeway.) Turn west (left) at Wilshire Boulevard for Beverly Hills. Continue north on La Cienega for West Hollywood.
- **Other Los Angeles-Area airports:** Bob Hope Airport (BUR; tel: 818/840-8840); LA/Ontario International Airport (ONT; tel: 909/937-2700); John Wayne Airport Orange County (SNA; tel: 949/252-5200).

San Diego

- **San Diego International Airport** (tel: 619/400-2404; www.san.org) is about 3mi (5km) from downtown. Pick up taxis, shuttles or buses at the Transportation Plaza at Terminal 1 or 2, or curbside at the commuter terminal (mostly for in-state flights).
- **Taxis** pick up passengers at all terminals for trips to downtown ($) and beyond.
- **Cloud 9 Shuttle** (tel: 858/505-4998 or 800/258-3826) operates a shared-ride van service ($–$$) to San Diego and beyond.
- **San Diego Transit** (tel: 619/233-3004) bus 992 heads from the airport to downtown.
- **If you're driving,** take North Harbor Drive east for downtown and west for Shelter Island and Point Loma. Harbor Island is across from the airport. To get to La Jolla take I-5 north. For Mission Valley, take I-8 east.

Train Stations

Amtrak (tel: 800/872-7245; www.amtrak.com) trains serve California. San Francisco-bound passengers must disembark at the Emeryville station (5885 Horton Street) in the East Bay and take a shuttle bus to the city. Amtrak stops in Los Angeles at Union Station (800 North Alameda Street) and in San Diego at the Santa Fe Depot (1050 Kettner Boulevard).

Bus Stations

Greyhound (tel: 800/231-2222; www.greyhound.com) is the state's main long-distance bus company, serving San Francisco (200 Folsom Street), Los Angeles (1716 E. 7th Street), San Diego (1313 National Avenue), Sacramento (420 Richards Boulevard) and many other cities.

Orienting Yourself

San Francisco

Union Square is the hub of downtown San Francisco. Many hotels are here, on Market Street or in nearby SoMa (South of Market Street area).

Finding Your Feet

San Francisco Visitor Information Center

✉ Hallidie Plaza, Lower Level, Powell and Market streets ☎ 415/391-2000; www.sanfrancisco.travel

🕐 May–Oct Mon–Fri 9–5, Sat, Sun 9–3; Nov–Apr closed Sun, 1 Jan, Thanksgiving and 25 Dec

🚇 Muni Metro J, K, L, M, N and BART (Powell Street) 🚌 Muni Bus 5, 6, 21, 27, 30, 31, 38, 45; F-line trolley; Powell-Mason and Powell-Hyde cable cars

Los Angeles

Downtown Los Angeles is favored more by business travelers than leisure travelers, who tend to gravitate toward Hollywood, West Hollywood, Beverly Hills or beach towns such as Santa Monica.

Los Angeles Visitor Information Center

✉ 900 Exposition Boulevard ☎ 213/763-3466; www.discoverlosangeles.com 🕐 Daily 9:30–5

🚇 Metro Red Line (7th & Figueroa) 🚌 MTA Bus 20, 460; DASH A, E, F

Hollywood and Highland Visitor Information Center

✉ 6801 Hollywood Boulevard ☎ 323/467-6412 🕐 Mon–Sat 10–10, Sun 10–7

🚇 Metro Red Line (Hollywood & Highland) 🚌 MTA Bus 163, 210, 212, 217; DASH Hollywood

San Diego

San Diego sprawls outward from its downtown waterfront. Most tourist attractions are north of downtown

International Visitor Information Center:

✉ 996 N Harbor Drive ☎ 619/737-2999; www.sandiegovisit.org 🕐 Summer and fall daily 9–5; winter and spring daily 9–4 🚇 Trolley (American Plaza) 🚌 Bus 30, 992

Getting Around

Driving

You can get by without a car in San Francisco and parts of San Diego, but driving is the easiest way to see most of California. I-5 and US 101 are the major north–south highways. Scenic, winding (i.e., the going's often slow) Highway 1 runs north–south along the coast, merging several times with US 101. I-80 runs east–west through the middle of Northern California. I-10 and I-15 travel east–west through Southern California.

On the Road

- You need a **valid driver's license** from your home state or country to drive in California. The minimum age for drivers is 16, though the license is provisional, with restrictions, until age 18; car-rental companies usually require that drivers be 21 or older (some charge more if you're under 25). There are sometimes restrictions about the type of car you can rent if you're under 25.
- Drivers and passengers must **wear seat belts at all times.**
- Children under 8 years of age or 4.75ft (145cm) in height must **ride in safety seats**; most car-rental agencies supply them for an additional charge.
- Except where indicated otherwise, **right turns are permitted on red lights** after you've come to a full stop. Turns onto intersecting one-way streets are permitted in the same circumstances.

- Driving with a **blood-alcohol level** higher than .08% is illegal.
- **The speed limit on freeways** is 65 or 70mph (105/112km/h) on rural roads and from 55 to 65mph (88–105km/h) on city freeways. In cities, the speed limit is generally 25 or 30mph (40/48km/h) unless posted otherwise.
- In the San Francisco Bay Area, Los Angeles and San Diego, **avoid commuting hours on the freeways** 7–10am and 4–7pm (longer in L.A.).

In-State Air Travel

If you plan ahead, fares can be competitive for flights between Northern and Southern California. If you have the time, though, you may still want to drive to take in the scenery.

City Transit

San Francisco Bay Area

- **Hotels charge a fortune for parking,** and spaces on the street are sometimes difficult to find – two good reasons to take advantage of public transportation. Rent a car for trips farther afield.
- The **Transit Information Line** (tel: 511 or 888/500-4636 from any area code in the Bay Area) has advice about public systems.
- **Muni** (tel: 311 or 415/701-2311) operates buses, light-rail vehicles, antique trolleys and cable cars in San Francisco. All cost the same amount except cable cars, for which you pay slightly more.
- For above-ground trips on Market Street up to Castro or along the Embarcadero, the **antique trolleys are convenient** (and fun). Exact change is required in dollar bills or coins.
- **Transfers** cost $2.25 (as many journeys as you like for 90 mins). **Visitor Passes** for 1–7 days ($6–$29) are often cheaper for some trips.
- **All-day passes** can be purchased at the Visitor Information Center (➤ 35) and elsewhere.
- **BART** trains (tel: 415/989-2278 or 510/465-2278) serve downtown and the southern part of San Francisco and travel to the East Bay and northern San Mateo County. You buy tickets in BART stations.

Los Angeles Area

- It is generally difficult to tour L.A. by public transit, but it can be done, and in some cases (going to the *Queen Mary,* for instance), it's preferable.
- If you're going to use public transportation, consider staying downtown – subways and bus routes fan out from here. **MTA** buses and **Metro Line** (tel: 323/466-3876) light-rail vehicles serve the metropolitan area. The MTA also operates **DASH** (tel: 213/808-2273) minibuses for short hops around downtown and elsewhere. Santa Monica and other nearby towns operate their own bus systems. Exact change is required except at light-rail stations.

San Diego

- Downtown, Balboa Park and Old Town are well served, and Coronado and SeaWorld receive adequate service, but to get to La Jolla and other places takes a long time, and some locales are under served or nearly ignored.
- **San Diego Transit** (tel: 619/233-3004) operates buses (all over) and trolleys (downtown, to Old Town and Mission Valley and to California's border with Tijuana, Mexico). Exact change is required on buses; you can purchase trolley tickets at vending machines in the stations.

Finding Your Feet

Taxis
Taxis are difficult to hail in all three cities. You're generally better off calling for one or joining the line at a hotel taxi stand.

- **San Francisco:** Yellow Cab (tel: 415/333-3333) and Luxor Cab (tel: 415/282-4141).
- **Los Angeles:** Yellow Cab (tel: 877/733-3305) and United Independent Taxi (tel: 323/653-5050).
- **San Diego:** Silver Cab (tel: 619/280-5555) and Yellow Cab (tel: 619/444-4444).

Accommodations

Standards are high throughout the state, but in general the best accommodations are available in San Francisco and Los Angeles and in resort areas such as the Wine Country, the Monterey Peninsula, Santa Barbara and Palm Springs.

Hotels and Motels
- Hotels and motels are the **most common types of lodgings**. Hotels tend to be the best options in big cities and motels are kings of the highways.
- **Full-service hotels** in California often include such amenities as fitness rooms, indoor pools, laundry service, in-room modems and safes, valet parking and concierges. Motels often offer outdoor swimming pools and hot tubs, along with amenities such as cable TV and hair dryers.
- Many hotels and motels allow children (of varying ages) **to stay free** with their parents in a room. Some allow pets. Most do not include meals in the rates – except for the occasional Continental breakfast.
- **One drawback with motels** is security because the door to your room opens directly to the outside world.

Bed and Breakfast Inns
B&Bs in California often charge high rates and generally require two-night minimum stays on weekends and three-night minimum stays on holidays. Many are also geared toward romantic couples. For more information visit the Californian Association of Bed & Breakfast Inns at www.cabbi.com.

Resorts
California has a number of high-end, full-service resorts, with such amenities as golf courses, tennis courts and multiple swimming pools.

Hostels
California has a number of hostels that charge $15–$30 per night per person. Most have dormitory-type rooms where sexes are segregated, some have rooms for couples or families. Most limit stays to a few days at a time. **Hostelling International – USA** (tel: 240/650-2100; www.hihostels.com).

Accommodation Prices
Expect to pay per double room, per night (excluding tax)
| $ under $100 | $$ $100–$175 | $$$ over $175 |

Food and Drink

California is one of the most cosmopolitan places to eat out in the world, and the vast array of cuisines available reflect its melting-pot population and generally high standards of culinary excellence.

Regional Specialties

- California's fertile fields provide local chefs with a **multitude of fresh produce and other ingredients** such as Sonoma lamb, Castroville artichokes, Gilroy garlic, Modesto almonds and Coachella Valley dates.
- **Seafood is another specialty.** One of the most savored local delicacies is the Dungeness crab, known for its sweetness. San Francisco is the home of cioppino, a richly seasoned shellfish stew.
- San Francisco is also **renowned for Asian food.** Dim sum – a selection of Chinese dumplings and other tasty morsels – is a must for lunch, as is phó, a delicious Vietnamese noodle soup usually containing beef and vegetables. In general, Asian restaurants offer some of the best bargains.
- Developed in California over the past quarter-century or so, and always evolving, **California cuisine** relies on fresh local ingredients to create innovative, often light fusion dishes that blend American, Asian, Mediterranean and Latin influences.
- **New American cuisine** can perhaps best be thought of as high quality comfort food with a twist. A pork chop, for instance, may be cooked fairly rare and served with a gravy containing fresh herbs; the mashed potatoes on the side may be infused with garlic. Regional and ethnic influences are sometimes evident, and organic ingredients are often highlighted.
- **Latin American food** is prevalent throughout the state, especially the areas closer to Mexico.

Drink Specialties

- **California wines** rank among the finest in the world. While vintages from the Napa and Sonoma valleys are best known, don't overlook those from other regions, such as near Monterey or Santa Barbara.
- **The martini,** said to have been invented in California, has regained its former cachet. Fine martini bars now dot the big cities. Irish coffee – coffee spiked with Irish whiskey and whipped cream – is claimed to have been born at the **Buena Vista Café** (▶ 73) in San Francisco. **Margaritas**, though a Mexican import, have virtually been adopted as the California state drink.
- Recent years have seen a renaissance of wonderful **local microbreweries** producing a variety of flavorful specialty beers, now available throughout the state.
- **Best brew pubs** include the **Beach Chalet,** San Francisco (▶ 63), **Beer Revolution**, Oakland (http://beer-revolution.com) and **Father's Office** (1018 Montana Avenue, Santa Monica; tel: 310/736-2224).

Dining Options

- California's trendiest restaurants are the new bistros and cafés springing up around the state that are often casual in look and feel but serious about good food. Celebrity chefs often helm the kitchens. Hot restaurants include **Delfina** (▶ 70) in San Francisco, **The French Laundry** in Napa Valley (▶ 100), and **Patina** and **Spago Beverly Hills** (▶ 157) in L.A.

Finding Your Feet

- Many of the hottest restaurants have **bars** where you can walk in without a reservation and order from the bar or, sometimes, the full menu.
- **Lounges and brew pubs** that offer a relaxing or upbeat atmosphere and specialize in drinks, but also serve excellent food, are another trend.
- **You can't always tell the quality** of a restaurant by its exterior. In Los Angeles, a fine restaurant may be hidden away in a small shopping mall. In San Francisco, what appears to be a modest neighborhood ethnic spot may serve some of the best food in the city.

Some Bests
The following restaurants are recommended for their special attributes:

Best for alfresco meals:
Copley's, 621 N Palm Canyon Drive, Palm Springs (➤ 185), George's at the Cove, San Diego (➤ 175) and Tra Vigne, St. Helena (➤ 100)

Best for California cuisine:
Café Beaujolais, Mendocino (➤ 99), Chez Panisse, Berkeley (➤ 70) and The French Laundry, Napa Valley (➤ 100)

Best neighborhood ethnic cuisine:
La Super-Rica, Santa Barbara (622 N Milpas Street; tel: 805/963-4940), The Slanted Door, San Francisco (➤ 71) and Ton Kiang, San Francisco (➤ 72)

A Practical Guide to Eating Out
- **You can dine very well for $15 a person or even less**, especially at a neighborhood ethnic restaurant. Keep in mind that tax, tip and drinks can add 50 percent or more to the total cost of a meal.
- Eating hours typically are: **breakfast** from about 7 to 9:30/10am (though some diners serve breakfast all day and night); **lunch** from 11:30/noon to 2/2:30pm; **dinner** from 5 to 9:30/10pm or until late.
- Call ahead. Restaurants **often change their opening hours** and days or occasionally close for private parties.
- Except for informal diners and cafés, **most restaurants accept reservations**, and it's a good idea to book well ahead at trendy restaurants in big cities.
- **Tipping is an expected practice in California**, though usually the amount is left to the discretion of the customer. Tips range between 15 and 20 percent. Some upscale restaurants routinely add a service charge (around 15 to 18 percent) for groups of six or more people.
- Even in the big cities, **casual dress is widely accepted**. However, some establishments do impose a dress code – a jacket or jacket and tie for men – or occasionally have a policy barring jeans, shorts or sneakers.
- By law, **smoking is banned indoors** in all California restaurants. Some allow cigarette smoking on outdoor patios. Indoor bars are now also legally nonsmoking, though some are lax in their enforcement.
- **Credit cards are accepted** at most restaurants, but not all. If you aren't sure, it's wise to carry plenty of cash or traveler's checks.

Restaurant Prices
Expect to pay per person for a meal, excluding drinks and service:
| $ under $15 | $$ $15–$25 | $$$ over $25 |

Shopping

In California you can get everything from Asian silks to Mexican pottery. If you're looking for more homegrown products, consider handmade jewelry from local artists, Native American baskets, or California wines, almonds or dates.

Local Specialties

On the North Coast, especially in the Mendocino area, look for beautifully crafted paintings and jewelry by local artists. Carmel, along the Central Coast, is another town lined with art galleries. The San Joaquin Valley is good for buying almonds and, in the town of Reedley, near Fresno, Mennonite quilts (Mennonite Quilt Center; 1012 G Street, Reedley; tel: 559/638-3560). San Francisco offers a bonanza of Asian imports in its Chinatown and Japantown districts. Los Angeles is the place to buy movie memorabilia, while L.A.'s Olvera Street and San Diego's Old Town are good for Mexican and Central American imports. The Palm Springs area is strong on Native American crafts.

Pricing

Full retail-price clothing is not particularly good value in California, though factory outlet shops do provide bargains on designer fashions. Imports from Asia and Latin America are often very good buys. And you won't find better prices on local products such as California wines.

Practicalities

■ **Hours:** Shops and stores may open anywhere from 9am to noon; the latter is most common among small specialty shops, and on Sundays for many stores. Most stores stay open until 5 or 6pm. though stores in malls or shopping plazas often don't close until 9pm or even later. Some stores stay open late one night a week, usually a Thursday or Friday, and a fair number of smaller stores close on Sunday or Monday.

■ **Payment methods:** Most stores accept credit cards and traveler's checks.

■ **Etiquette:** Browsing is permissible almost everywhere, and most sales-persons do not rely on high-pressure tactics. In fact, service in stores is often too relaxed – it's not always easy to find someone to wait on you.

Top Shopping Districts

■ **For chic shopping,** the ultimate is Rodeo Drive in Beverly Hills (➤ 143).

■ **For good-value standard shopping,** you'll usually do best at a big-city or suburban mall. But one district that can provide surprising value, con-sidering its popularity with tourists, is **San Francisco's Fisherman's Wharf** (➤ 45). There you'll find a huge Cost Plus World Market store (2552 Taylor Street; tel: 415/928-6200), loaded with inexpensive imports of all kinds, as well as several big shopping complexes – Ghirardelli Square, Anchorage Square and Pier 39 among them (➤ 69 for all) – that, combined, offer hundreds of specialty shops, food courts, bay views, and free street performers and other entertainment. Though you'll have to hunt down the good value stuff among the overpriced schlock, they're there.

■ **For the best department stores, San Francisco's Union Square** (➤ 72) is the place to go. Macy's, Neiman-Marcus and Saks Fifth Avenue are here, while Nordstrom and Bloomingdale's are nearby at the Westfield San Francisco Centre (➤ 72).

Entertainment

The state's varied terrain lends itself to a wide variety of outdoor activities, while the cities and resort areas are centers for nightlife and the arts.

Information
- The best sources for current entertainment listings are **local newspapers**.
- Several cities and resort areas have **24-hour, toll-free, hot-line numbers** that give upcoming events.
- **Most regional visitor bureaus and information centers** (➤ 36) produce annual guides or seasonal brochures that list groups offering music, theater and dance. Check the local phone directory for details.

Nightlife
Los Angeles, San Francisco and, to a lesser extent, San Diego and Palm Springs, are the nightlife capitals of California.
- **Bars:** The best selection is in San Francisco and Los Angeles, ranging from classy hotel lounges and sleek bars in trendy restaurants to atmospheric dives in colorful neighborhoods (➤ 73).
- **Nightclubs:** For sheer raucous entertainment, Los Angeles, especially the Sunset Strip, has the top nightclubs and dance clubs (➤ 160).
- **Culture:** San Francisco's Civic Center area, with world-class opera and symphony, and its nearby Theater District, which presents touring productions of Broadway-style shows along with other stage plays, is a top site for the performing arts (➤ 73 for information). In Los Angeles the cultural divisions are more dispersed but center on several downtown performing arts venues (➤ 160).

Spectator Sports
California has five major league baseball teams, three National Football League teams and four National Basketball Association teams. In addition, the state has women's professional basketball teams, three National Hockey League teams, several thoroughbred racing tracks, a number of professional and amateur soccer teams and numerous college teams in many sports.

Outdoor Activities
- Thousands of miles of scenic and often **challenging hiking trails** crisscross the state's mountains and forests.
- Dozens of **top-flight downhill ski and snowboarding resorts**, as well as thousands of miles of scenic cross-country ski and snowshoe trails, are located in the Sierra Nevada and other mountain ranges.
- **Mountain biking, horseback riding and rock climbing** are other sports popular in rugged California landscapes.
- **Water sports** – canoeing, fishing, kayaking, river rafting, sailing, swimming, surfing, waterskiing and windsurfing among them – thrive along the ocean coastline, as well as in the rivers and lakes.
- **Whale watching expeditions** set out in winter from Monterey and other coastal communities during gray whale migrations.
- **Road biking, running and jogging** are favorite pastimes along many paved trails, such as the 32-mile (51km) Jedediah Smith Memorial Bicycle Trail along the American River Parkway near Sacramento.
- **Hot-air ballooning**, most common in the Wine Country but also found in Southern California and the Sierra, offers a bird's-eye perspective on it all.

San Francisco &
The Bay Area

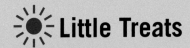 Little Treats

Behind Bars
Alcatraz (➤ 50), the high-security prison out in San Francisco Bay, became famous thanks to a host of Hollywood creations.

A Cultural Melting Pot
Hip young things coexist peacefully with a selection of Spanish shops and bookstores in the happening **Mission District** (➤ 65).

Studying in Style
Berkeley's (✚ 206 C1) lively combination of cafés, restaurants, parks and booksellers is perfect for a chilled afternoon.

Getting Your Bearings

Good food, carefree living and an active cultural scene have been San Francisco trademarks since the frisky Gold Rush days. Writing in 1880, Robert Louis Stevenson credited the city's convivial ambiance to its international citizenry. "The town is essentially not Anglo-Saxon; still more essentially not American," he wrote. "The shops along the streets are like the consulates of different nations. The passers-by vary in features like the slides of a magic lantern."

Elsewhere in his writings Stevenson acknowledged the clashes of culture that characterized 19th-century San Francisco. More than almost anywhere in America, though, this city of shapely hills and water views has been a place that tolerates and even celebrates eccentricity and diversity. It's no accident that Beat writers, psychedelic rockers and budding performance artists all flourished here, not to mention the pioneers in the feminist, personal development and gay-liberation movements.

The agreeable climate attracted the earliest settlers, Ohlone people who lived near what is now Mission Dolores. Spanish seafarers discovered what one called a "very noble and very large harbor" beyond the strait later named the Golden Gate. But it took the discovery of gold to prompt mass migration. San Francisco boomed for 50 years, until the earthquake and fire of 1906 destroyed it.

By the time the city recovered, Los Angeles was on the rise and business had begun moving south. San Francisco continued to attract entrepreneurs and artists, though, and it has remained the hub of Northern California life. The sense of history is palpable, but with multimedia and internet companies thriving, a 21st-century dynamism is amply evident as well.

17 Golden Gate Bridge

Marina Blvd

18 Palace of Fine Arts

Lincoln B

101

California St

16 California Palace of the Legion of Honor

Geary Boulevard

15 Cliff House

SAN FRANCISCO

Fulton St

Golden Gate Park

14

Lincoln Way

1

19th Ave

7th Ave

0   2 km

0   1 mi

Getting Your Bearings

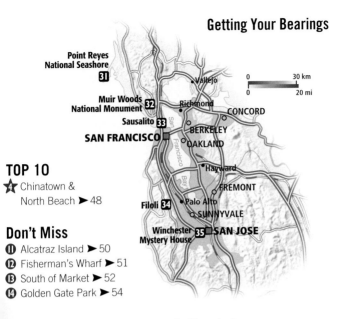

TOP 10

★ Chinatown &
North Beach ➤ 48

Don't Miss

⑪ Alcatraz Island ➤ 50
⑫ Fisherman's Wharf ➤ 51
⑬ South of Market ➤ 52
⑭ Golden Gate Park ➤ 54

At Your Leisure

⑮ Cliff House ➤ 58
⑯ California Palace of the Legion
of Honor ➤ 58
⑰ Golden Gate Bridge ➤ 58
⑱ Palace of Fine Arts ➤ 59
⑲ Lombard Street ➤ 59
⑳ Coit Tower/Telegraph Hill ➤ 59
㉑ Ferry Building ➤ 62
㉒ Haas-Lilienthal House ➤ 62
㉓ Nob Hill ➤ 62
㉔ Union Square ➤ 63
㉕ Civic Center ➤ 63
㉖ Hayes Valley ➤ 64
㉗ Haight Street ➤ 64
㉘ Mission Dolores ➤ 64
㉙ Castro District ➤ 65
㉚ Mission District ➤ 65
㉛ Point Reyes National
Seashore ➤ 66
㉜ Muir Woods National
Monument ➤ 66
㉝ Sausalito ➤ 66
㉞ Filoli ➤ 67
㉟ Winchester Mystery House ➤ 67

San Francisco & The Bay Area

Three Perfect Days

If you're not quite sure where to begin your travels, this itinerary recommends a practical and enjoyable three days exploring San Francisco and the Bay Area, taking in some of the best places to see. For more information see the main entries (►48–67).

Day 1

Morning
A hearty breakfast will fortify you for an early-morning ferry ride to **⓫ Alcatraz Island** (below; ►50), home to the famous prison.

Afternoon
Head into **❹ North Beach** (►48), where you can lunch Italian at **Tommaso's** (►71) or **L'Osteria al Forno** (519 Columbus Avenue; tel: 415/982-1124) and browse through the shops on Columbus and Grant avenues. From North Beach, continue into **★ Chinatown** (►48).

Evening
Catch the sunset or beautiful twilight views from the **Top of the Mark** (►73) cocktail lounge. Dinner is a real event at **Gary Danko** (►70). For a delightful time that's less of a splurge, head to the always bustling **Zuni Café** (►72).

Point Reyes
National Seashore
31
32 Muir Woods
National Monument
33
Sausalito

Filoli **34**

35 Winchester
Mystery House

Day 2

Morning
Take the Powell-Mason line to the **Cable Car Museum** (▶ 63). Walk north or hop on another cable car and get off at Greenwich Street. Walk east four blocks to visit **20 Coit Tower** (▶ 59), afterward descending the Greenwich and Filbert steps.

Afternoon
Have lunch at **Fog City Diner** (1300 Battery Street; tel: 415/982-2000; $$). Walk south along the waterfront side of the Embarcadero, savoring the East Bay views and breezes. Then catch an F-line antique trolley and head up Market Street. Disembark at 3rd Street and walk south into the **13 South of Market (SoMa)** district (▶ 52), where you can sit in Yerba Buena Gardens or enjoy cultural and entertainment options that include museums, galleries, a video arcade, the **Children's Creativity Museum** and an old-fashioned carousel.

Evening
Tea at the café or a cocktail at the bar of the swank **West San Francisco hotel** (181 Third Street; tel: 415/777-5300) should revive you in time for dinner at the Cajun-infused **Town Hall** (342 Howard Street; tel: 415/908-3900) that offers an energetic taste of New Orleans in San Francisco.

Day 3

Morning
The hubbub of the city recedes in gorgeous **14 Golden Gate Park** (below; ▶ 54). Begin your explorations with the flora in the park's eastern section at the Conservatory of Flowers and the nearby Rhododendron Dell, then walk west to Strybing Arboretum and stroll through the botanical exhibits there. Don't miss the two biggest attractions, the de **Young Memorial Museum** (▶ 56) and the **California Academy of Sciences** (▶ 54).

Afternoon
Have lunch at the Beach Chalet (▶ 69), then walk north along the Ocean Beach sidewalk to the **15 Cliff House** (▶ 58).

Evening
Have an early Chinese seafood dinner at the reasonably priced **Yuet Lee** (1300 Stockton Street; tel: 415/982-6020). After dinner, watch San Francisco have a laugh at itself at the long-running *Beach Blanket Babylon* show (▶ 74). Order your tickets in advance, especially during summer.

★4 Chinatown & North Beach

Chinese settled Chinatown and Italians populated adjacent North Beach in the 19th century. More so than any other immigrants, both groups clung with pride to old-country traditions. People from all over Southeast Asia now call Chinatown home and few Italians remain in North Beach, but the influence of these captivating neighborhoods' pioneers remains palpable.

Broadway, just north of the Financial District, is the traditional border between Chinatown and North Beach. From Columbus Avenue and Broadway the area is perfect for a leisurely walk.

Chinatown

In recent decades, Chinatown has burst beyond its traditional borders of Broadway and Bush, Kearny and Stockton streets. Some residents complain that little here is authentic, least of all the architecture, which has been called a travesty of Chinese design. Keep this in mind on touristy Grant Avenue, whose shopkeepers proffer mostly tacky souvenirs and overpriced jewelry (the gems and prices are better on Stockton Street). To see the "real" Chinatown, such as it exists, meander down the side streets and alleys.

Insider Tip

At 56 Ross Alley you can watch the bakers at **Golden Gate Fortune Cookies Co**. whip up batch after batch. A little further south at 837 Washington is the **Superior Trading Co.**, a large herbal pharmacy, which specializes in Chinese

Chinatown delicacies include the familiar and the exotic

medicine. Just east of Superior Trading is Waverly Place and the authentic **Tin How Temple**, where incense fills the air. A flier explains the history of the small Buddhist temple.

Other temples on Waverly include **Jeng Sen Temple** (No. 146) and **Norras Temple** (No. 109); remember to be respectful and quiet when you enter.

If you want to shop for Chinese food, head to Stockton Street, where you will find Peking duck, soy-sauce chicken and barbecued pork hanging in shop windows. Some stores specialize in dried delicacies such as black and white fungus, shark fin, sea scallops and abalone.

North Beach
On Columbus Avenue, beat writers such as Jack Kerouac (▶ 22) read or sold their works at still-bohemian **City Lights Books** (▶ 73) and hung out at nearby **Vesuvio** (▶ 73).

Designer boutiques and quirky shops line Grant Street, along with a few old-timers such as the **Italian French Baking Co.** at 1501 Grant Avenue, which sells terrific breads.

You can rest in Washington Square park, heart of North Beach during its Italian heyday, and still a neighborhood nexus. From here you can either walk south down Columbus Avenue toward Chinatown or head to **Coit Tower** (▶ 59).

Across from Washington Square on Filbert Street is **Saints Peter and Paul Church,** a Roman Catholic church, which featured in the 1971 Clint Eastwood movie *Dirty Harry*.

City Light Books in North Beach, a former hangout of beat generation author Jack Kerouac

TAKING A BREAK
Rest your feet at **Ten Ren Tea Co.** (949 Grant Street), where you can sample exotic tea blends. Continue north on Grant to Broadway to reach **Caffe Trieste** (601 Vallejo Street), a beat haunt, serves invigorating espressos, as does **Caffe Puccini** (411 Columbus). **Golden Gate Bakery** (1029 Grant Avenue) sells tasty mooncakes, egg tarts and other Chinese pastries. Chinese dim sum – meat-filled dumplings and other morsels – is served from early morning until mid-afternoon at **New Asia** (772 Pacific Avenue).

🚇 Chinatown: 214 C4; North Beach: 214 B4
🚎 1 California (Chinatown only), 30-Stockton, 45-Union/Stockton

Tin How Temple
✉ 125 Waverly Place, 3rd floor
☎ 415/391-4841 🕐 Daily 10–4
🎫 Free (donation)

⓫ Alcatraz Island

Many people declare the ferry ride and visit to Alcatraz Island and its former maximum-security penitentiary to be the highlight of their trip to San Francisco. The 15-minute ferry ride, breezy setting and city vistas supply some of the thrills, but what fascinates even more is the tour of "The Rock," where notorious gangsters such as Al "Scarface" Capone, "Machine Gun" Kelly and Robert Stroud, the "Birdman," did time, because other prisons couldn't handle them.

Tours of Alcatraz provide a vivid (yet never grim) portrait of prison life, and the self-guided audio tour includes enlightening – at times even heartwarming – commentary by former guards and inmates.

The **federal prison** operated from 1934 to 1963, and during this period there were 14 attempted escapes. Three prisoners in 1962 made it to the water, where they used raincoats as flotation devices, but they were presumed to have drowned in their attempt to reach San Francisco. No executions occurred on Alcatraz, though there were eight murders and five suicides. In 1963, the U.S. Attorney General, Robert F. Kennedy, ordered the prison closed. Alcatraz Island's illustrious history also includes a stint as a military post and an occupation from 1969 to 1971 by Native Americans who claimed the island on behalf of all U.S. Indian tribes. Allot four hours minimum for the ferry ride and tour, and in summer make reservations a few days ahead.

Many inmates tried to escape "The Rock," but none succeeded

TAKING A BREAK

Insider Tip
There are no restaurants or cafes on Alcatraz, but there is a **picnic area**. It is worth noting that you are only allowed to eat and drink in the designated areas.

➕ 214 off C5 ✉ Fisherman's Wharf, Pier 41 ☎ 415/981-7625 (boat schedules and information); www.alcatrazcruises.com; www.nps.gov/alcatraz
🕐 Ferries (approx. every 30 minutes) Oct–March 8:45–1:30 (evening tour 3:50) Mar–Oct daily 9:30–3:55 (evening tours 6:10 and 6:45)
🚌 30-Stockton, 19-Polk; Powell-Hyde cable car; F-line antique trolleys (east on Market Street and around the Embarcadero)
💲 $38 (ferry, admission & audio guide); children $26.25

⑫ Fisherman's Wharf

The tiny fleet that sails into the wharf with the morning catch is among the few remnants of San Francisco's once prosperous fishing industry. Today, T-shirt and trinket shops, street vendors and artists, and seafood restaurants keep things frenetic at Pier 45, a few piers west of Pier 39.

Head to Pier 39 to enjoy an al fresco snack under the open sky accompanied by a fresh breeze and the song of seagulls

You can't escape the commercial tourist attractions of the wharf, but several fine **nautical attractions** still dock here. The more interesting of the two World War II-era vessels docked here is the U.S.S. *Jeremiah O'Brien* (tel: 415/544-0100). The warship took part in the D-Day invasion of Normandy (June 6, 1944) in France, and the 50th-anniversary festivities in 1994. The engine room appeared in the movie *Titanic*. The gadgetry aboard the U.S.S. *Pampanito* (tel: 415/775-1943), a submarine that served with distinction in the Pacific, seems amusingly antiquated.

Shops, restaurants, Aquarium of the Bay, Hard Rock Café and a carousel lure millions of people to Pier 39 (Powell Street and Embarcadero). The most entertaining attraction, though, is free: highly photogenic **sea lions** on the pier's western side that loll, bark and vie for supremacy.

Insider Tip

PIER 39 PIER 39

TAKING A BREAK
Outdoor stands near Pier 47 and Pier 39 sell fried clams, shrimp cocktails and other seafood offerings.

✚ 214 B5 ☎ 415/674-7503; www.fishermanswharf.org
🚃 30-Stockton, 19-Polk; F-line antique trolleys (east on Market Street and around the Embarcadero); Powell-Hyde cable car

INSIDER INFO

■ At the **Hyde Street Pier** you can board a schooner and a side-wheel ferry. The pier is part of the **San Francisco Maritime National Historical Park**.

■ Along the waterfront, **boats and ferries depart** for bay cruises and excursions to Sausalito (▶ 66) and other points along the coast. For a great nature-oriented day trip, pack a picnic lunch and head to **Angel Island**, a state park that previously served as a processing center for immigrants. Once on the island, you can ride a tram or bike (rentals at dock available seasonally), or take a hike past historic and scenic sites.

Insider Tip

⓭ South of Market

Business, culture and entertainment converge in the South of Market area (SoMa). Trade shows and conventions take place at Moscone Center, the San Francisco Museum of Modern Art tops an eclectic roster of cultural institutions and the diversions range from a century-old carousel to virtual-reality games. With several of its highlights less than a decade old, SoMa has become a hot hangout for locals and visitors.

SoMa stretches from just west of the Embarcadero to Division Street. The western part contains some top nightclubs and restaurants, but SoMa's core is the **Yerba Buena Gardens** complex, home to restaurants, a bowling alley, a skating rink and the 🎠 **Children's Creativity Museum**. **Moscone Convention Center** is here as well. The 🎠 **Metreon complex** contains IMAX and conventional theaters, along with the UltraBowl (video bowling). Willows, pines and other trees border the grassy knoll within the tranquil East Garden, perhaps the city's most pleasant small park. At the garden's southern edge is a waterfall dedicated to Martin Luther King Jr. that provides a scenic and sonic backdrop.

Insider Tip

San Francisco Museum of Modern Art

Swiss architect Mario Botta designed the **San Francisco Museum of Modern Art (SFMOMA)**, a snazzy 1995 modernist structure. Matisse, O'Keeffe, Warhol and Richard Diebenkorn

SFMOMA hosts a world-famous collection of modern art

(a Bay Area resident for many years, ➤ 22) are among the painters represented. The photography collection is one of California's finest. Don't miss the new Rooftop Garden that features sculptures and the Rooftop Coffee Bar.

Head to the edge of the Yerba Buena Gardens to find, among other things, such cultural institutions as the ⛩ **Yerba Buena Center for the Arts** with its very own theater that promotes local culture, the ⛩ **Children's Creativity Museum** that makes art and technology exciting for kids and teens alike, and the **Museum of the African Diaspora**, which uses interactive exhibits to share stories about Africa and its global impact. **The Contemporary Jewish Museum**, designed by architect Daniel Libeskind, has exhibits exploring Jewish culture, history, art and ideas.

TAKING A BREAK

Metreon's ground floor contains several restaurants, including the **Firewood Café** and **Sanraku** (Japanese). On a fine day, you can eat in the **East Garden** or on a terrace overlooking it.

Yerba Buena Gardens
🔢 214 C2 ✉ Bordered by Mission, 4th, Folsom and 3rd streets
☎ 415/820-3550; www.yerbabuenagardens.com 🕐 Daily 6–10
🚇 Muni Metro J, K, L, M, N and BART (New Montgomery)
🚌 9-San Bruno, 14-Mission, 15-Kearny, 30-Stockton

San Francisco Museum of Modern Art (SFMOMA)
🔢 214 D2 ✉ 151 3rd Street ☎ 415/357-4000; www.sfmoma.org
🕐 Late May to early Sep Thu–Tue 10–5:45 (also Thu 6–8:45); mid-Sep to late May 11–5.45 💵 $18

⛩ Yerba Buena Center for the Arts
🔢 214 D2 ✉ 701 Mission Street ☎ 415/227-8666; www.ybca.org
🕐 Tue–Sun 11–6 💵 varies

⛩ Children's Creativity Museum
🔢 214 C2 ✉ 221 Fourth Street ☎ 415/820-3320; http://creativity.org
🕐 Tue–Sun 10–4 (summer); Wed–Sun only rest of year 💵 $12

Museum of the African Diaspora
🔢 214 D2 ✉ 685 Mission Street ☎ 415/358-7200; www.moadsf.org
🕐 Wed–Sat 11–6, Sun noon–5 💵 $10

The Contemporary Jewish Museum
🔢 214 C2 ✉ 736 Mission Street ☎ 415/655-7800; www.thecjm.org
🕐 Thu 1–8, Fri–Tue 11–5 💵 $12

INSIDER INFO

To appreciate Yerba Buena, **sit for at least a few moments in the East Garden** – one entrance is off Mission Street, mid-block between 3rd and 4th.

Insider Tip

⓮ Golden Gate Park

About 75,000 people drop by Golden Gate Park on a sunny weekend, just one indication of this more than 1,000-acre (405ha) urban getaway's vital role in city life.

Magical without being showy about it, the Golden Gate Park is a place where the whole is greater than the sum of its parts – in this case lakes, gardens, groves, playgrounds, a herd of buffalo, windmill and a brew pub with ocean views. The main reasons to come here are to stroll amid nature both rustic and manicured, and to visit the **de Young Memorial Museum**, which reopened to much fanfare in 2005 and the 🔲 **California Academy of Sciences**, which returned in 2008 after several years of renovation, during which the museum was banished to a temporary location South of Market. Pritzker Prize-winning architect Renzo Piano designed the new "green" museum – the building's sustainable design earned it the highest LEED rating – creating a living roof that houses the planetarium, aquarium, natural history museum and rainforest dome.

Planetarium and Aquarium

The all-digital, state-of-the-art **Morrison Planetarium** has popular shows about the stars and planets every half hour during the week and every 45 minutes on weekends. There is no extra cost for the shows, but you will need a separate ticket, which is handed out on a first-come, first-served

Visitors enjoy a quiet moment on Stow Lake, one of the highlights of Golden Gate Park

basis. It's advisable to get your tickets before you start exploring the museum, as the next show time might not be available.

Downstairs is the superb **Steinhart Aquarium**, which houses 38,000 animals from 900 different species. Back upstairs is the Kimball Natural History Museum and the interesting hall of dioramas, which is worth checking out.

The Victorian-style Conservatory of Flowers

First-rate chefs helm both the dining options in the museum, the Academy Café and the fancier Moss Room. On Thursday evenings (6–10pm), the museum hosts an enjoyable event for adults, who are invited to drink, dance, and take in the exhibits.

Park Highlights

The main sights are in the park's eastern and western ends. John F. Kennedy Drive passes by or near several of the park's delights along the 3mi (5km) from Stanyan Street to Ocean Beach. Greenery is such a trademark of Golden Gate Park it's hard to imagine that nearly the entire area was once sand dunes. Much of the credit for the landscaping goes to John McLaren, the park's intrepid superintendent from 1890 to 1943, but he was partly just lucky: Golden Gate Park sits atop several underground streams, which

he tapped as water sources for the vegetation he nurtured so creatively.

Insider Tip If your time is limited, concentrate on the eastern part. Drive or take the 5-Fulton bus to 8th Avenue, walk east on John F. Kennedy Drive to the Conservatory Garden, then loop back west on Kennedy Drive past the Rhododendron Dell to the attractions between 8th Avenue and Cross-Over Drive. These include the **Japanese Tea Garden** and **San Francisco Botanical Garden at Strybing Arboretum**. If you have more time, drive or catch the 5-Fulton bus west to the ocean. At 36th Avenue walk south on Kennedy Drive to the **Buffalo Paddock** or continue on to 47th Avenue, near the **Dutch Windmill** and **Cliff House**.

The **Conservatory of Flowers**, a copy of the original at the Royal Botanical Gardens in Kew, England, has been refurbished since being damaged in a mid-1990s rainstorm. The 19th-century structure merits a peek, however, as do the tropical and subtropical plants inside the seasonal gardens. To the west, on the other side of the street, is the peaceful Rhododendron Dell. South of the conservatory, on Bowling Green Drive, lies the National AIDS Memorial Grove, and beyond that the 🎠 **Children's Playground** with a carousel dating from 1912.

The **de Young Memorial Museum** was designed by the architectural firm of Herzog & de Meuron, among whose other commissions are the Tate Modern in London. The de Young's strengths include the works of the John D. Rockefeller III Collection of American Paintings and the African and Native American holdings. A public observation tower offers stunning Bay Area views. There is a public sculpture garden and the museum hosts lively Friday Nights at the de Young from 5 (April–Nov) with live entertainment.

The well-groomed Japanese Tea Garden

Japanese Tea and Botanical Gardens

Ponds, pagodas and bamboo-lined paths create a tranquil atmosphere at the **Japanese Tea Garden**. Magnolias, camellias, azaleas, Japanese maples, dwarf pines and other plants and trees grow in the garden, which was developed for Golden Gate Park's 1894 Midwinter Exposition. You can contemplate the scene over a cup of tea in the teahouse.

Crowds of summer tourists can shatter the tea garden's calm, so you may find things more peaceful at the nearby **San Francisco Botanical Garden at Strybing Arboretum**. The 55-acre (22ha) arboretum contains biblical, fragrance, succulent and primitive plant gardens, along with the trees and other vegetation of several continents. One entrance is about 100ft (30m) west of the Japanese Tea Garden.

TAKING A BREAK

The wide windows of the 1925 Spanish Colonial-style **Beach Chalet** (►69) look out on Ocean Beach. Lucien Labaudt's stunning wraparound mural, painted in the fresco style, depicts 1930s San Francisco.

🚌 214 off A1 🚇 N-Judah (south side) 🚌 5-Fulton (north side)

California Academy of Sciences
🚌 197 off A1 ✉ 55 Music Concourse Drive
☎ 415/321-8000; www.calacademy.org
🕐 Mon–Sat 9:30–5, Sun 11–5 💲$30

Conservatory of Flowers
🚌 197 off A1 ✉ John F. Kennedy Drive at Conservatory Drive
☎ 415/831-2090; www.conservatoryofflowers.org
🕐 Tue–Sun 10–4:30 (last entry 4pm) 💲$7

de Young Memorial Museum
🚌 197 off A1 ✉ 50 Tea Garden Drive, off John F. Kennedy Drive
☎ 415/750-3600; http://deyoung.famsf.org
🕐 Tue–Sun 9:30–5:15 (until 8:45 on Fri April–Nov) 💲$10

Japanese Tea Garden
🚌 197 off A1 ✉ Tea Garden Drive, off John F. Kennedy Drive
☎ 415/752-1171; http://japaneseteagardensf.com
🕐 Mar–Oct daily 9–6; Nov–Feb 9–4:45 💲$7

San Francisco Botanical Garden at Strybing Arboretum
🚌 197 off A1 ✉ 9th Avenue at Lincoln Way
☎ 415/661-1316; www.sfbotanicalgarden.org
🕐 Daily from 7:30am; Nov–Jan until 4; mid-March–Sep until 6; Oct, Feb–mid-March until 5 💲$7

INSIDER INFO

- Weekends are great days to come to the park because many streets are closed to traffic.
- If you're planning to visit the Japanese Tea Garden in summer, be sure to **arrive by 9:30am** to beat the crowds. If you're feeling energetic you can rent bicycles and skates at several shops on Stanyon Street between Page and Waller streets.
- From east to west, **additional park highlights** include the Music Concourse and its bandshell (bandstand), the Rose Garden, Stow Lake, the Buffalo Paddock and the Dutch Windmill.

At Your Leisure

15 Cliff House

Folks have been coming to the Cliff House complex for more than a century to have a drink or a meal and enjoy the ocean view. Just offshore is **Seal Island**, a favorite hangout of birds and, despite the name, sea lions. Fun to roam through – if it's not too windy – are the ruins of the **Sutro Baths**, a gigantic swimming and bath-house facility (just north of the Cliff House) that burned down in5the 1960s. As regards the food, expect no-great-shakes American fare – though brunch isn't bad – and you really can't beat those amazing vistas.

➕ 214off A1 ✉ 1090 Point Lobos Avenue
☎ 415/386-3330; www.cliffhouse.com
🕑 Mon–Sat 9–9:30, Sun 8:30–9:30
(bar open until 11 Sun–Thu, midnight Fri–Sat)
🚌 18-46th Avenue; 38-Geary (but only the ones marked Point Lobos or Fort Miley)

16 California Palace of the Legion of Honor

The French neoclassical Legion of Honor, completed in 1924, is a tasteful three-quarter-scale adaptation of the 18th-century Palais de la Légion d'Honneur in Paris. The windswept cliff-top setting itself rates a stop, with views of the city unfolding to the east and south, and glimpses through gnarled cypress and pines of the Golden Gate to the north. But the museum's collection also entices. Key holdings include prints and drawings, pre-20th-century European art, English and European porcelain and sculptures by Auguste Rodin.

Insider Tip

➕ 214 off A1
✉ 34th Avenue at Clement Street
☎ 415/750-3600; http://legionofhonor.famsf.org
🕑 Tue–Sun 9:30–5:15 (last ticket 4:30)
🚌 2-Clement, 18-46th Avenue, 38-Geary
🎟 $10

17 Golden Gate Bridge

One of San Francisco's most exhilarating views (► 60-61) is that of the 1.7-mile (2.7km) icon that connects the city with Marin County. The suspension bridge's towers taper slightly as they rise gracefully to a height of 746ft (227m). The distinctive color, international orange, complements the surroundings: blue sky, the often dark-gray waters of the bay, the brown to green hillsides, and the San Francisco skyline. (The U.S. Navy wanted to paint the bridge

The windswept cliff-top setting of the California Palace of the Legion of Honor

black and yellow so ships could see it better.) A stroll across this sturdy yet elegant structure can be superb on a sunny day, but if it's cloudy or the wind is gusting, be ready for one bone-chilling excursion. The vista points at either end have magnificent views, but for a loftier perspective – with the bridge's cables framing the city – take the Alexander Avenue exit from the Marin side and take the first left. You will pass under US 101; turn left again and head up Conzelman Road to the Marin Headlands.

➕ 214 off A4 ☎ www.goldengatebridge.org
🕐 Cars, bicycles 24 hours; pedestrians summer 5am–9pm; winter 5am–6:30pm

🔟 Palace of Fine Arts

San Francisco's civic leaders produced the lavish Panama-Pacific International Exposition of 1915 to proclaim the city's recovery from the 1906 earthquake and fire. The fair's temporary buildings were later torn down, leaving only the classical-style palace. This was so beloved by locals that it was replicated in permanent materials in the 1960s. The **Exploratorium**, a warehouse-like space full of amusing interactive displays that elucidate principles of natural and applied science, has moved from its site here down to Pier 15.

➕ 214 off A4 ✉ Beach and Baker streets
☎ 415/561-0360 (Exploratorium); www.palaceoffinearts.org; www.exploratorium.edu
🕐 Exploratorium: Tue–Sun 10–5 (also most Mon holidays)
💲 Moderate (free first Wed of month)
🚌 30-Stockton

🔟 Lombard Street

You've got better things to do with your time. But, hey, you're on vacation, so go ahead, take the irresistible plunge down San Francisco's novelty block, where eight switchbacks

Take a cable car to the top of the "Crookedest Street in the World"

deliver cars from the top of the hill to the bottom. It's one-way only.

➕ 214 A4 ✉ Lombard Street between Hyde and Leavenworth streets (enter on Hyde)
🚌 19-Polk; Powell–Hyde cable car

🔟 Coit Tower/Telegraph Hill

Lillie Hitchcock Coit, a rather eccentric fan of city firefighters, bequeathed the money that built the 210ft (64m) Coit Tower in their honor. The bay and downtown views from the 1933 structure are unparalleled, and interior murals depict Depression-era California. Now fully restored, these wall paintings are open to visitors once again. If you find yourself suddenly feeling amorous, you'll know why readers of a local newspaper voted Coit Tower the city's premier spot for lovers. Two sets of plant- and flower-lined steps lead past Craftsman bungalows and other lodgings down the east slope of Telegraph Hill from the base of the tower itself. The **Greenwich Steps** descend to Montgomery Street, where, if you look south, you'll see the wood-plank **Filbert**

The Golden Gate Bridge

The Golden Gate Bridge, which celebrated its seventy-fifth anniversary in 2012, stretches across the "Golden Gate" strait between the San Francisco Peninsula and Marin County on the opposite side. It's the longest and most beautiful suspension bridge in the world and the most celebrated symbol of San Francisco. Approximately 14 million tourists make the pilgrimage to the bridge every year and 112,000 cars traverse it every single day.

❶ **Measurements** The bridge, which is lavishly illuminated at night, is 1.7mi (2.7km) long, clears the water by 220ft (67m), and boasts a span of 4,200ft (1,280m). Its towers are 745ft (227m) in height.

❷ **Towers** A 154ft (47m)-high concrete shell was built around the base of the towers during the construction process to protect them from the tides. The seawater was then pumped away to create a dry space to work. The foundations that each of the 21,500-ton towers rest on have to withstand tides of nearly 62mph (100km/h).

❸ **Tower foundations** The towers' foundations are 66ft (20m) thick and sunk approximately 98ft (30m) deep into the seabed about 1,132ft (345m) offshore. The concrete poured into the supporting foundations during construction would be enough to build a 5ft (1.5m)-wide, 2485mi (4,000km)-long road that could stretch all the way from New York to San Francisco.

❹ **Roadway** The roadway runs 220ft (67m) above the surface of the ocean that's 318ft (97m) deep at this point. Made of reinforced concrete, it was built out from both towers simultaneously so that the tension on the suspension steel cables would be evenly distributed.

The bridge traverses the Golden Gate Strait that connects San Francisco Bay with the Pacific Ocean

San Francisco & The Bay Area

Steps continuing east. At the bottom of Telegraph Hill you can catch a bus on Battery Street to downtown or walk north a few blocks to Fisherman's Wharf. A fine few hours can be had wandering from North Beach (➤ 49) to Coit Tower.

➕ 214 C4 ✉ Telegraph Hill Boulevard and Greenwich Street ☎ 415/362-0808
🕐 May–Oct daily 10–6 (5 rest of year)
🚌 39-Coit (from Washington Square park, Union Street side) 💲 $7

21 Ferry Building

The 1896 Ferry Building amazingly survived San Francisco's two major earthquakes, not to mention the in-dignity of having its facade blocked by a freeway for three decades, only to emerge – after a complete makeover that shows off the struc-ture's spectacular skylit nave – as a popular upscale marketplace. Local purveyors of gourmet pro-duce, meats, fish and prepared foods have permanent bodegas, and a farmers' market is held year-round on Tuesdays and Thursdays (10–2) and Saturdays (8–2). This is a great place to pick up a gourmet snack for an impromptu waterfront picnic.

➕ 214 off C3 ✉ Embarcadero and Market Street ☎ 415/983-8030; www.ferrybuilding marketplace.com, www.cuesa.org
🕐 Mon–Sat 10–6, Sun 11–5 (individual business hours vary; some restaurants open later)
🚇 Embarcadero Station (BART and all Muni)
🚌 1-California; F-line antique trolleys

22 Haas-Lilienthal House

Many mansions along broad Van Ness Avenue were dynamited in 1906 to halt the advance of the fires that followed the earthquake. The imposing Queen Anne-style Haas-Lilienthal House, one block west, was one of the beneficiaries of this strategy. With 24 period-decorated rooms,

the home, built in 1886 for German-born immigrant William Haas, a prominent merchant, was modest compared to the destroyed mansions. But it's still a grand setting, and on the one-hour, guided tours you'll get a feel for the taste and style of prosperous San Franciscans of the late 19th century. Walking tours of Pacific Heights leave from the house on Sundays at 12:30.

➕ 214 A3
✉ 2007 Franklin Street, near Washington Street
☎ 415/441-3000; www.sfheritage.org
🕐 Wed, Sat noon–3, Sun 11–4
🚌 1-California, 27 Bryant, 47–49 Van Ness/Mission
💲 $8

23 Nob Hill

Nob Hill, a mostly residential neigh-borhood, has some of the city's finest views. It became the place to live when the 19th century's "Big Four" railroad barons – Charles Crocker, Leland Stanford, Mark Hopkins and Collis Huntington – spent thousands of dollars erecting mansions near California and Mason streets. **Grace Cathedral** (California and Taylor streets; www. gracecathedral.org) stands on the site of Crocker's mansion, which, like those of his friends, was destroyed in the 1906 earthquake and fire. The Fairmont Hotel (California and Mason streets), just about to open, was gutted, but its shell survived, as did that of the brownstone James Flood Mansion (now the Pacific Union Club), across Mason Street. To take in the views, head to the Top of the Mark (➤ 73), the upscale sky-line bar at the Mark Hopkins-Intercontinental hotel (California and Mason streets).

Insider Tip

➕ 214 A3 🚌 1-California; all cable-car lines

WHAT MAKES A CABLE CAR GO?

Cables loop continuously beneath Powell, Hyde, Mason and California streets. To get a cable car going, the operator uses a long pole called a grip, which grabs the cable, causing the car to move along with it. To stop, the operator releases the grip. In the basement of the **Cable Car Museum**, you can view the wheels moving the cables. (Mason and Washington streets; tel: 415/474-1887; www. cablecarmuseum.org; open: Apr–Sep daily 10–6; Oct–Mar 10–5. Bus: 1-California; Powell-Hyde and Powell-Mason cable cars. Admission: free.)

24 Union Square

The hub of downtown's shopping and financial districts is home to Niketown, Tiffany & Co., and the Neiman-Marcus and Macy's department stores. On the west side of the square is the Westin St. Francis, the scene of the party that ended Fatty Arbuckle's career. On the opposite side of the square to the east is Maiden Lane, a 19th-century red-light district that's now the locale of fancy shops. The circular ramp at the gallery at 140 Maiden Lane is said to have been architect Frank Lloyd Wright's test run for the Guggenheim Museum in New York City. Three blocks south of Union Square on Powell Street are the San Francisco Visitor Information Center (➤ 35) and the turnaround for San Francisco's two iconic cable-car lines.

➕ 214 C2

🚋 3-Jackson, 30-Stockton, 38-Geary; Powell-Hyde and Powell-Mason cable cars

25 Civic Center

Shafts of golden light and the marble stairs of its massive rotunda seem to cascade from above onto the main floor of San Francisco's debonair **City Hall**, a French High-Baroque Revival-style edifice from 1915 where baseball player Joe DiMaggio once married actress Marilyn Monroe. Free tours of the Hall take place daily (tel: 415/554-6139). Across from the Civic Center Plaza is the superb **Asian Art Museum**, with fascinating objects on display from more than three dozen countries.

Insider Tip

➕ 214 A1 ✉ Polk and McAllister streets

☎ 415/554-6023; http://sfgsa.org

🕐 Mon–Fri 8–8

🚇 Civic Center (BART and all Muni); Van Ness (all Muni)

🚋 5-Fulton, 19-Polk, 21-Hayes, 47-Van Ness

Take a tour of San Francisco's grand Civic Center with its massive rotunda

One of the many beautifully painted residences in the Haight/Ashbury area

Asian Art Museum
✚ 214 A1
✉ Larkin and McAllister streets
☎ 415/581-3500; www.asianart.org
🕙 Tue–Sun 10–5 (also 5–9 Thu Feb–Sep)
💵 $12

🅺 Hayes Valley
Shops and galleries – smart, but not too fancy, offbeat but not too funky – lie west of Van Ness Avenue along Hayes Street. To revive yourself after your shopping excursion drop by La Boulange (500 Hayes Street; tel: 415/863-3376, daily 7–7) for a latte and a delicious fresh pastry or sandwich.
✚ 214 A1

🅺 Haight Street
A San Francisco rock critic wrote that the "Summer of Love" never happened in 1967 – journalists dreamed it up, he claimed. Which would make it all the more ironic that the corner of Haight and Ashbury streets, ground zero during the Flower Power days, remains a major pilgrimage for San Francisco visitors. Whether there was a "Summer of Love" or not, except for waifs in tie-dye shirts seeking spare change and haggard-

looking characters who breeze by proffering joints, there's precious little evidence of it today. At the Ben and Jerry's store at Haight and Ashbury you can, however, buy Cherry Garcia ice cream, named for the late Grateful Dead musician Jerry Garcia, who lived nearby at 710 Ashbury Street. One oasis of 1960s idealism and activism is the **Red Victorian Bed, Breakfast & Art** (1665 Haight, near Cole Street). At its Peace Center Arts Gallery are posters, T-shirts, Haight Street hagiographies and even a meditation room. The most interesting stretch of Haight Street is between Masonic Avenue and Shrader Street.
✚ 214 off A1
🚌 33-Stanyan, 71-Haight-Noriega

🅺 Mission Dolores
San Francisco's oldest standing structure, erected in 1791 of wood and stucco, is officially called Mission San Francisco de Asis. The 4ft (1.2m) thick adobe walls of the chapel have survived numerous major earthquakes. The original bells, which were cast in Mexico, remain, as do some of

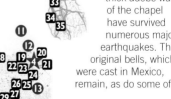

the original redwood roof support beams. Vegetable dyes were used to create the superb ceiling design, which is based on the beautiful Ohlone Indian baskets.

🚹 214 off C1 ✉ Dolores/16th streets
☎ 415/621-8203; www.missiondolores.org
🕐 Daily 9–4 (4:30 May–Oct) 🚋 J-Church (Muni); BART (16th and Mission streets)
🚌 22-Fillmore; F-line antique trolley 🎟 $5

OFF THE BEATEN TRACK

You can see north to Marin County and east to Oakland from **Twin Peaks**, the second highest spot in San Francisco. It can get windy up here, but the views are sublime. (Twin Peaks Boulevard off Portola Drive; take Market Street west from Castro. Bus: 37-Corbett from north side of Market Street west of Castro Street.)

🟥29 Castro District

Gay folk settled this middle-class neighborhood in the 1970s, and before long it had garnered an international reputation as a homosexual mecca. The new residents helped elect Harvey Milk, who ran a camera shop on Castro Street, the first openly gay member of the San Francisco Board of Supervisors. Another supervisor, Dan White, murdered Milk and Mayor George Moscone in 1978. White had resigned from the board and when he wanted to be reinstated – something only the mayor could do – they had declined to support the notion, igniting his murderous rage. A huge rainbow flag, a symbol of the gay community, flies above Harvey Milk Plaza, at Castro and Market streets, and two landmarks can be found across Castro from it. The **Twin Peaks Tavern** (401 Castro) was one of the first gay bars whose windows looked out on the street. The need to hide behind curtains

The Mission District is known for its buildings adorned with dramatic murals

or shutters became less pressing in the early 1970s as San Francisco became more tolerant. A few doors down stands the Spanish baroque-style **Castro Theatre** (429 Castro), built in 1922 as a silent-movie house. An organist plays the Mighty Wurlitzer between shows almost every night.

🚹 214 off A1 🚋 Muni (K, L, M)
🚌 24-Divisadero, 33-Stanyan, 37-Corbett; F-line antique trolleys

🟥30 Mission District

Mission Dolores anchors the northern edge of the Mission District, for many years a major Latin American neighborhood but now evolving as Asians, Arabic people and upwardly mobile professionals have moved in. One popular section is the Valencia Corridor, the eight blocks of Valencia Street between 16th and 24th streets, where thrift stores, cheap eateries and bookstores thrive. On 24th Street, between Mission and Bryant streets, the Latin American influence remains strongest. At the Precita Eyes Mural Arts & Visitors Center (2981 24th Street, near Alabama Street; tel: 415/285-2287, open: daily), you can pick up a map with directions to the area's murals, many by Latino artists. Galeria de la Raza/Studio 24 (2857 24th Street, at Bryant Street; tel: 415/826-8009, open: Wed–Sun), exhibits and sells the work of American-born and international Latino artists.

🚹 197 off B1
🚋 BART (16th Street, 24th Street)
🚌 14-Mission, 22-Fillmore, 27-Bryant, 48-Quintara/24th Street

San Francisco & The Bay Area

31 Point Reyes National Seashore

Quite possibly the most beautiful wilderness in the entire Bay Area, what is now the Point Reyes National Seashore was settled centuries ago by Coast Miwok Indians. A good first stop is Bear Valley Visitor Center, 38mi (61km) northwest of San Francisco, off Highway 1 in Olema, where you can pick up maps and view exhibits about the seashore's wildlife and vegetation. The shortest of two easy-to-walk paths that leave from the center's parking lot ends at **Kule Loklo**, a re-created Miwok village. On the slightly longer Earthquake Trail, part of which passes over the San Andreas Fault, stands a fence that shifted 16ft (25m) during San Francisco's 1906 earthquake. Solitary Point Reyes Lighthouse, a 21-mile (34km) drive from the visitor center, sits on a rocky promontory at the bottom of 308 very steep steps. The bluff above it is billed, correctly it would seem, as the windiest spot on the American West Coast. A visit to Point Reyes and Muir Woods National Monument makes for a fine day trip from San Francisco.

➕ 206 B2 ✉ Highway 1 (from San Francisco take US 101 north to Mill Valley/Stinson Beach exit and follow signs) ☎ 415/464-5100; www.nps.gov/pore ⏰ Park: daily from sunrise to midnight (or overnight with a camping permit); Visitor centers: opening times vary; Lighthouse: Fri–Mon 10–4:30 💲 free

32 Muir Woods National Monument

The coastal redwood grows to heights of 200ft (60m) or more in this forest 11mi (18km) north of the Golden Gate Bridge. If your California travels won't be taking you past the state's other redwood groves, visit Muir Woods. The only drawback is the park's popularity (from May to October it's best to visit before 10am or after 4pm), but most visitors don't leave the paved and boardwalked trails. For a good introduction to the park's flora and fauna, walk the main trail to Bridge 4, but loop back to the entrance via the less-traveled Hillside Trail. The 2-mile (3km) hike (trail maps at the park entrance) takes a little more than an hour.

➕ 206 B1 ✉ Muir Woods Road, off Panoramic Highway (from San Francisco take US 101 north to Mill Valley/Stinson Beach exit and follow signs) ☎ 415/388-2595; www.nps.gov/muwo ⏰ Daily 8–dusk 💲 $10/per car & week (annual pass for all NP $80)

Windswept Point Reyes is a beautiful spot for an exhilarating seashore walk

Admiring the immensely tall redwoods in the Muir Woods National Monument

33 Sausalito

This town across the bay from San Francisco has gotten so gosh darn cute that few traces of its risqué past remain. Rumrunners and sailors hung out in the 19th century, and during the mid-20th century artists and other bohemian types settled here. It costs too much for most artists to live in Sausalito now, but the superb San Francisco views and jolly atmosphere remain. A great way to visit the walkable town is via boat – either the **Golden Gate Ferry** (tel: 511 (toll-free) or 415/455-2000 from outside the Bay Area) from the Ferry Building (Market Street and the Embarcadero in San Francisco) or the **Blue & Gold Fleet** (tel: 415/705-8200) from Pier 41. Bridgeway, the town's main drag, contains shops and restaurants.

✚ 206 B1 ✉ Off US 101 (take Alexander Avenue exit at north end of Golden Gate Bridge, follow signs to downtown)
🚌 Route 10/Golden Gate Transit

34 Filoli

Sixteen acres (6.5ha) of formal gardens surround the 43-room home, 26mi (42km) south of San Francisco, built for William Bowers Bourn II, whose holdings included the **Empire Mine** (➤ 93). The exterior of the Georgian Revival-style structure stood in for the Carrington mansion on the opening credits of the long-running drama series *Dynasty*. If you've visited European manors or even Hearst Castle, you may find the house tour (only the first floor is open to the public) less than spectacular. The gardens, though, designed as a series of "rooms," are among America's most outstanding.

Insider Tip

✚ 206 B1 ✉ Canada Road, west of Edgewood Road exit off I-280 ☎ 650/364-8300; www.filoli.org 🕐 Mid-Feb to Oct Tue–Sat 10–2:30, Sun 11–2:30 (guided tours; reservations recommended) 💷 Feb–May $20, June–Oct $18

35 Winchester Mystery House

The gun-manufacturing heiress Sarah Winchester believed the mediums who said she'd die if construction stopped on her mansion, so from 1884 until she died 38 years later, her workers kept building. The resulting 160 rooms contain such oddities as staircases that dead-end into ceilings but also include stylish touches such as Tiffany windows and parquet floors with many inlaid woods.

✚ 208 B5 ✉ 525 S Winchester Boulevard, off I-280, San Jose ☎ 408/247-2101; www.winchestermysteryhouse.com 🕐 Sep–May 9–3 (estate tour), 9–5 (mansion tour); June–Aug 9–5 (estate tour), 9–7 (mansion tour) 💷 $30

AMUSE YOURSELF

Tech Museum of Innovation (201 S. Market Street, San Jose; tel: 408/294-8324; $20) features interactive exhibits in communications, medical, computer, outer-space and other fields.
🎡 **Six Flags Discovery Kingdom** (1001 Fairgrounds Drive, off Highway 37, Vallejo; tel: 707/643-6722; www.sixflags.com, $64.99), 35mi (56km) northeast, has rides and marine shows.
🎡 **California's Great America** (Great America Parkway off US 101, Santa Clara; tel: 408/988-1776; www.cagreatamerica.com; $62,99), south of the city, has thrill rides and entertainment. Both parks are closed in winter.

Where to…
Stay

Prices
Expect to pay per double room, per night (excluding tax)

$ under $100 $$ $100–$175 $$$ over $175

SAN FRANCISCO

Chancellor Hotel $$
The 15-story Chancellor is a moderately priced bargain hotel, offering comfort without extra-vagance. Rooms are of medium size, with high ceilings and fans. Deep tubs add a touch of luxury to the bathrooms. Most of the rooms sleep three people, but a few two-room connecting suites are available. The hotel also has an excellent restaurant and bar.

🚩 214 B5
✉ 433 Powell Street, CA 94102
☎ 415/362-2004 or 800/428-4748;
www.chancellorhotel.com

Cow Hollow Motor Inn & Suites $–$$
Conveniently situated near Union and Chestnut streets, the Cow Hollow Inn is well-kept and offers accommodations at a reasonable price. Amenities include AC, free wireless and parking.

🚩 214 C4 ✉ 2190 Lombard Street, CA 94123
☎ 415/921-5800; www.cowhollowmotorinn.com

Hotel Del Sol $$
Motels for the budget-conscious line Lombard Street, but this one, part of the Joie de Vivre chain, is a few blocks south on a quieter street and has more personality. The rooms are comfortable and amenities include a complimentary town car service and a heated swimming pool. The Marina District location means it is close to the stores and restaurants on Chestnut and Union streets.

🚩 214 off A4
✉ 3100 Webster Street, CA 94123
☎ 415/921-5520 or 877/433-5765; www. jdvhotels.com/hotels/sanfrancisco/del_sol

Hotel Diva $$
Conveniently located a block from Union Square, in the theater district, this pet-friendly, hotel offers modern rooms and decor at good value. Stainless steel features throughout the hotel, and rooms are furnished with cobalt blue carpeting, up-to-date bedding, and lighting. Amenities include high-speed internet, iPod docking stations and a fitness room.

🚩 214 B2 ✉ 440 Geary Street, CA 94102
☎ 415/885-0200 or 800/553-1900;
www.hoteldiva.com

The Marker San Francisco $$$
Near Union Square, the Marker makes one of the most striking impressions in the city. From its beaux arts facade to its eye-catching lobby – where you can sip complimentary evening wine beside a huge fireplace – to its 208 vividly decorated rooms, some with whirlpool tubs.

🚩 214 B2 ✉ 501 Geary Street, CA 94102
☎ 415/292-0100 or 866/622-5284;
www.monaco-sf.com

Hotel Rex $$$
Replicating the sophisticated appearance of San Francisco's stylish 1920s-era artistic and literary salons, the Rex has a lobby lined with walls of old books and guest rooms filled with restored walnut armoires and original art-

works. Marble baths add a touch of luxury to its rooms. The lobby harbors a clubby lounge.

➕ 214 B2 ✉ 562 Sutter Street, CA 94102 ☎ 415/433-4434 or 800/433-4434; http://thehotelrex.com

Ritz-Carlton $$$
The Ritz-Carlton may be San Francisco's finest hotel. Everything here bespeaks luxury: The neo-classical building, the lobby and hallways lined with antiques and paintings, the ample and richly furnished rooms, the Italian marble baths and the gracious service.

➕ 214 C3 ✉ 600 Stockton Street, CA 94108 ☎ 415/296-7465 or 800/241-3333; www.ritzcarlton.com

Taj $$$
Intimate, quiet, luxurious and not far from Union Square, the Taj helps set the standard for top-flight service among San Francisco hotels. Elegance surrounds you from the moment you enter the lobby until you settle into your comfortable

room, equipped with an antique armoire, writing desk and marble bath. Many rooms have sitting areas. The hotel's restaurant, Campton Place (5) is one of the city's top places to dine.

➕ 214 C2 ✉ 340 Stockton Street, CA 94108 ☎ 415/781-5555 or 866/332-1670; www.tajhotels.com/sanfrancisco

White Swan Inn $$–$$$
Of San Francisco's many bed-and-breakfast inns, the White Swan is the most elegant in the downtown area. Inside this 1908 building, just a few blocks from Union Square, the decor is reminiscent of an English Edwardian townhouse. That feel extends more informally to the 26 rooms, which have fireplaces, four-poster beds and floral wallpapers, and in the clubby library, where afternoon hors d'oeuvres are served. Buffet-style breakfasts may be taken in your room or in the parlor.

➕ 214 B2 ✉ 845 Bush Street, CA 94108 ☎ 415/775-1755 or 800/999-9570; www.whiteswaninnsf.com

Where to...
Eat and Drink

Prices
Expect to pay per person for a meal, excluding drinks and service:
$ under $15 $$ $15–$25 $$$ over $25

Absinthe $$$
This sophisticated French bistro in the Civic Center area is one of the best places for a drink or a meal before a performance of a symphony, opera or ballet. The appetizers and entrées are generous and well prepared. Treat yourself to one of the tempting cold seafood platters.

➕ 214 A1 ✉ 398 Hayes Street, San Francisco ☎ 415/551-1590; www.absinthe.com 🕐 Tue–Fri 11:30–midnight, Sat 11–midnight, Sun 11–10 (Thu–Sat bar open until 2am)

Beach Chalet $$
Occupying the upper floor of a historic building on the western edge of Golden Gate Park, this combination brew pub and restaurant is one of the most scenic and good-natured spots in San Francisco. You might have to fight the crowds, especially around sunset or at Sunday brunch. Choose from an eclectic, if not overly imaginative, American menu of seafood, pastas, sandwiches

and bar snacks. The attractive Park Chalet Garden Restaurant is around back, facing the park.

✚ 214 off A1

✉ 1000 Great Highway, Golden Gate Park, San Francisco

☎ 415/386-8439; www.beachchalet.com

🕒 Mon–Thu 9am–10pm, Fri 9am–11pm, Sat 8am–11pm, Sun 8am–10pm

Bix $$$

This stylish art-deco supper club on the fringes of North Beach seems right out of the 1930s. Find a spot at the bar, order a cocktail, and listen to live piano jazz; or ask for a table downstairs or on the mezzanine and savor Bix's updated and often inventive versions of traditional American dishes. The menu changes seasonally.

✚ 214 C3

✉ 56 Gold Street, San Francisco, between Montgomery and Sansome streets

☎ 415/433-6300; www.bixrestaurant.com

🕒 Lunch Fri 11:30–2:30; dinner Mon–Thu 5:30–11, Fri–Sat 5:30–midnight, Sun 5:30–10

Boulevard $$$

Both inside and out, Boulevard is one of San Francisco's most beautiful restaurants. It occupies the ground floor of the Audiffred Building, an 1889 jewel on the Embarcadero, and the decor could have been lifted right out of Paris. But Chef Nancy Oakes's menus, which change frequently depending on seasonal ingredients, are primarily Californian, with Mediterranean, Latin and Asian influences. Weekday lunches offer inventive pizzas and more informal service.

✚ 214 off C2

✉ 1 Mission Street, San Francisco

☎ 415/543-6084; www.boulevardrestaurant.com

🕒 Lunch Mon–Fri 11:30–2; dinner Sun–Thu 5:30–10, Fri–Sat 5:30–10:30

Chez Panisse $$$

Since the 2140s, Alice Waters' temple of gastronomy in Berkeley has defined and redefined California cuisine, and it remains one of the Bay Area's top restaurants for a special occasion. Each night, in two seatings, one menu is served, based on the freshest seasonal ingredients. While this is always a high-end destination, Mondays are considerably less expensive than other nights. Upstairs, a casual, more moderately priced café (tel: 510/548-5049) serves both lunch and dinner, with exceptional salads, tasty pizza and other fare.

✚ 206 C1

✉ 1517 Shattuck Avenue, Berkeley

☎ 510/548-5525; www.chezpanisse.com

🕒 Chez Panisse: Mon–Sat 6–10.30. Café: lunch Mon–Thu 11:30–3:45, Fri–Sat 11:30–3; dinner Mon–Thu 5–10:30, Fri–Sat 5–11:30

Delfina $$–$$$

This lively Italian trattoria, in San Francisco's slightly gritty but increasingly gentrified Mission District, continues to be popular and consistently delicious. What the neighborhood lacks in charm the food makes up for in taste and quality. The menu changes seasonally, but may include steelhead with melted leeks and Meyer lemon-caper butter or roasted leg of lamb with cannellini beans and black olives. The wine list focuses on Italy and California. Delfina's pizza café is next door and is a good place for an informal meal.

✚ 214 off B1

✉ 3621 18th Street, San Francisco

☎ 415/522-4055; www.delfinasf.com

🕒 Dinner Mon–Thu 5:30–10, Fri–Sat 5:30–11, Sun 5–10

Gary Danko $$$

Considered by many to be the best dining experience in San Francisco, this popular Fisherman's Wharf restaurant lets diners choose a three-, four- or five-course meal of New American fare, with a number of delicious choices for each course. Don't skip the cheese course, which showcases 16 to 20 selections from California and abroad. Food, wine selection and service are unparalleled.

⊞ 214 A5
✉ 800 North Point Street, San Francisco
☎ 415/749-2060; www.garydanko.com
🕐 Dinner daily 5:30–10

Greens $$

This longtime favorite vegetarian restaurant also enjoys a big following among carnivores, who may not even notice that the delicious pizza is topped with Swiss chard rather than sausage or that the terrific enchilada is stuffed with goat's cheese instead of chicken. Greens also serves up some of the city's most soul-stirring bay views. Saturday nights are reserved for special five-course fixed-price dinners; other nights, and lunches, are à la carte. Sunday brunches are a big hit here.

⊞ 214 off A4 ✉ Fort Mason Center, Building A, San Francisco ☎ 415/771-6222; www. greensrestaurant.com 🕐 Lunch Tue–Sat 11:45–2:30, Sun 10:30–2; dinner daily 5:30–9

The House $–$$

Shielded from some of North Beach's bustle, this minimalist Asian fusion restaurant is helmed by a local chef, influenced by Asian cuisine. The inventive menu includes dishes such as blue lake bean tempura and sesame soy glazed salmon in a bonito sake broth. The tables are a tight fit, but the service is friendly and attentive.

⊞ 214 C4 ✉ 1230 Grant Avenue, San Francisco ☎ 415/986-8612
🕐 Lunch Mon–Sat 11:30–2:30; dinner Mon–Thu 5:30–10, Fri 5:30–11, Sat 5–11, Sun 5–10

La Mar Cebicheria Peruana $$–$$$

International chef, Gaston Acurio, chose San Francisco as the location for his first restaurant in North America, and serves his traditional Peruvian cuisine in this gorgeous setting on the Embarcadero. The restaurant is popular with locals, and the extensive menu includes a variety of *ceviches* (fresh fish and shellfish) dishes and *lomo saltado*, a traditional Peruvian stir-fry of sautéed beef tenderloin, onions, tomatoes, and cilantro (coriander) with fried potatoes and rice. Cocktails include, of course, the pisco sour (a traditional Peruvian cocktail made with brandy) and pisco punch, invented in San Francisco in the early 1800s).

⊞ 214 off C4
✉ Pier 1.5 (Embarcadero), San Francisco
☎ 415/397-8880 🕐 Lunch daily 11:30–2:30; dinner Sun–Wed 5:30–9:30, Thu– Sat 5:30–10

The Slanted Door $$$

In a city where good Vietnamese food is taken for granted, The Slanted Door ranks at or near the top. Located at the Ferry Building (▶ 62), it draws diners from across San Francisco eager to sample chef Charles Phan's imaginative dishes. Expect a fair amount of clamor inside the airy space and to have to wait for a table, even with a reservation. The menu, which changes frequently, makes good use of local, seasonal ingredients. Fresh spring rolls, spicy squid and shaking beef all explode with flavor.

⊞ 214 off C4 ✉ Embarcadero and Market Street, San Francisco ☎ 415/861-8032; www. slanteddoor.com 🕐 Lunch daily 11:30–2:30 (till 3pm Sun); dinner daily 5:30–10pm

Tommaso's Restaurant $$–$$$

Bustling, loud and always crowded, this old-fashioned, family-run North Beach Italian restaurant draws locals primarily for its wood-fired pizzas (touted as the oldest oven on the West Coast), plus an extensive selection of pastas, salads, and oven-baked specials. Tiramisu is usually on the dessert menu. The restaurant doesn't take reservations, so be prepared to wait for a table – the food is worth it.

⊞ 214 C3 ✉ 1042 Kearny Street, San Francisco ☎ 415/398-9696
🕐 Tue–Sat 5–10:30, Sun 4–9:30

Ton Kiang Restaurant Dim Sum-Seafood $–$$

This is one of San Francisco's most beloved neighborhood Chinese restaurants, located along Asian Geary Boulevard, a few blocks from Golden Gate Park. Come for outstanding dim sum at lunchtime or Chinese-style seafood at night. Salt-baked chicken and clay-pot seafood dishes are specialties.

✚ 214 off A1 ✉ 5821 Geary Boulevard, San Francisco ☎ 415/387-8273; www.tonkiang.net 🅖 Mon–Thu 10–9, Fri 10–9:30, Sat 9:30–9:30, Sun 9–9

Zarzuela $–$$

It would be hard to match the charming setting of this Spanish restaurant in Russian Hill: the Hyde Street cable car meanders past regularly, and it gives views of the Coit Tower and Alcatraz. Authentic seafood paella, tapas and sangria are the main draws, and the service is friendly. Reservations aren't accepted, and parking here is close to impossible.

✚ 214 A4 ✉ 2000 Hyde Street, San Francisco ☎ 415/346-0800 🅖 Tue–Thu 5:30–10, Fri–Sat 5:30–10:30

Zuni Cafe $$–$$$

Some customers come for the people-watching – which goes into high gear at the sleek copper bar – and others for the top-notch Mediterranean food orchestrated by chef Judy Rodgers. But eventually, it seems, almost everyone comes to the Zuni, a café that has been a local San Francisco institution for more than three decades. The wood-burning oven turns out a great whole roasted chicken, while the Caesar salad and hamburger on focaccia are classics. Sit on the balcony for an overview, or opt for oysters, washed down by a martini or Bloody Mary, at the ground-level bar.

✚ 214 off A1 ✉ 1658 Market Street, San Francisco ☎ 415/552-2522; www.zunicafe.com 🅖 Tue–Thu 11:30–11, Fri–Sat 11:30–midnight, Sun 11–11

Where to…
Shop

In San Francisco, one of America's great shopping cities, each neighborhood has a distinct personality.

Union Square is the heart of the downtown shopping district. Major department stores include Macy's, Neiman-Marcus, Barneys and Saks Fifth Avenue. Upscale boutiques such as Armani, Gucci, Polo, Vuitton, Hermés, Tiffany and Cartier also dot the area.

Wilkes Bashford (375 Sutter Street; tel: 415/986-4380; www.wilkesbashford.com), a men's clothier, and **Gump's** (135 Post Street; tel: 415/982-1616; www.gumps.com), which carries high-quality antiques, glassware and porcelains, are local favorites. Giant chain stores, such as Apple, Sephora, Williams-Sonoma, Niketown and Victoria's Secret, are also on hand.

Nearby, the **Westfield San Francisco Centre** (865 Market Street; tel: 415/495-5656; www.westfield.com/sanfrancisco) has dozens of specialty shops, as well as Bloomingdale's and Nordstrom department stores.

In the **Financial District**, the glass-domed **Crocker Galleria** (50 Post Street; tel: 415/393-1505; www.thecrockergalleria.com) has three levels of shops and restaurants, plus rooftop gardens.

Near the waterfront, the **Embarcadero Center's** office buildings (www.embarcaderocenter.com/ec) contain more than 100 shops on the lower levels, including book, travel and clothing stores.

Jackson Square, on the fringes of the Financial District, is home to several stores selling fine antiques.

Union Street in the Marina District is known for its boutiques, antiques and fine jewelry stores.

Three major shopping complexes stand out in the **Fisherman's Wharf** area: **Ghirardelli Square** (900 North Point Street; tel: 415/775-5500; www.ghirardellisq.com), **Anchorage Square** (2800 Leavenworth Street; tel: 415/775-6000; www.anchoragesquare.com) and **Pier 39** (Embarcadero at Beach Street; tel: 415/981-7437; www.pier39.com). All have specialty shops where you'll find everything from kites to redwood furniture. Fisherman's Wharf is also the easiest place to find a souvenir T-shirt.

North Beach is known for its Italian delis and bakeries, as well as quirky boutiques, art galleries and bookstores.

City Lights Books (261 Columbus Avenue; tel: 415/362-8193; www.citylights.com) is the city's most famous.

Hayes Valley, along Hayes Street near the Civic Center, has become a center for trendy art galleries and shops selling vintage collectibles.

Budget shoppers can head to discount and factory outlet stores in the **South of Market** area.

Among them are **Jeremy's** (2 South Street Avenue; tel: 415/882-4929; www.jeremys.com) and **Nordstrom Rack** (555 Ninth Street; tel: 415/934-1211). Chinatown and Japantown are other good areas to search for bargains, mostly Asian imports.

The **Haight-Ashbury** is the place to rummage for retro-chic items such as 1960s vintage apparel and art-deco home accessories.

Wasteland (1660 Haight Street; tel: 415/863-3150; www.shopwasteland.com) has a good selection. The cutting-edge shops in the Castro district are geared toward gays and lesbians.

Where to...
Go Out

Check the two free weeklies, the *Bay Guardian* (www.sfbg.com) and the *SF Weekly* (www.sfweekly.com), and the Sunday edition of the *San Francisco Chronicle* (www.sfgate.com).

BARS

In the **Top of the Mark** in the Mark Hopkins Intercontinental hotel atop Nob Hill (999 California Street; tel: 415/392-3434; www.intercontinentalmarkhopkins.com) enjoy dance music and city views.

The art-deco **Redwood Room** at the Clift Hotel (495 Geary Street; tel: 415/929-2372; www.clifthotel.com) and the **Americano** (Hotel Vitale, 8 Mission Street; tel: 415/278-3777; www.americanorestaurant.com), with its terrace, are also popular.

The **Buena Vista Café** (2765 Hyde Street; tel: 415/474-5044, http://thebuenavista.com), near the Wharf, is credited with inventing Irish coffee.

Specs' (12 Saroyan Place, off Columbus Avenue; tel: 415/421-4112) and **Vesuvio** (255 Columbus Avenue; tel: 415/362-3370; www.vesuvio.com) both exude old-time North Beach ambiance.

Trendsetters crowd into **Sightglass Coffee Bar** (270 7th Street; tel: 415/861-1313; https://sightglasscoffee.com) in the **SOMA** area, and the **Balboa Café** (3199 Fillmore Street; tel: 415/921-3944; www.balboacafe.com), in the Marina District.

Gay bars are centered in the Castro, Lower Polk Street and South of Market areas, while lesbian bars can be found on Valencia Street in the Mission District.

San Francisco & The Bay Area

For jazz, head to the **Café du Nord** (2170 Market Street; tel: 415/861-5016; www.cafedunord.com) in the Castro, where you need to dress up; or to San Francisco's historic jazz district in the Fillmore area.

Here, try **Sheba Piano Lounge** (1419 Fillmore; tel: 415/440-7414; www.rasselasjazzclub.com) or **Yoshi's San Francisco** (1330 Fillmore; tel: 415/655-5600; www.yoshis.com). For blues and jazz, try the **Boom Boom Room** (1601 Fillmore; tel: 415/673-8000; www.boomboomblues.com).

The **Great American Music Hall** (859 O'Farrell Street; tel: 415/885-0750; www.gamh.com), the **Fillmore** (1805 Geary Boulevard; tel: 415/346-6000) and **Slim's** (333 11th Street; tel: 415/255-0333; www.slims-sf.com) all present top rock, blues or country-music acts.

The **San Francisco Symphony** (201 Van Ness Avenue; tel: 415/864-6000; www.sfsymphony.org) and the **San Francisco Opera** (301 Van Ness Avenue; tel: 415/864-3330, http://sfopera.com) are in the Civic Center area.

Pick up half-price, same-day tickets (daily) for theater performances at **TIX Bay Area** (www.tixbayarea.com) on the western edge of Union Square.

Several theaters host productions of Broadway musicals and plays, including the **Orpheum** (1192 Market Street; www.shnsf.com), the **Golden Gate** (1 Taylor Street, opposite 6th Street/Market Street) and the **Curran** (445 Geary Street). Check shows at all three by calling 888/746-1799. The **American Conservatory Theater** stages plays at the Geary Theater (415 Geary Street; tel: 415/749-2228; www.act-sf.org).

Club Fugazi (678 Green Street; tel: 415/421-4222) in North Beach hosts the long-running **Beach Blanket Babylon** (www.beach blanketbabylon.com), an outlandish and popular revue.

Mezzanine (444 Jessie Street; tel: 415/625-8880) has stylish dance, gallery and performance spaces, while **DNA Lounge** south of Market (375 11th Street; tel: 415/626-1409; www.dnalounge.com) showcases alternative rock and hip-hop. **Ruby Skye** hosts a selection of top DJs who play their electronic beats in a former Victorian theater decorated in a futuristic style (420 Mason Street; tel: 415/693-0777; www.rubyskye.com).

The **San Francisco Giants** baseball team (tel: 415/972-2000 for tickets, http://sanfrancisco.giants.mlb.com) plays at AT&T Park in China Basin.

The **East Bay's Oakland A's** (tel: 510/638-4627 for tickets, http://oakland.athletics.mlb.com) play baseball at Oakland-Alameda County Coliseum, the same stadium that hosts the **Oakland Raiders** (tel: 510/864-5000; www.raiders.com) of the National Football League.

The NFL's **San Francisco 49ers** (tel: 415/656-4900; www.49ers.com) play football at Candlestick Park, but tickets are difficult to obtain.

Call **Ticketmaster** (tel: 800/745-3000; www.ticketmaster.com).

The **Golden State Warriors** (tel: 510/986-2200 for tickets; www.nba.com) play NBA basketball at the Oracle Arena in Oakland.

Golden Gate Park has 20 public tennis courts (tel: 415/753-7001) and a par-3 golf course.

Alternatively, head for the links at **Lincoln Park** (tel: 415/221-9911; www.lincolnparkgc.com), or one of two options in **Harding Park**, e.g. the **Fleming 9 Course** (99 Harding Road; tel: 415/664-4690; https://tpc.com/hardingpark).

Northern California

 **Little Treats**

Geology: Live!
The bubbling mud pots in **Lassen Volcanic National Park** (▶ 95) show just how lively the earth is deep beneath the surface.

Adventures on the River
Snow meltwater sends the rivers rushing through **Gold Country** (▶ 92) – climb aboard a rubber raft and hold on tight!

The Land of the Giants
Head to **Humboldt Redwoods State Park** (▶ 94) and you'll feel completely dwarfed by the gigantic 330ft (100m)-tall trees.

Northern California

Getting Your Bearings

Northern California beyond the Bay Area encompasses a vast territory, and some of world's most expensive real estate. The natural wonders here include craggy coastal bluffs and wonderfully remote beaches, soaring redwoods, hot springs, superb wildlife and state parks, the granite cliffs of the Sierra Nevada, spectacular caverns and the allegedly magical Mount Shasta.

A travel writer in the 1960s characterized Northern California as "not seductive," by which he meant it's not flashy and doesn't nurture a swinging social scene. The region has its upscale locales – the chic Wine Country for one – and handsome bed-and-breakfast inns dot the coastal and inland areas. But Northern California is composed mainly of farming areas and small towns with regular folks going about their business. Their activities just happen to have one of the world's most scenic backdrops.

US 101, I-5 and I-80 lead to most of the region's attractions. US 101 heads north from San Francisco, skirting the western edge of the Wine Country before continuing into Redwood Country. More or less parallel to the coast, US 101 is inland for the first 260mi (418km) north of San Francisco, then hugs the shore for another 100mi (160km) until right before the California–Oregon border.

I-5 parallels US 101 up the approximate center of Northern California. The road travels through the Shasta Cascade area, which includes the magical Mount Shasta and Lassen Volcanic National Park.

I-80 heads east from San Francisco to the state capital, Sacramento. Farther east off I-80 are the Gold Country and Lake Tahoe. Yosemite National Park and Mono Lake are due east of the Bay Area by various routes.

Orick
Eureka
Garbervil
0 50 km
0 50 mi
Fort Brac
Sonoma
Me

The graceful California State Capitol Building in downtown Sacramento

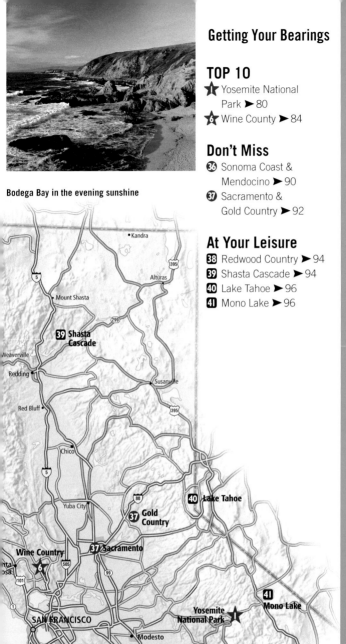
Bodega Bay in the evening sunshine

Getting Your Bearings

TOP 10
⭐ Yosemite National Park ➤ 80
⭐ Wine County ➤ 84

Don't Miss
36 Sonoma Coast & Mendocino ➤ 90
37 Sacramento & Gold Country ➤ 92

At Your Leisure
38 Redwood Country ➤ 94
39 Shasta Cascade ➤ 94
40 Lake Tahoe ➤ 96
41 Mono Lake ➤ 96

Kandra

Alturas

Mount Shasta

39 Shasta Cascade

Weaverville

Redding

Susanville

Red Bluff

Chico

Yuba City

40 Lake Tahoe

37 Gold Country

Wine Country **6**

37 Sacramento

Santa Rosa

SAN FRANCISCO

41 Mono Lake

Yosemite National Park

Modesto

San Jose

Merced

Five Perfect Days

Perfect Days in...

If you're not quite sure where to begin your travels, this itinerary recommends a practical and enjoyable five days exploring Northern California, taking in some of the best places to see. For more information see the main entries (➤ 80–96).

Day 1

Morning
Drive north from San Francisco on US 101 and west (at Santa Rosa) on Highway 12. Loosen your limbs at **Bodega Bay** (➤ 90) then continue north on Highway 1 to **Goat Rock Beach** (left; ➤ 74), where sea lions do their stretching.

Afternoon
Lagoon and ocean views make lunch at River's End in Jenner a memorable experience. Take a scenic history lesson at **Fort Ross Historic State Park** (➤ 20) before heading east on Fort Ross Road and south on Cazadero Road to Highway 116. In Guerneville pick up River Road – it's the town's main street – and continue east into the Russian River Valley wine region.

Evening
Have dinner at Healdsburg's Bistro Ralph (➤ 100); if you're lucky there'll be an evening band concert in Healdsburg Plaza.

Day 2

Morning
After a leisurely breakfast, take a 11am tour in the ⭐**Wine Country** (➤ 84).

Afternoon
Pick up some picnic items at the Oakville Grocery (➤ 102) in Healdsburg. Drive south on Healdsburg Avenue and Eastside Road. Veer left (you're still heading south) on Trenton–Healdsburg Road. Just before River Road is the Mark West Estate (7010 Trenton–Healdsburg Road; tel: 707/836-9647) with its great pinot noir wines. Head east on River Road past US 101 to **Calistoga** (➤ 84, Wine Country).

Evening
Have dinner at a restaurant in downtown Calistoga.

Day 3

Morning
Take a hot-air balloon ride and view the vineyards from above or a hike through Robert Louis Stevenson State Park, 7mi (11km) north of downtown Calistoga on Highway 29.

Afternoon
Have lunch at **Tra Vigne** (➤ 100), then head south to Rutherford. Stop into **Mumm Napa Valley** (➤ 80) in the ⭐ **Wine Country**, then continue south on Highway 29 and east on Highway 12 and I-80 to 🕗 **Sacramento** (➤ 92), a two-hour drive.

Evening
Have dinner in Sacramento at Rio City Café (➤ 100).

Day 4

Morning
Stroll around Old Sacramento and tour the **California State Railroad Museum** and **Sutter's Fort** (➤ 92).

Afternoon
Shoot east on I-80 and north on Highway 49 and have lunch in **Nevada City** (➤ 92) at Café Mekka (237 Commercial Street; tel: 530/478-1517). Head south on Highway 49, stopping at 🕗 **Gold Country** (➤ 92) attractions; don't miss the **Empire Mine** if it's open.

Evening
Spend the night in one of the hotels in scenic Sutter Creek.

Day 5

Morning
Drive south on Highway 49 to Highway 120 and head east into ⭐ **Yosemite National Park** (right, ➤ 80).

Afternoon
Visit Glacier Point and Yosemite Valley. If it's summer, catch the sunset at Hetch Hetchy Reservoir.

Evening
Have dinner at the **Majestic Yosemite Dining Room** (➤ 101).

★Yosemite National Park

What is there to say about Yosemite National Park except don't miss one of America's scenic superstars. The park's waterfalls, the granite monoliths Half Dome and El Capitan, Mariposa Grove with its giant sequoias, and the view of Yosemite Valley and beyond from Glacier Point are all stunners, as is that man-made standard-setter for mountain-rustic chic, the Majestic Yosemite Hotel.

Seeing the Park

Most visitors charge straight into Yosemite Valley, but consider heading first to **Glacier Point** (take Wawona Road south to Glacier Point Road) for an unforgettable glimpse of the valley – you'll be standing 3,000ft (915m) above it – and perspectives on the major sights except El Capitan. When you see them up close they'll stagger you all the more.

From Glacier Point, head toward Yosemite Valley, back down Glacier Point Road (closed in winter) and north on Wawona Road. After you pass through a tunnel, park in the lot to the right and walk across the road to the vista point,

Insider Tip

El Capitan (left) and Cathedral Rocks from Valley View in Yosemite National Park

HAPPY TRAILS TO YOU

Yosemite's system of trails includes short and easy hikes and moderately difficult ones such as the 1.25-mile (2-kilometer) path to **Sentinel Dome** or the half loop (6.5mi/10km) or full loop (13mi/21km) around Yosemite Valley. The Four Mile Trail between **Yosemite Valley** and **Glacier Point** is a relatively short but strenuous climb, though it's easier in the reverse direction, most of which is downhill. If you're heading into the backcountry, stop by the Wilderness Center (it's near the valley visitor center; open May until October) for permits and information.

which has a head-on view of El Capitan. Then continue a short way to the parking lot for **Bridalveil Fall,** so called because the slightest wind moves the misty cascade a dozen feet or more from its center.

As you continue east, the name of the road you're on becomes Southside Drive. Stop along the way to enjoy the breathtaking views. Follow signs to Sentinel Bridge and make a left off Southside Drive to reach the Valley Visitor Center. Viewing the exhibits here, you'll learn how to distinguish which of Yosemite's features were formed by erosion and which by volcanic eruption. Ancient waters rose to about 9,000ft (2,745m), rounding the rock domes below this

Northern California

elevation. Massive upheavals from beneath the earth's crust – assisted much later by Ice-Age glaciers, which ever so slowly tore through weaker sections of granite – produced the gigantic slabs that jut willy-nilly out of the landscape.

Drop by the **Majestic Yosemite Hotel**, tucked away to the east of the visitor center. The deluxe lodge contains wide wood-beam ceilings, stone fireplaces and Indian artifacts. Head west from the Ahwahnee on Northside Drive to the parking lot for **Yosemite Falls** – actually three falls that appear almost as one when winter snows are melting. The easy hike to the base of the bottom section, Lower Falls, is a half-mile (0.8km) round trip. **El Capitan**, a bit farther west on Northside Drive, shoots nearly 3,600ft (1,100m) straight up from the valley floor. It's so sturdy that even glaciers, which over millennia ripped ever so slowly through the valley, couldn't reshape its facade.

From El Capitan you can head south on Wawona Road past the cutoff for Glacier Point to the giant sequoias of **Mariposa Grove**, of which two of the trees are among the largest in the world. During busy times, instead of driving you'll have to take a shuttle bus that leaves from the Wawona Store, near the Wawona Hotel.

It takes a full day just to breeze past Yosemite's highlights. To truly appreciate the natural setting, though, take your time and venture off the beaten path, if not for a back-country hike or a bike or horseback ride through the valley, at least to **Hetch Hetchy Reservoir** (►opposite) or verdant **Tuolumne Meadows** (Highway 120/Tioga Road east from Big Arch Rock Entrance; Tioga Road closed late fall to late spring).

Getting There
From the San Francisco area take I-580 and Highway 132 east. At Modesto head south on Highway 99. At Merced take Highway 140 east into the park. From the Los Angeles area take I-5 north and Highway 99 north to Fresno; from there, Highway 41 heads north into the park.

Winter in Yosemite enchants as much as summer does

TAKING A BREAK
Your splurge in Yosemite Valley is the **Majestic Yosemite Dining Room** (►98); take a peek at the high-ceilinged room even if you don't stop for a meal, or have a drink in the lobby bar. Fast food is available near the visitor center. There is also fine dining at the Wawona Hotel's main restaurant.

🚹 209 D5 ✉ Entrances: South Entrance (Highway 41), Arch Rock (Highway 140), Big Oak Flat (Highway 120, west side of park), Tioga Pass (Highway 120, east side of park; open only in summer)
☎ 209/372-0200; www.nps.gov/yose for park information; 801/559-5000 for lodging reservations; 800/436-7275 for campground reservations (301/722-1257 from outside the US or Canada); 209/372-1208 for bicycle rentals; 209/372-8348 for horseback riding
💵 $30/per car & week (annual pass for all NP $80)

INSIDER INFO

- Try to **avoid summer weekends**, when park visitation is highest. Summer weekdays aren't as bad. The weeks just before Memorial Day and after Labor Day are even less trafficked and the weather is mild.
- If you can, **spend at least one night in Yosemite**, either camping (facilities range from comfortable to primitive) or at the plush **Majestic Yosemite Hotel**, the historic Wawona Hotel or the casual Yosemite Lodge. You'll also find log cabins and safari-style tents.
- On the valley floor you can **rent a bicycle** (there are 12mi (19km) of mostly flat paths in the valley alone) or arrange **guided horseback rides**.
- You can drive to each sight in Yosemite Valley or **hop aboard the free shuttle bus** that serves each of them and Glacier Point.
- Visit the re-created **Indian Village of the Ahwahnee** (➤ 20).
- A 1-mile (1.6km) path (formerly a park road) in the Crane Flat section leads to **Tuolumne Grove**, a stand of 25 giant sequoias. The hike to the grove is easy, but the trip back is moderately strenuous (Highway 120 and Tioga Road).
- A huge valley was dammed to create the **Hetch Hetchy Reservoir**, which supplies San Francisco with much of its water. Steep granite cliffs surround most of the reservoir.

Northern California
⭐6 Wine Country

The chardonnays, zinfandels, cabernets and other vintages produced in Sonoma and Napa counties are among the finest in the US, and the setting – dense green in much of Sonoma, more arid and a little Mediterranean in quality in Napa – dazzles as much as the wines.

Even if you don't drink wine, the scenery alone is worth an excursion. Diversions that aren't wine-oriented include hiking, cycling, canoeing, primping at luxurious spas and dining at trend-setting restaurants. But wine is the main attraction, and the two counties contain more than 400 wineries. **Napa** and **Sonoma** are the names of towns, valleys and counties. All are north of San Francisco, with Sonoma County due west of Napa County.

Calistoga, at the northern edge of the fertile Napa Valley, is a compact area, less than a mile (1.6km) wide at some points. It contains America's foremost appellation (viticulture region) and makes an excellent base for visiting the wine-makers in the area, while Healdsburg provides a perfect base for expeditions, with shops and restaurants bordering the town plaza. From here, some first-rate wine tastings in the beautiful Alexander Valley, Dry Creek Valley and the Russian River Valley are within easy reach.

The Wineries and Other Attractions

Buena Vista Carneros Winery
Modern California winemaking started at what is now the Buena Vista Carneros Winery, founded in 1857 by Agoston Haraszthy, a Hungarian immigrant. You can peek into fascinating 19th-century caves on guided or self-guided tours. Specialties include pinot noirs and chardonnays.

➕ 206 C2 ✉ 18000 Old Winery Road, off E Napa Street, Sonoma
☎ 800/926-1266; www.buenavistawinery.com
🕐 Daily 10–5; food and wine pairing daily 11–3 🍷 $30

Ripe grapes in
Sonoma Valley

Benziger Family Winery

A tram travels into the vineyards as part of the tour at Benziger Family Winery, known for its fine chardonnays and cabernets. The unpretentious tour is a good one to take if winespeak intimidates you.

Insider Tip

✚ 206 C2 ✉ 1883 London Ranch Road, west off Arnold Drive, Glen Ellen
☎ 888/490-2739; www.benziger.com
🕐 Trips on the tractor trailer 11–3:30, every 30 min, except noon 💲 $40

Jack London State Historic Park

The park's museum contains London memorabilia. A 1-mile (1.6km) hike ends at the ruins of the dream house the author built but never occupied (it was destroyed by fire).

✚ 206 C2 ✉ 2400 London Ranch Road ☎ 707/938-5216; www.parks.ca.gov
🕐 Daily 10:30–5; closed Dec–Feb Tue & Wed 💲 $10

Kunde Family Estate

Homelike Kunde produces an excellent zinfandel from grapes grown on 19th-century vines.

✚ 206 C2
✉ 9825 Sonoma Highway (north from north end of Arnold Drive), Kenwood
☎ 707/833-5501; www.kunde.com 🕐 Daily 10:30–5; reservation only 💲 $20

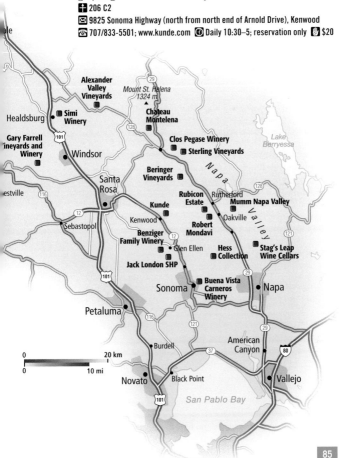

Northern California

Simi Winery
Founded in the 19th century but employing the latest viticulture technology, Simi Winery has built its reputation on producing excellent cabernets, chardonnays and sauvignon blancs. At the large winery, a good first stop in the Healdsburg area, you can pick up a copy of the free Russian River Wine Road map which will help you to locate the vineyards.

Insider Tip

The Domaine Carneros vineyard in Napa Valley

🚩 206 B2 ✉ 16275 Healdsburg Avenue (Dry Creek Road exit off US 101, left at second light), Healdsburg ☎ 707/433-6981; www.simiwinery.com
🕐 Daily 10–5; tours 11 and 2 💵 $15

Alexander Valley Vineyards
Just 6mi (9.6km) from Healdsburg Plaza, this family-owned winery is known for its cabernet sauvignon and its "sin zin."

🚩 206 B2 ✉ 44 Highway 128, Healdsburg
☎ 707/433-7209; www.avvwine.com 🕐 Daily 10–5 💵 $15

Gary Farrell Vineyards and Winery
Along Westside Road lie several other fine wine producers, including Rochioli, Porter Creek and, farthest west, Gary Farrell. The winemaker's specialty is pinot noir and a full-bodied, yet crisp, chardonnay.

🚩 206 B2 ✉ 10701 Westside Road, Healdsburg
☎ 707/473-2909; www.garyfarrellwines.com
🕐 Daily 10:30–4:30; tours by appointment 💵 $15

Chateau Montelena

The oldest sections of the main stone structure here date from 1882. The winery took first prize for its chardonnay at the 1976 blind tasting in France, but over the years its cabernets have garnered more awards.

➕ 206 C2 ✉ 1429 Tubbs Lane, off Highway 29, Calistoga
☎ 707/942-5105; www.montelena.com
🕐 Daily 9:30–4; numerous tours and tastings available 👆 $20

Clos Pegase

The postmodern architect Michael Graves designed Clos Pegase, where the top varietals are chardonnays, merlots and cabernets.

➕ 206 C2 ✉ 1060 Dunaweal Lane, Calistoga ☎ 707/942-4981; www.clos pegase.com 🕐 Daily 10:30–5; wine tastings at 10:30, noon and 1:30 👆 $20

Sterling Vineyards

An enclosed gondola whisks you to the hilltop head-quarters of Sterling Vineyards, whose specialties include merlots and chardonnays. Choose the "Sterling Silver Experience" to view the house's very own art collection as you taste their wines. Picasso, Chagall, Frasconi and Ansel Adams are all represented.

Insider Tip

➕ 206 C2 ✉ 1111 Dunaweal Lane, Calistoga
☎ 707/942-3345; www.sterlingvineyards.com
🕐 Mon–Fri 10:30–4:30, Sat, Sun 10–5; self-guided tours only 👆 $28

Beringer Vineyard

Elegant gables, turrets and ornate carvings set a vaguely Gothic tone at the Beringer Vineyards, which were founded in 1876. The tours of this winery, best known for its chardonnays, cabernets and merlots, include the tunnels Chinese laborers dug into the side of Spring Mountain.

➕ 206 C2 ✉ 2000 Main Street, St. Helena ☎ 707/963-8989; www.beringer.com
🕐 June–Oct 10–6; Nov–May 10–5; numerous tours and tastings available 👆 $40

Culinary Institute of America

Greystone, the Institute's West Coast campus, has a shop, a restaurant and a corkscrew display with some technologically

Insider Tip

INSIDER INFO

You can take a **mud bath** at one of **Calistoga's spas**. Some folks swear by the usual regimen (the cost runs to about $100): Shower, 10 minutes in the mud, a soak in a hot mineral bath, some time in the steam room, a blanket wrap and a massage. The "mud" is actually volcanic ash, and in most spas is mixed with peat. It's heated to boiling point after each use to keep things sanitary. The purists at **Indian Springs** (1712 Lincoln Avenue; tel: 707/942-4917; www.indianspringscalistoga.com) use 100 percent volcanic ash. The **Mount View Spa** (1457 Lincoln Avenue; tel: 707/942-5789; www.indianspringscalistoga.com) and **Health Spa Napa Valley** (1030 Main Street, St. Helena; tel: 707/967-8800; www.napavalleyspa.com), two upscale establishments, offer mudless, state-of-the-art treatments.

EXCURSIONS ALOFT AND EARTHBOUND

- **Adventures Aloft** (tel: 800/944-4408; www.nvaloft.com) conducts sunrise balloon rides in the Napa Valley.
- **Sonoma Thunder** (tel: 707/829-9850; www.balloontours.com) does the same in the Sonoma Valley. Rates run to around $225 per person, which includes breakfast (most flights take place in the early morning).
- **Triple Creek Horse Outfit** (tel: 707/887-8700) leads guided horseback rides through the state parks in Sonoma and Napa valleys.
- **Getaway Adventures** (tel: 800/499-2453; www.getawayadventures.com) rents bikes and leads hiking, cycling, sea-kayaking and canoe trips in Napa and Sonoma. Some bike trips include vineyard tours.

amazing specimens. Cooking demonstrations in combination with a wine tasting (book ahead!) take place at 1:30 at the weekends.

🔢 206 C2 ✉ 2555 Main Street, St. Helena
☎ 707/967-1100; www.ciachef.edu/california

Frog's Leap

This vineyard complete with its distinctive red barn from 1884 uses traditional growing techniques to produce a selection of organic wines.

🔢 206 C2 ✉ 8815 Conn Creej Road, Rutherford
☎ 707/963-4704; www.frogsleap.com
🕐 Daily 10–4; tours Mon–Fri at 10:30 and 2:30 💵 $20

Mumm Napa Valley

Winemaking photographs by Ansel Adams (➤ 22), a well-conceived tour and the chance to sip effervescent sparkling wines make Mumm Napa Valley a worthy stop. Guests can sample "flights" (three glasses) of a recent vintage in the tasting salon.

🔢 206 C2 ✉ 8445 Silverado Trail, Rutherford
☎ 800/686-6272; http://mummnapa.com
🕐 Daily 10–4:45; tours at 10, 11, 1 and 3 💵 $25

Robert Mondavi

You'll get the best overview of the winemaking process and taste some superb wines at Robert Mondavi, the winery of the man who created fumé blanc. Mondavi is often crowded in summer.

🔢 206 C2 ✉ 7801 St. Helena Highway, Oakville
☎ 888/766-6328; www.robertmondaviwinery.com
🕐 Daily 10–5; tour times vary 💵 $30

Hess Collection

At the Hess Collection, a mountain hideaway, top-notch modern art (Bacon, Stella and others) vies for attention with valley views and full-bodied cabernets and chardonnays.

🔢 206 C2 ✉ 4411 Redwood Road, west of Highway 29, Napa
☎ 707/255-1144; www.hesscollection.com
🕐 Daily 10–5:30; tour times vary 💵 $25

For a very special experience, embark on a hot air balloon adventure over the endless grapevines of Sonoma County

INSIDER INFO

- To get to the **Napa Valley** from San Francisco, take US 101 north to Highway 37, east to Highway 121, east to Highway 29, then continue north.
- Wineries along the **Silverado Trail** tend to be less busy than their counterparts along the more or less parallel Highway 29.

- To get to the **Sonoma Valley**, take US 101 north to Highway 37, east to Highway 121, north to Highway 12, then continue north.
- North of San Francisco off US 101 are the **Alexander Valley** (take the Healdsburg exit) and the **Russian River Valley** (take the River Road exit and head west).
- Most wineries in Napa and some in Sonoma **charge tasting fees** ($10 or more), which are almost always deducted from purchases.
- In summer **it's best to make tour reservations** because some wineries limit the number of participants.
- If you're driving, keep in mind that a **blood-alcohol level of over .08%** qualifies you as legally drunk. Though results vary from individual to individual, the average person reaches that level drinking more than one 4oz (118ml) glass of wine.
- Take at least one winery tour. **Robert Mondavi**, **Beringer** and **Simi** provide a good overview of the winemaking process.

③⑥ Sonoma Coast & Mendocino

A cross-section of Northern California's wildlife and vegetation – whales, sea lions, ospreys, wildflowers and redwoods – inhabits the coastline near Highway 1 as it slithers north through Sonoma and Mendocino counties. The attractions in this land of rock-strewn beaches and fishing and former logging towns are simple yet simply delightful, among them 19th-century Point Arena Lighthouse and the Mendocino Coast Botanical Gardens.

Only Alfred Hitchcock could have turned the placid village of **Bodega**, just off Highway 1 along Highway 12, and the equally peaceable fishing town of **Bodega Bay**, on Highway 1 itself, into the terror-filled setting for *The Birds* – the church and schoolhouse buildings in Bodega still stand. The remodeled bar and eating areas at the **Tides Wharf Restaurant** (835 Highway 1; tel: 707/875-3652) aren't as atmospheric as they were when Hitchcock filmed on the site, but the fish dishes are tasty. Head north to the **Terrapin Creek Cafe** (1580 Eastshore Road/Highway 1; tel: 707/875-2700) for a California menu with international influences.

🐾 Sea Lions and Sea Views
Sea lions loll on windswept **Goat Rock Beach**, 10mi (16km) north of Bodega Bay in Jenner. Trappers in search of sea otters established **Fort Ross** (▶ 20), 9mi (14km) beyond that. During blooming season (usually May), pink blossoms brighten nearby **Kruse Rhododendron State Reserve** (www. parks.ca.gov). Here's how Jack London described this part of the coast in *The Human Drift*: "Especially in the Fort Ross section did we find the roads thrilling, while all the way along we followed the sea. At every stream, the road skirted dizzy cliff-edges, dived down into lush growths of forest and ferns and climbed out along the cliff-edges again."

The Pacific coast by Navarro Point in Mendocino County

INSIDER INFO

- On the first day of a two- or three-day excursion from San Francisco you could **drive up the Sonoma Coast**, stopping at a few sights before ending up in Mendocino.
- You can reach Highway 1 at Bodega Bay by driving west from US 101 in Santa Rosa on Highway 12. The **quickest way to Mendocino** from San Francisco is via US 101 north to Cloverdale, west on Highway 128 and then north on Highway 1. In both cases the longer but more scenic option is to take Highway 1 the entire way.

About 58mi (93km) north of Fort Ross is **Point Arena Lighthouse** for dizzying views of crashing waves as they spout through a rocky blowhole. The attractive town of Point Arena itself is worth a look. Just 20mi (32km) beyond lies the tiny down-home **Elk**, a good pit stop with upscale shops and cafés.

Artists flocked to **Mendocino**, about 13mi (21km) north of Elk, in the 1950s and 1960s. The town's headlands setting, restaurants and B&Bs make it a superlative place to stop. Explore its shops and museums, walk the headlands and pay a visit to the **Mendocino Coast Botanical Gardens**, whose mild maritime climate supports an astonishing array of plant life (there's also a good café here). A beach and miles of dunes are among the draws at **MacKerricher State Park**.

The grape-growing region due east of Mendocino, amid the redwoods along Highway 128, has become known for chardonnay, pinot noir and sparkling wines; you'll often have the tasting rooms all to yourself. **Husch** (4400 Highway 128, Philo; tel: 800/554-8724;www.husch vineyards.com) and the **Roederer Estate** (4501 Highway 128, Philo; tel: 707/895-2288; www.roedererestate.com) are good first stops.

TAKING A BREAK

The best of several fine Mendocino restaurants is **Café Beaujolais** (►99), although the clifftops are usually crowded the views and food make for a memorable meal.

✚ 206 B2/3

Point Arena Lighthouse
✉ 45500 Lighthouse Road, Mendocino Coast off Highway 1
☎ 707/882-2777; www.pointarenalighthouse.com ◷ Daily 10–3:30 💵 $7.50

Botanical Gardens
✉ 18220 N Highway 1, Fort Bragg ☎ 707/964-4352; www.gardenbythesea.org
◷ Mar–Oct daily 9–5; Nov–Feb 9–4 💵 $14

MacKerricher State Park
✉ Highway 1, north of Fort Bragg
☎ 707/964-964-9112; www.parks.ca.gov/?page_id=436
◷ Call ahead for opening hours 💵 Free

③⑦ Sacramento & the Gold Country

After gold was discovered in the Sierra foothills, California's politicians moved the state capital to Sacramento. As always, they went where the money went – and there was plenty of it. Sacramento's city yields clues about Gold Rush life, but to see real mines and former mining towns, venture east into the Gold Country.

Sacramento

Sacramento's finest attraction, the 🎌 **California State Railroad Museum** exhibits 150 years of railroad cars and locomotives. The museum is the highlight of slightly too manicured Old Town Sacramento, where wooden sidewalks, restored buildings and old-fashioned signage recall the Gold Rush.

Gold, silver and commerce financed the Corinthian-style State Capitol (10th and L streets) with its rotunda and fine gardens. **Sutter's Fort State Historic Park** and the on-site **State Indian Museum** survey local history, as does the **California Museum**.

A historic train at Sacramento's California State Railroad Museum

Best of the Gold Country

From Sacramento you can explore the Gold Country. I-80 east connects with Highway 49, running north–south through the region. North of the interstate on Highway 49, 60mi (97km) from Sacramento, is Nevada City, whose walkable historic district has many Gold Rush buildings. North of town is **Malakoff Diggins State Historic Park** (▶21).

Many mines dried up quickly, but the **Empire Mine,** now in **Empire Mine State Historic Park**, whose lode yielded nearly 6 million ounces (170 million grams) of gold, remained open until the 1950s. Highway 49 winds south for 24mi (38km) from Grass Valley back to I-80 and the town of Auburn. Just 18mi (29km) farther south lies **Marshall Gold Discovery State Historic Park**. James Marshall (▶17) set off the Gold Rush when he spotted a nugget here in 1848.

Hangtown

🏴 **Placerville,** south of Coloma on Highway 49 and 44mi (70km) east of Sacramento on US 50, was known during Gold Rush days as Hangtown, a nod to its townsfolk's preferred method for dispensing justice. The self-guided tour of Hangtown's **Gold Bug Mine**, a rock-walled horizontal mine, shows the conditions miners experienced.

Saloons, a Wells Fargo express office and other period buildings at **Columbia State Historic Park**, 70mi (113km) south of Placerville, re-create Gold Rush life.

TAKING A BREAK

Try **Paragary's** (1401 28th Street; tel: 916/457-5737, $$) for happy hour or dinner.

➕ 207 D2

Sacramento Visitor Center
➕ 1002 2nd Street, Old Sacramento
☎ 916/442-7644; www.
visitsacramento.com 🕐 Daily 10–5

California State Railroad Museum
✉ 125 I Street ☎ 916/445-6645;
www.csrmf.org 🕐 Daily 10–5
✋ $9

Sutter's Fort State Historic Park
✉ 2701 L Street ☎ 916/445-4422;
www.parks.ca.gov/?page_id=485
🕐 Daily 10–5 ✋ $5

California Museum
✉ 1020 O Street ☎ 916/653-7524;
www.californiamuseum.org
🕐 Tue–Sat 10–5, Sun noon–5 ✋ $9

Empire Mine State Historic Park
✉ 10791 E Empire Street, south from Highway 49, Grass Valley
☎ 530/273-8522; www.parks.ca.
gov/?page_id=499
🕐 Daily 10–5 ✋ $7

Marshall Gold Discovery State Historic Park
✉ 310 Back Street, Highway 49, Coloma ☎ 530/622-3470;
www.parks.ca.gov/?page_id=484
🕐 Daily. Park: late Mai to early Sep 8–8, until 5 rest of year; Museum: Nov–March 9–4, until 5 rest of year
✋ $8

Gold Bug Mine
✉ From Highway 49 take US 50 east and Bedford Avenue north, Placerville
☎ 530/642-5207;
www.goldbugpark.org
🕐 Apr–Oct daily 10–4;
Nov–Mar Sat, Sun 12–4
✋ $5

Columbia State Historic Park
➕ 207 D1
✉ 11255 Jackson Street, off Hwy 49, Columbia
☎ 209/588-9128;
www.parks.ca.gov/?page_id=552
🕐 Daily 10–4
✋ Free

INSIDER INFO

- Highway 49 **twists and turns** and the going can sometimes be slow.
- **If you've only a day** get a feel for the region by touring Nevada City, Grass Valley, Coloma and Placerville. Alternatively, spend the night in Sutter Creek and explore its downtown before continuing southward.
- Don't miss **Calaveras Big Trees State Park**, off Highway 4 near Arnold.

Insider Tip

At Your Leisure

38 Redwood Country

Northern California's tallest red-woods grow in Mendocino County and points north. The 31-mile (50km) **Avenue of the Giants** (Highway 254) snakes north from US 101 from north of Garberville to Pepperwood, where it rejoins US 101. (Garberville is just over 200mi (320km) north of San Francisco.) Along the avenue, north of Weott, is **Humboldt Redwoods State Park**, where you can tour redwood groves.

A few interesting towns north of the park off US 101 are **Ferndale**, **Eureka** (the best town to stay over-night) and **Arcata**, all of whose downtown historic districts (follow highway signs) contain Victorian-era homes. Still farther north, past

Trinidad, is Patrick's Point State Park, where the ocean views are superb.

Insider Tip

About 17mi (27km) beyond **Patrick's Point** is the entrance to **Redwood National and State Parks**. Stop by the Thomas H. Kuchel Visitor Center (US 101, south of Orick; tel: 707/465-7765) for direc-tions to Tall Trees Grove and the redwoods within Lady Bird Johnson Grove. **Crescent City**, about 40mi (64km) north of Orick, is the last big town before the Oregon border. If you get up this far, check out **Battery Point Lighthouse**, which was completed in 1856.

Humboldt Redwoods State Park

➕ 206 B4 ☎ 707/946-2409; www.parks.ca. gov/?page_id=425 ⚙ Apr–Oct daily 9–5; Nov–Mar 10–4 ✋ Free

Patrick's Point State Park

➕ 206 B2 ☎ 707/677-3570; http://www.parks. ca.gov/?page_id=417 ⚙ Call for opening times ✋ Free

Redwood National and State Parks

➕ 206 B5 ☎ 707/464-6101; www.nps.gov/redw) ⚙ Park: all year daily. Crescent City & Thomas H Kuchel Visitor Center: 9–5, until 4 in winter ✋ Free

Battery Point Lighthouse

➕ 206 C5
✉ Battery Point Island, end of A Street
☎ 707/464-3089; www.delnortehistory.org/ lighthouse
⚙ Apr–Sep daily 10–4; Oct–Mar Sat, Sun 10–4 (tides permitting, call ahead) ✋ $3

39 Shasta Cascade

In the far north of California, **Mount Shasta** dominates the terrain be-tween the coastal redwoods and the Cascade Range. With its crisp,

Avenue of the Giants Redwoods in Humboldt Redwoods State Park

Pine trees surround the gigantic Lake Tahoe, a paradise for fans of outdoor sports

clear air and easy to strenuous trails, Mount Shasta is perfect for hikes of a day or longer. The upper slopes of the 14,162ft (4,317m) peak remain snow-covered year-round. Call **Mount Shasta Visitors Bureau** (tel: 530/926-4865, http:// visitmtshasta.com) for hiking, camping and information.

South of Mount Shasta off I-5 are the **Lake Shasta Caverns**, well worth touring. Off I-5 at the lake's southwestern tip is **Shasta Dam** (tel: 530/275-4463, free). You can tour the dam, one of the largest in the US (times vary, call ahead).

An interesting stop in **Weaverville**, 47mi (75km) west of Redding, is the ornate **Joss House** (Oregon and Main streets; tel: 530/623-5284), a Taoist temple completed by Chinese immigrants in 1874 (Thu–Sun 10–5).

Lassen Volcanic National Park, 49mi (79km) east of Red Bluff (take Highway 36 east to Highway 89 north), contains bubbling sulfuric hot springs, cinder cones, lava beds and boiling mud pots. The strenuous Lassen Peak Hike yields spectacular views of the lakes and trees and beyond to Mount Shasta. The easier Bumpass Hell Trail leads to areas of geothermal activity.
➕ 207 D4 ✉ I-5 ☎ 530/365-7500 or 800/326-6944 for tourist information about the Shasta Cascade area; www.nps.gov; www.parks.ca.gov

Lake Shasta Caverns
➕ 206 C4
✉ 20359 Shasta Caverns Road, Lakehead
☎ 530/238-2341 or 800/795-2283; http://lakeshastacaverns.com
🕐 Apr, May and Sept daily 9–3 (tours every hr); late May to early Sep 9–4 (tours every 30 min); Oct–Mar tours 10, 12 and 2 💲$24

Lassen Volcanic National Park
➕ 207 D3 ☎ 530/595-4480; www.nps.gov/lavo/index.htm
🕐 Park: all year daily. Visitor center: April–Oct daily 9–5; closed Dec–March and Mon, Tue in Nov
💲$20/per car & week (annual pass for all NP $80)

Northern California

40 Lake Tahoe

The border between California and Nevada slices right through Lake Tahoe, the largest alpine body of water in North America. Hikers, swimmers and sightseers flock to the lakeside beaches and nearby mountains in summer, and when the weather turns cold, skiers slalom down the slopes at what has long been California's premier ski region. Squaw Valley, near Tahoe's west shore, hosted the 1960 Winter Olympics. All year round, millions eschew the scenic beauty and head straight into the Nevada-side gambling casinos.

To get the lay of the land, ride the Gondola at **Heavenly** (Ski Run Boulevard, off US 50, South Lake Tahoe; tel: 800/220-1593 or 775/586-7000; www.skiheavenly.com). The whole Tahoe basin unfolds before you as the gondola climbs the slopes of **Heavenly Ski Resort** to 9,123ft (2,780m) above sea level; at the top you can dine or hike.

You can drive the lake's 72-mile (116km) circumference in a day, though in summer, when traffic's heavy, it's generally a better strategy to explore just a short section, such as the **Pope-Baldwin Recreation Area** and **Emerald Bay**, both along Highway 89 on the south side. If you head to delightful Emerald Bay, visit **Vikingsholm** (www.vikingsholm.org), a rustic estate built in the 1920s. Or you could instead drive north, to **Sand Harbor Beach** (Highway 28) or **Tahoe City** (Highway 89).

🔲 207 E2

✉ US 50 (South Lake Tahoe and Nevada-side casinos); Highway 89 (Tahoe City and lake's western and northern shores)

☎ 530/541-5255 (south), 775/588-4591 (Nevada) and 530/581-6900 (north, visitor and lodging information); www.visiting laketahoe.com

41 Mono Lake

Crusty, coral-like tufa juts out of this beautiful lake, 13mi (21km) east of Yosemite National Park. Take the South Tufa Trail (Highway 120, 5mi (8km) east of US 395) to see the most dramatic spires and some of the millions (literally) of migratory birds that flock here. The ghost town of **Bodie** (▶21) is 31mi (50km) northeast of **Lee Vining.**

🔲 209 E5 ✉ Scenic Area Visitor Center, US 395, Lee Vining ☎ 760/647-3044; www.monolake.org 🕐 Daily 8–5

The lunar landscape of Mono Lake's tufa

Where to...
Stay

Prices
Expect to pay per double room, per night (excluding tax)
$ under $100   **$$** $100–$175   **$$$** over $175

SONOMA COAST & MENDOCINO

Jenner Inn & Cottages $$–$$$
The gorgeous Sonoma Coast town of Jenner is one of those settings where the tribulations of travel recede in the face of sweeping vistas and terrain that seems to tumble into the sea. A fitting place to enjoy the scenery and set out for coastal hikes, winery visits and other activities, is this lodging with rooms, suites and cottages, some set amid the trees, others along the waterfront. Some rooms have fireplaces, spas, saunas and kitchens, and to enhance the getting-away-from-it all ambiance, only a few rooms have phones or a TV.
✚ 206 B2 ✉ 10400 Coast Route 1, Box 69, Jenner, CA 95450
☎ 7707/865-2377 or 800/732-2377; www.jennerinn.com

MacCallum House Inn $$–$$$
As you stroll around Mendocino, you're almost sure to notice MacCallum House Inn. Built in 1882, it is a beautifully restored Victorian house with a gingerbread trim. A total of 19 rooms in three different accommodations – the main house, seven cottages and the Barn – are sympathetically furnished with antiques. Some rooms have decks, fireplaces and kitchenettes, and many have water or garden views. The hotel also has a good restaurant and café-bar.
✚ 206 B3 ✉ 45020 Albion Street, Box 206, Mendocino, CA 95460 ☎ 707/937-0289 or 800/609-0492; www.maccallumhouse.com

Stanford Inn by the Sea & Spa $$$
If you're an active – and upscale – traveler, you'll find this woodsy yet stylish lodge a great choice; you can even rent a canoe here for a trip down the nearby Big River. Overlooking the river and ocean, just south of town off Highway 1, the two-story inn has roomy accommodations with cozy fireplaces and decks that allow you to drink in the views. After a day in the outdoors, return for wine and hors d'oeuvres served by the fire in the lounge, and wake up the next morning to a big organic vegetarian breakfast, all included in the rates.
✚ 206 B3 ✉ Coast Highway and 44850 Comptche-Ukiah Road, Box 487, Mendocino, CA 95460 ☎ 707/937-5615 or 800/331-8884; www.stanfordinn.com

WINE COUNTRY

Comfort Inn Calistoga $$$
This no-frills motel on the edge of Calistoga offers reliable accommodations for the price. The rooms have the look you might expect, but they're comfortable and you can unwind from wine touring in the steam room, a small heated pool, or the hot tub. Rates include a modest Continental breakfast.
✚ 206 C2 ✉ 1865 Lincoln Avenue, Calistoga, CA 94515 ☎ 707/942-9400 or 800/652-5130; www.comfortinncalistoga.com

Gaige House Inn $$$
Though this bed-and-breakfast is housed in an 1890 Italianate Queen Anne building, some of the sunny

rooms inside are decorated with distinctive Southeast Asian touches. You can stretch out in the hammock on the backyard deck overlooking Calabazas Creek, or sip premium complimentary wines in the book-lined living room in the evenings. Some rooms have cozy fireplaces, spacious private decks and whirl-pool baths or clawfoot tubs. Service is solicitous, a concierge is on hand to answer any queries and the full breakfasts are top quality.

✚ 206 C2 ✉ 13540 Arnold Drive, Glen Ellen, CA 95442 ☎ 707/935-0237 or 800/935-0237; www.gaige.com

Villagio Inn & Spa $$$

For a Wine Country splurge, check into this luxury resort in the lower Napa Valley. With prices like these (rooms start at around $350 per night), pampering is the order of the day, and the amenities include a bottle of wine upon arrival, a champagne breakfast buffet, and afternoon tea. The spa is worth a visit whether you stay here or not.

Insider Tip

✚ 206 C2 ✉ 6481 Washington Street, Yountville, CA 94599 ☎ 707/944-8877 or 800/351-1133; www.villagio.com

SACRAMENTO & GOLD COUNTRY

Amber House Bed & Breakfast $$$

The architectural styles of the two homes that form this charming inn near the State Capitol are Craftsman to Dutch Colonial, but what is consistent here, is the attention to detail. The rooms are all named for famous artists and writers and decorated accordingly. If you're in a romantic mood, reserve the Lord Byron room; for something more cozy the Brahms room might be the ticket (only the jolly Dickinson room goes against the biographical grain). The ensuite bathrooms are as grand as the rooms.

✚ 206 C2 ✉ 1315 22nd Street, Sacramento, CA 95816 ☎ 916/444-8085 or 800/755-6526; www.amberhouse.com

Murphys Historic Hotel and Lodge $–$$

With its historic section and saloon, this hotel offers a brush with the gold rush but also convenient access to more current pastimes, such as shopping for art and antiques (though you can still pan for gold nearby if you wish). The hotel is also a good anchor for a Sierra Foothills winery tour: tasting rooms for the fine Black Sheep, Milliaire and Stevenot wineries are nearby. The nine rooms in the historic section have period antiques and share baths; past guests include Mark Twain and the bandit Black Bart. The rooms in the modern section all have private baths and more contemporary furnishings.

Insider Tip

✚ 206 C2 ✉ 457 Main Street, Murphys, CA 95247 ☎ 209/728-3444 or 800/532-7684; www.murphyshotel.com

YOSEMITE

Majestic Yosemite $$$

Opened in 1927, the Ahwahnee is one of the grandest hotels of America's national park system. The public rooms have enormous fireplaces and memorable views of the park; a highlight is afternoon tea in the Great Lounge. Guest rooms are on the small side, but tastefully decorated, with Native American accents. Twenty-four cottages are scattered in nearby woods.

✚ 209 D5 ✉ Ahwahnee Drive, Yosemite National Park, CA 95389 ☎ 888/413-8869; www.yosemitepark.com/the-ahwnee.aspx

Best Western Yosemite Gateway Inn $

If you can't stay within the National Park, try this well-run motel on a woodsy hillside 15mi (24km) from the park's southern entrance. The rooms are pleasing if nondescript. Some have mountain views, balconies or patios, and some have kitchens. The units with two bedrooms and a kitchen are a great bargain for families (six-person maximum). There is a garden, heated indoor and outdoor pool, a hot tub, an exercise room and a coin-operated laundry.

🏨 209 D4 ✉ 40530 Highway 41, Oakhurst, CA 93644 ☎ 559/683-2378 or 888/256-8042; www.yosemitegatewayinn.com

Yosemite Valley Lodge & Half Dome Village $$$

The lovely Yosemite Lodge has 249 motel-like rooms, as well as restaurants, a bar and an Olympic-size pool, while rustic Curry Village has 161 cabins with and without baths, 319 canvas-walled tent cabins with shared baths, 18 motel rooms and eating facilities. There is no air-conditioning. Reservations are often easier to obtain here than at the Majestic, but you'll still need to reserve well in advance.

🏨 209 D5 ✉ Northside and Southside drives, Yosemite National Park, CA 95389
☎ 888/413-8869 (reservation number for all hotels in Yosemite); www.travelyosemite.com/lodging/yosemite-valley-lodge/, www.travelyosemite.com/lodging/half-dome-village/

Aston Lakeland Village Resort $$–$$$

This modern complex rests amid secluded forested grounds with its own stretch of sandy beach on the southern shores of Lake Tahoe. Nearby are Nevada casinos and ski resorts (free shuttles). Accommodations range from hotel-type rooms to four-bedroom town-houses with sleeping lofts, but most units come with kitchens, fireplaces and balconies. Two pools, two hot tubs, a sauna, two tennis courts, and beach volleyball in the summer, are among the facilities.

🏨 207 E2 ✉ 3535 Lake Tahoe Boulevard, South Lake Tahoe, CA 96150
☎ 800/530/544-1685 or 800/822-5969; www.astonlakelandvillage.com

Where to...
Eat and Drink

Prices
Expect to pay per person for a meal, excluding drinks and service:
$ under $15 $$ $15–$25 $$$ over $25

Café Beaujolais $$–$$$

Mendocino's best-known restaurant fits the local look: rustic and relaxed. It is set in a Victorian farmhouse surrounded by gardens. But Café Beaujolais' reputation for pure, fresh ingredients and innovative California country cooking, accented by cuisines from around the world, extends far beyond the Mendocino-Sonoma region. While the menu changes seasonally, you can count on locally grown organic produce, freshly caught seafood, meat from free-range animals and breads baked on the premises. An excellent wine list complements the menu.

🏨 206 B3 ✉ 961 Ukiah Street, Mendocino
☎ 707/937-5614; www.cafebeaujolais.com
🕐 Lunch Wed–Sun 11:30–2:30; dinner daily from 5:30

Mendo Bistro $$–$$$

This popular Fort Bragg spot features New American fare made with local, seasonal ingredients. Chef and owner Nicholas Petti and his wife, Jaimi, earn points for

Northern California

winning hospitality, and the prices are reasonable. Menu items include a variety of house-made pasta, a selection of meat and chicken from sustainable ranches (you can select the preparation and sauce), and fresh fish, including mussels and oysters on the half shell.

🞧 206 B3 ✉ 301 North Main Street, 2nd floor, Fort Bragg ☎ 707/964-4974; www.mendobistro.com 🕐 Daily 5–9

WINE COUNTRY

Bistrot Don Giovanni $$–$$$

This casual restaurant, situated on the plaza in the heart of Healdsburg, is building a big reputation for home-style California cooking. The owner-chef, Ralph Tingle, makes good use of Sonoma lamb and local produce. Service is welcoming, and the bar is a popular gathering place for Wine Country residents. The outdoor patio is pleasant on warm evenings.

🞧 206 C2 ✉ 4110 Howard Lane, Napa ☎ 707/224-3300; http://bistrodongiovanni.com 🕐 Sun–Thu 11:30–9:30, Fri, Sat until 10

Downtown Bakery $–$$

Heavenly selections of breakfast treats with freshly baked breads, tasty pastries and sinfully delicious cakes. Mouth-watering sandwiches and focaccia pizzas served at lunchtime.

🞧 206 B2 ✉ 308 A Center Street, Healdsburg ☎ 707/431-2719; http://downtownbakery.net 🕐 Mon–Fri 6–5:30, Sat 7:30–5, Sun 7–4

The French Laundry $$$

Worth every penny of its very expensive price tag, Thomas Keller's French-American Yountville establishment serves a nine-course chef's tasting menu or a nine-course vegetarian tasting menu. Both change daily based on the season's produce, but highlights may include glazed white quail with smoked *foie gras* essence, savoy cabbage and Maine lobster tail served with buckwheat spatzle

(soft egg noodles) and red beet vinaigrette. Reservations are accepted two months in advance.

🞧 206 C2 ✉ 6640 Washington Street, Yountville ☎ 707/944-2380; www.frenchlaundry.com 🕐 Lunch Fri–Sun 11–1; dinner daily 5:30–9:15

The Girl & the Fig $$–$$$

Occupying precious real estate, off the charming Sonoma Plaza, this welcoming restaurant serves rustic Provençal fare in the heart of the Wine Country. From the *charcuterie* platter and the *fromage* to the *croques monsieur* and the shellfish and saffron stew, the ingredients are fresh, local and seasonal, and the wine list focuses on Rhone-style California wines. Enjoy the food, while seated on the terrace.

🞧 206 C2 ✉ 110 W. Spain Street, Sonoma ☎ 707/938-3634; www.thegirlandthefig.com 🕐 Mon–Thu 11:30–10, Fri, Sat 11–11, Sun 10–10

Pizzeria Tra Vigne $$–$$$

Many Napa Valley habitués consider Tra Vigne the quintessential Wine Country restaurant. The service is friendly and efficient. The surrounding landscape is superb (ask for a seat on the outdoor terrace when you make your reservation), as is the food: fresh pasta, grilled meats and seafood. The inspired wine list, however, concentrates on local vintages. Inside, in the high-ceilinged dining room, there's an attractive bar; try one of the house-made grappas.

🞧 206 C2 ✉ 1016 Main Street, St. Helena ☎ 707/963-4444; www.pizzeriatravigne.com 🕐 Sun–Thu 11:30–9

SACRAMENTO & GOLD COUNTRY

Rio City Café $$

Located on the bank of the Sacramento River in Old Town, Rio City Café serves reliably good Californian cuisine with global (mainly Asian, Southwestern, Italian) influences. The varied menu includes jambalaya, ahi nachos, pasta dishes, fresh fish and burgers. It's a fun and lively atmosphere; opt for outdoor seating by the river on a warm summer evening, or a table by the fireplace in winter.

➕ 206 C2
✉ 1110 Front Street, Sacramento
☎ 916/442-8226; www.riocitycafe.com
🕐 Mon–Thu 11–9, Fri 11–10, Sat 10–10, Sun 10–9

YOSEMITE NATIONAL PARK

The Majestic Yosemite Dining Room $$–$$$

The Majestic Yosemite Dining Room, the main restaurant of Majestic Yosemite Hotel doesn't break any culinary ground but the well-prepared American dishes, such as grilled steaks and lightly sauced fish, are well suited to the classic lodge surroundings. As you admire the vaulted ceiling that soars 34ft (10m) above, the sparkling chandeliers and the tables set with linen and china, you'll hardly believe that, shortly before, you were out hiking in jeans – which, by the way, violate the dress code here, along with shorts and sneakers. Try to make your dinner reservations well in advance. Special Christmas and New Year's feasts are so popular that you have to enter a lottery to be chosen. Reservations are accepted 60 days in advance.

➕ 209 D5
✉ Ahwahnee Road, Yosemite National Park
☎ 209/372-1489; www.travelyosemite.com/lodging/dining/the-majestic-yosemite-hotel
🕐 Mon–Sat breakfast 7–10, lunch 11:30–2, Sunday brunch 7–2, daily dinner 5:30–9

Erna's Elderberry House & Restaurant $$–$$$

One of the state's finest restaurants, Erna's Elderberry House is well worth a drive down from Yosemite; it's in the town of Oakhurst, about 15mi (24km) south of the park's southern entrance via Highway 41.

Erna's offers a French-California menu that changes daily to reflect the freshest ingredients. The indoor dining areas have attractive contemporary touches.

➕ 209 D4 ✉ 48688 Victoria Lane, Oakhurst
☎ 559/683-6800; www.elderberryhouse.com
🕐 Dinner daily 5:30–8:30; Sunday brunch 11–1. Closed first 3 weeks Jan

Mountain Room Restaurant $$–$$$

The best restaurant in Yosemite Lodge at the Falls (▶ 93), open for dinner only, serves up Continental cuisine – steak, seafood and pasta – along with some incredible views of Yosemite Falls. You can also opt for the less formal Mountain Room Lounge, where appetizers are served, or have a casual breakfast, lunch or dinner at the food court.

➕ 209 D5 ✉ Off Northside Drive, Yosemite National Park ☎ 209/372-1274; www.yosemitepark.com/dining_mountainroom.aspx
🕐 Daily 5:30–9

LAKE TAHOE

Sunnyside Restaurant & Lodge $$–$$$

This spot draws masses of visitors, summer and winter, with its stunning location, set on the edge of Lake Tahoe. Steaks are the main feature on the menu in the more upscale dining room, while the casual lakeside grill features starters, such as crispy zucchini (courgette) sticks and fried calamari, and there are plenty of burgers, sandwiches, and salads to choose from, on the mains. Don't miss the famous hula pie (chocolate cookie pie crust, macadamia nut ice cream, hot fudge, whipped cream and chopped macadamia nuts). Children are welcome and dress is casual.

➕ 207 E2
✉ 1850 W Lake Boulevard, West Shore
☎ 530/583-7200; www.sunnysidetahoe.com
🕐 Mountain Grill: Daily 11–9; Lakeside Room: 5–9

Where to...
Shop

Arts and crafts, wines, gourmet foods and antiques are among shopping highlights of the region.

MENDOCINO

It's easy to wander Mendocino's compact streets and window shop for art, crafts and handmade jewelry. At the **Mendocino Art Center** (45200 Little Lake Street; tel: 707/937-5818; www.mendocinoartcenter. org), shows highlight works of local artists.

SONOMA

On the main plaza in Sonoma, you'll find several specialty food shops and bakeries, including the **Sonoma Cheese Factory** (2 Spain Street; tel: 707/996-1931; www. sonomacheesefactory.com), which carries stocks of local cheeses.

SACRAMENTO

Restored Old Sacramento has a number of arts and crafts shops tucked among the historic riverfront buildings. At the **Huntington, Hopkins & Co. Store** (113 I Street; tel: 916/323-7234) you can shop for Victorian-era items in a replica mid-19th-century hardware store.

WINE COUNTRY

You can buy wines at any winery open for tastings or tours. Two branches of the historic **Oakville Grocery** carry fine selections of wines and gourmet foods. The original is in the Napa Valley (7856 St. Helena Highway, Oakville; tel: 707/944-8802); the second is in the Russian River area (124 Matheson Street, Healdsburg; tel: 707/433-3200; www.oakville grocery.com).

Where to...
Go Out

Northern California is not known for its nightlife. Most entertainments in the region involve the rugged outdoors.

MUSIC

Northern California hosts several annual music festivals, among them **Mendocino Music Festival** (July; tel: 707/937-2044; www.mendocino music.com), Lake Tahoe's **Arts Music Theatre Festival** (Valhalla, June to September; tel: 530/541-4975; www.valhallatahoe.com/ events.html) and the **Russian River Jazz and Blues Festival** (September; weekend event at Johnson's Beach in Guerneville; tel: 949/362-3366; http://russianriverfestivals.com).

In Sacramento you can check the entertainment listings in the *Sacramento Bee* newspaper, or visit www.sacramento365.com.

SPORT

Sacramento's National Basketball Association team, the **Kings,** plays at Sleep Train Arena (1 Sports Parkway; tel: 916/928-6900; www.nba.com).

Northern California is a wonderland for participant sports. During the warm months, hikers, mountain bikers and horseback riders can take to hundreds of miles of trails, while canoeists, kayakers and river rafters can test the region's many waterways. In winter, Northern California is a haven for skiers and snowboarders.

The Central Coast

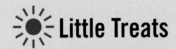 Little Treats

Kelp Forests and Giant Octopuses
The **Monterey Bay Aquarium** (➤ 114) offers an impressive insight into the underwater world at the edge of the Pacific Ocean.

Old Spanish Days Fiesta St. Barbara
Santa Barbara (➤ 109) celebrates its Spanish heritage during this opulent five-day festival in August.

A Gigantic Colony of Elephant Seals
Head to various viewpoints to observe up to 10,000 animals lounging on the beach near **San Simeon** (➤ 120).

The Central Coast

Getting Your Bearings

The revved-up pace of California's large cities relaxes considerably along the state's less populated Central Coast. Murky urban waters give way to aqua-blue clarity, powerful foamy-white waves crash against a mostly rocky shoreline and wildflowers sprout from steep slopes that plunge straight into the Pacific. You can bask in the windswept glory of it all from ocean-view bars and restaurants or hike the beaches and explore their tide pools. The best way to travel is by car, although buses serve parts of the area.

The highlights lie along winding, scenic Highway 1. The going can be slow in summer, but fortunately you've got that fabulous view. Highway 1's vistas are half the fun of a Central Coast visit, but if you're the driver, pay attention: On the curvy sections, one false move and you'll turn your automobile into a submarine.

Monterey is 116mi (187km) south of San Francisco and 335mi (540km) north of Los Angeles, near the southern tip of crescent-shaped Monterey Bay. The Monterey Peninsula's other towns of note, Pacific Grove and Carmel, are nearby, and Big Sur is less than 30mi (48km) to the south. The quickest route to the Monterey Peninsula from San Francisco is I-280 south to Highway 85 heading southeast to US 101 south to Highway 68 west. If you're coming up from Los Angeles, take I-5 north to Highway 46 west to US 101 north to Salinas; at Salinas pick up Highway 68 west. Hearst Castle is just off Highway 1, and Santa Barbara is on a joint stretch of Highway 1 and US 101.

Highway 1 affords spectacular views out over California's Pacific coast

The magnificent pool at Hearst Castle

TOP 10

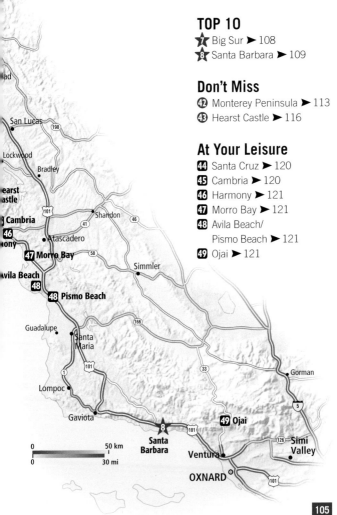

San Lucas (198)

Lockwood

Bradley

earst
astle
(101)
Cambria
46
ony
Atascadero
Shandon
(41)
(46)
47 Morro Bay (58)
vila Beach
48
Simmler
48 Pismo Beach

Guadalupe
Santa
Maria
(166)
(101)

(1)
(101)
Lompoc

(33)
Gorman
(5)

Gaviota
49 Ojai
(101)
(126) Simi
Valley
8
Santa
Barbara
Ventura
0 ____ 50 km
0 ____ 30 mi
OXNARD
(101)

The Central Coast

Three Perfect Days

If you're not quite sure where to begin your travels, this itinerary recommends a practical and enjoyable three days exploring the Central Coast, taking in some of the best places to see. For more information see the main entries. (► 108–121)

Day 1

Morning
Begin on the ㊷ **Monterey Peninsula** (above) in Pacific Grove, where the bracing winds at **Asilomar State Beach** (► 114) will rouse you. If you're visiting during butterfly season, head over to the **Monarch Grove Sanctuary** (► 114, and then cruise the spectacular **17-Mile Drive** (► 114) – and don't forget your camera.

Afternoon
Lunch in Monterey on Euro-American bistro fare at sedate and tasteful **Montrio Bistro** (414 Calle Principal; tel: 831/648-8880). Sea creatures await at **Monterey Bay Aquarium** (► 114), where late-afternoon feedings always entertain. From the aquarium, drive south on Highway 1 to Carmel to browse downtown shops or walk through **Point Lobos State Natural Reserve** (► 115).

Evening
Return to Monterey where there are plenty of places to dine or opt for dinner at historic **Tarpy's Roadhouse** (► 124).

Day 2

Morning
Drive south on Highway 1 to ⭐ **Big Sur** (► 108), stopping for coffee at Café Kevah, part of the Nepenthe complex. Continue south on Highway 1, pulling into vista points.

Afternoon

Drop by the colony of northern elephant seals just north of Hearst Castle. Drive past the castle to **45 Cambria** (▶ 120) and have lunch with an ocean view at the **Sea Chest Restaurant** (▶ 125). Backtrack north to tour magnificent **43 Hearst Castle** (▶ 116). Later, check out tiny, intriguing **40 Harmony** (▶ 121), 5mi (8km) south of Cambria.

Evening

Check into your lodgings in **47 Morro Bay** (▶ 121), and walk a bit of the Embarcadero, before dinner.

Day 3

Morning

Highway 1 merges with US 101 at San Luis Obispo. Pause for a brief rest at **48 Pismo Beach** (▶ 121), strolling Pismo Pier or the beach, and then continue south on US 101 to ☆**Santa Barbara** (▶ 109).

Afternoon

Settle into your Santa Barbara lodgings and have lunch at **Toma**, overlooking the marina, which serves Italian-Mediterranean fare in a serene beachfront setting (334 W Cabrillo Boulevard; tel: 805/962-0777, www.tomarestaurant. com). **Stearns Wharf** (▶ 109) juts into the Santa Barbara Channel off Cabrillo Boulevard not far from Brophy Bros. Park east of the wharf; after walking it, continue east to sandy, quintessentially Californian **East Beach** (▶ 119). Make a short drive to stately **Mission Santa Barbara** (left; ▶ 109).

Evening

From the mission, head to one of the lots near the **State Street shopping district** (▶ 109). Later, have dinner on State Street at **Palazzio** (▶ 117).

The Central Coast

★ Big Sur

Nature rules in Big Sur, a land of fierce beauty immortalized in the photographs of Ansel Adams. The writer Henry Miller declared the terrain the "face of the earth as the Creator intended it to look." Almost every year winter floods wash out part of Highway 1, while in summer the winds howl and rocks tumble off steep cliffs onto the roadbed.

The Big Sur stretches from Carmel nearly to Hearst Castle. **Bixby Bridge,** about 13mi (21km) south of Carmel, is one of the world's highest single-span bridges. Park on the north side to view the structure's towering arches. South of Bixby, **Point Sur Lighthouse** sits atop a sandstone outcrop (tel: 831/625-4419; www.pointsur.org) and can be visited year-round on weekend tours (also, on some weekdays from April through October; $12) .

Nine miles (14km) south of the lighthouse is Big Sur Station. Rangers here dispense maps and advice about area hiking and sights, including nearby Pfeiffer Beach, where waves crash through a tall, doughnut-shaped rock offshore. The station is at the west entrance to **Pfeiffer Big Sur State Park** (tel: 831/667-2315; www.parks.ca.gov/?page_id=570). One of its trails passes through redwood groves to a 60ft (18m) waterfall. Another heads up Pfeiffer Ridge to unparalleled coastal panoramas. About 12mi (19km) south of Big Sur Station is **Julia Pfeiffer Burns State Park** (www.parks.ca.gov/?page_id=570). A 0.5-mile (0.8km) trail leads to a waterfall that flows out of a rocky cliff onto the beach.

Spectacular views of the Big Sur from the Pacific Coast Highway

TAKING A BREAK

Dine or drink indoors or out at **Nepenthe** (48510Highway 1; tel: 831/667-2345; www.nepenthebigsur.com), about 2.5mi (4km) south of Big Sur Station. The adjacent **Café Kevah** is a good spot for brunch or lunch.

✚ 208 B4 🚌 Bus 22 from Monterey to Big Sur and Nepenthe twice daily

⭐8 Santa Barbara

A mere 90-minute drive from Los Angeles, beautiful Santa Barbara has for decades been a hideaway for Hollywood's moneyed elite – Ronald Reagan, Michael Douglas, Oprah Winfrey and Michael Jackson have lived here. Yet the city remains remarkably down-to-earth.

The county courthouse, Mission Santa Barbara and the waterfront are among the important sights to see, but don't fight it. Linger over that harbor-view lunch, space out in the Santa Barbara Botanic Garden, or laze in the sand at East Beach or Butterfly Beach. Santa Barbara is a phenomenal place to relax and feel fabulous.

Insider Tip

The Wharf

Unlike the beaches and waterfronts of most West Coast towns, Santa Barbara's face south, not west. Wood-plank **Stearns Wharf,** which extends several hundred yards into the Santa Barbara Channel, is a good place to start a waterfront tour. Park along Cabrillo Boulevard, stroll to the end of the wharf, and you can sit on a bench and gaze out to sea or back at the city. The kids-oriented 👬 **Santa Barbara Museum of Natural History Sea Center** contains exhibits about the area's marine life. Restaurants and shops can also be found on the wharf.

East Beach with views of Santa Ynez Mountains in background

Around the Waterfront

From the wharf head east 2mi (3km) on Cabrillo Boulevard to the **Andree Clark Bird Refuge.** Signs along the foot and bicycle path identify the native and migratory species that

The Central Coast

frequent this serene lagoon and gardens that are great to pedal around. You can see the grounds of the Santa Barbara Zoo (no great shakes but a pleasant diversion for families) from the refuge.

Across Cabrillo Boulevard from the refuge is **East Beach**, which is usually busy with tanned, toned Santa Barbarans playing Frisbee or sand volleyball. The Cabrillo Pavilion Bathhouse has showers and lockers, but no towel concession.

Past Stearns Wharf is the **Santa Barbara Yacht Harbor.** The fleet comes in with the day's catch – including thousands of sea urchins for import to Japan – at this long breakwater.

Downtown Santa Barbara

From the waterfront you can take the State Street Shuttle up State Street or drive up Chapala Street and park in any of the public lots north of Gutierrez Street. **State Street,** Santa Barbara's downtown spine, is so convivial that folks from as far away as Los Angeles come for shopping weekends, visiting boutiques, antiques shops, outlet stores and other businesses. Two small malls are **El Paseo** (Cañon Perdido and State Street), whose core section dates from the early 20th century, and the newer **Paseo Nuevo** (700–800 blocks of State Street). Some of Santa Barbara's best restaurants and nightclubs are also on or near State.

County Courthouse with clock tower

Santa Barbara Courthouse and Mission

A hint of silent-era Hollywood excess enlivens the interior of the otherwise somber **Santa Barbara County Courthouse,** one block east of State Street at the corner of Anapamu and Anacapa streets. The Spanish-Moorish-style structure was completed in 1929. Take a tour or poke around a bit, then ride the elevator to the clock tower for a 360-degree city view. The **Red Tile Tour** (➤ below) begins here.

RED TILE TOUR

This 12-block, self-guided tour of adobes, parks, museums and other historic downtown sights is named for the curved terra-cotta roof tiles of the many Spanish-style buildings along the way. Pick up a map at the Santa Barbara Visitor Center (Garden Street and Cabrillo Boulevard; tel: 805/965-3021), a few blocks east of Stearns Wharf. Then walk, drive or take the Downtown Shuttle to the tour's starting point (about 0.5mi/0.8km away), the **County Courthouse** (➤ above).

INSIDER INFO

- **You can park easily** in lots on either side of State Street or on city streets elsewhere.
- Downtown and the waterfront are **within walking distance of each other**, but during the day (9–6; until 9 on Friday and Saturday in summer) inexpensive **shuttles** serve the waterfront and the main State Street shopping district. Another option is to **rent a bicycle (▶112).**
- Take one of the tours around the lavishly eccentric gardens at **Lotusland** (695 Ashley Road; tel: 805/969-9990; www.lotusland.org; tours mid-Feb to mid-Nov Wed–Sat 10am and 1:30pm (book in advance); $45), the **Montecito estate** of the late Madame Ganna Walska, a Polish opera singer. You will need to make an appointment to see the Egyptian lotuses, water lilies, topiary and dragon trees in the gardens, which are open Wed–Sat, mid-February to mid-November. Tours last approximately 1.5 hours.
- The heart of the **wine country** lies about an hour's drive (▶193) north of the town.

You'll need to drive or take the bus to visit **Mission Santa Barbara.** If you're only going to visit one California mission, make it this one. The padre overseeing the design of this 1820 structure (the mission was established in 1786) based its facade on that of an ancient Roman temple. Santa Barbara's 1925 earthquake devastated the mission, but care was taken during reconstruction to preserve the original 1820 design. Among the rooms are the main church, a chapel, a bedroom and a kitchen. The grounds include two well-tended gardens with succulents and other indigenous plants.

You'll need a car to get to the **Santa Barbara Botanic Garden,** with 78 acres (32ha) of plant life from California's varied regions. Guided tours are available.

TAKING A BREAK

Brophy Bros. Clam Bar and Restaurant (119 Harbor Way; tel: 805/966-4418, open Sun–Thu 11–10, Fri–Sat 11–11) is a popular dining spot or stop by **D'Angelo** Bread (25 W. Gutierrez Street; tel: 805/962-5466, open daily till 2pm) for pastries or a light snack.

✚ 208 C2 ▣ Downtown Shuttle (waterfront to Sola Street)

Stearns Wharf
✉ E. Cabrillo Boulevard, southern end of State Street
☎ www.stearnswharf.org ▣ Waterfront or Downtown Shuttle ▦ Free

SBMNH – Santa Barbara Museum of Natural History Sea Center
✉ 211 Stearns Wharf ☎ 805/962-2526; www.sbnature.org
🕐 Daily 10–5 ▦ $8.50

Andree Clark Bird Refuge
✉ 1400 E. Cabrillo Boulevard off US 101 ☎ 805/564-5418
🕐 Daily 8–10 ▣ Waterfront Shuttle (to zoo; short walk to refuge or transfer at Milpas Street to Bus 14) ▦ Free

The Central Coast

Santa Barbara Yacht Harbor
⊠ West end of Cabrillo Boulevard 🚌 Waterfront Shuttle

East Beach
⊠ E. Cabrillo Boulevard and Milpas Street 🚌 Waterfront Shuttle 🖐 Free

County Courthouse
⊠ 1100 Anacapa Street ☎ 805/568-3959; http://sbcourthouse.org
🕐 Mon–Fri 8–5, Sat, Sun 10–5; tours Mon–Sat at 2, also Mon, Tue and Fri at 10:30
🚌 Downtown Shuttle (to Anapamu Street; walk one block east)
🖐 Free, donation

Old Mission Santa Barbara
⊠ 2201 Laguna Street
☎ Tour: 805/682-4713 ext. 166; www.santabarbaramission.org
🕐 Daily 9–4:15
🚌 Bus 22 (from downtown transit center, Chapala and Carrillo streets) 🖐 $9

Santa Barbara Botanic Garden
⊠ 1212 Mission Canyon Road (from the mission take E. Los Olivos Street north to
Mission Canyon Road, make a right on Foothill Road and a left on Mission Canyon)
☎ 805/682-4726; www.sbbg.org 🕐 Mar–Oct daily 9–6; Nov–Feb 9–5
🚌 No bus service 🖐 $10

PEDAL AWAY

Excellent bicycle paths crisscross Santa Barbara. The waterfront
area is generally flat, and a popular and scenic trail slithers through
the nearby **Andree Clark Bird Refuge** (tel: 805/564-5433). The ride
from the waterfront to the mission takes about an hour (the terrain
becomes a little hilly near the mission), and from there it's only
2 miles (3km) to the botanic garden. **Wheel Fun Rentals** (tel: 805/
966-2282) has maps, information and a variety of wheel rentals.

The waterfront
area is popular
with cyclists
and walkers

㊷ Monterey Peninsula

"Please don't tell anyone!" pleaded a 19th-century painter extolling the beauty of Monterey to a newly arrived friend. The artist's worst fears – that people would discover the town and overdevelop it – all came to pass, but the area's natural attributes are so compelling even the most egregious encroachments of civilization can't diminish them. The Monterey Peninsula's two must-sees are the Monterey Bay Aquarium and 17-Mile Drive.

Enjoying the Pacific Grove waterfront area in Monterey Bay

Monterey

A good place to start a tour of Monterey is at the **Monterey State Historic Park Visitor Center** (Custom House Plaza), which has brochures for the 2-mile (3km) Path of History and sells tickets to the historic adobes and other sites along it. At touristy **Fisherman's Wharf,** a few hundred yards north of Custom House Plaza, you'll find T-shirt shops, seafood restaurants (some of them good) but precious few fishermen. They've all retreated to other piers.

The **Monterey Bay Recreational Trail** winds northwest for about a mile from Fisherman's Wharf to **Cannery Row**. You can walk the trail or take the bus. Many buildings that formerly housed smelly sardine-processing plants still line Cannery Row, whose quirky habitués inspired John Steinbeck to write the novel of the same name. The street's been too gussied up with mostly unmemorable shops and restaurants to evoke the past. One shop that reflects current industry is A **Taste of Monterey** (700 Cannery Row; www.atasteofmonterey.com), where you can sample wines by local vintners.

The Central Coast

The 🐠 **Monterey Bay Aquarium** sits at the western end of Cannery Row. This nearly complete survey of the bay's marine life merits a two-hour visit at the absolute minimum. The highlights include the sea otter habitat, a three-story kelp forest and the mesmerizing octopuses, but the pièce de résistance is the 1,200-gallon (4.5 mio. liter) "Open Seas Galleries" tank filled with sharks, stingrays and other denizens of the Pacific Ocean.

The Monterey Bay Aquarium's fantastic home by the bay of the same name

Pacific Grove

West of the aquarium, Cannery Row becomes Ocean View Boulevard, your signal that you've entered **Pacific Grove.** The attractive mellow town is known for its Victorian houses and bayside points of interest: among them sheltered Lovers Point Park Beach (a fine place to picnic) and Point Piños Lighthouse. **Asilomar State Beach** (tel: 831/646-6440; http://www.parks.ca.gov/?page_id=566), south of the lighthouse, epitomizes the untamed splendor of this section of California's Pacific coast. Between October and March, migrating monarch butterflies inhabit the **Monarch Grove Sanctuary** on Lighthouse Avenue and Ridge Road.

17-Mile Drive

With all the eye-catching coastline to the north and south, it might seem absurd to pay to see the stretch named **17-Mile Drive,** but it is special. Isolated and dramatic, the drive winds past breezy beaches battered by sometimes fierce waves. Rocks beneath the water create the peculiar phenomenon at the Restless Sea, where opposing ocean currents crash into each other and the waves appear to break in two directions. Other highlights along 17-Mile Drive include **Bird Rock,** a granite outcrop populated by seals, sea lions, gulls, cormorants and other wildlife, and the two-century-old **Lone Cypress,** sculpted by mighty winds that whip in from the sea. The booklet you receive at the entrance booth describes the key stops.

Other Attractions

Carmel is quaint, flooded with boutiques and mobbed on sunny weekends, but once again the setting saves the day. You may find the Ocean Avenue shopping area west of Highway 1 too precious, but both **Carmel River State Beach** (Scenic Road, off Highway 1; tel: 831/649-2836) and **Point Lobos State Natural Reserve** (Highway 1; tel: 831/624-4909) have great trails (pick up maps at the park entrances). At Point Lobos you can view sea lions from **Sea Lion Point Trail** or wander among the trees of **Cypress Grove Trail.** The handsome **Carmel Mission** (Rio Road and Lasuen Drive; tel: 831/624-3600; www.carmelmission.org) was command central for the 21 Franciscan missions established in California by Fra Junipero Serra.

TAKING A BREAK

Sample pasta, pizza, and seafood at Monterey's casual **Café Fina** (47 Fisherman's Wharf; tel: 831/372-5200; www.cafefina.com), a harbor-view Italian restaurant.

✚ 208 B4

Monterey State Historic Park Visitor Center
✉ 20 Custom House Plaza ☎ 831/649-7118; www.parks.ca.gov
🕐 Gardens daily May–Sep 9–5; Oct–April 10–4. Museums and History sites hours vary 🚐 Wave shuttle (summer only); Bus 1

Monterey Bay Recreational Trail
✉ Between Drake and David avenues 🚐 Wave shuttle (summer only); Bus 1

Monterey Bay Aquarium
✉ 886 Cannery Row ☎ 831/648-4800; www.montereybayaquarium.org
🕐 Daily 9:30–6 🚐 Wave shuttle (summer only); Bus 1 💵 $49.95

17-Mile Drive
✉ Five entrances, including Sunset Drive in Pacific Grove and Highway 1 in Carmel ☎ www.pebblebeach.com 🚐 Bus 1 💵 $10

Carmel Mission
✉ Rio Road and Lasuen Drive ☎ 831/624-1271; www.carmelmission.org
🕐 Daily 9:30–5 💵 $6.50

INSIDER INFO

■ From late May to early September, the **Wave shuttle bus** connects the major sights in historic Monterey. **Monterey-Salinas Transit** (tel: 888/678-2871) serves the area year-round. Take the company's Bus 1 from Fisherman's Wharf for an inexpensive scenic tour of Monterey and Pacific Grove.

■ **Carmel Walks** is a 2-hour walking tour that leads from the courtyard of the Pine Inn (corner of Lincoln Street/Ocean Ave) to various hidden backyards, gardens and little houses and teaches you all about the authors and film stars who live here (Tue–Sat 10, also Sat 2, $30; tel: 831/642-2700; carmelwalks.com).

㊸ Hearst Castle

Party central for early Hollywood's elite and among the most elaborate private homes in America, Hearst Castle reposes in hazy majesty amid the Santa Lucia Mountains. The castle was indeed fit for a king – nearly what newspaper magnate William Randolph Hearst (1863–1951) had become by 1919, when he began building his fantasy house. When construction finally ceased in 1947, the place still wasn't complete, though by then the massive spread included 165 rooms, 127 acres (51ha) of gardens and two luxurious pools.

The pine, oak and walnut furnishings of the 115-room main house, Casa Grande, lend the interior a heavy feel but reflect the California-Mediterranean style of the day and Hearst's memories of European castles he had visited. The guest cottages, by contrast, have an airier ambience.

The Neptune Pool, with its marble statues and colonnades

A FINE COLLABORATION

Hearst collaborated on his castle with Julia Morgan (1872–1957), whose knowledge of civil engineering came in handy building in earthquake country. The structure was built largely of reinforced concrete, a boon when the earth trembled, but a nightmare given Hearst's penchant for changing his mind. One example: Casa Grande originally had one bell tower. Hearst had it ripped out and replaced by the two seen today.

Magnificent furniture in the guest house at Hearst Castle

The Collection

"The Chief," as friends and employees called Hearst, was an avid collector of art and antiques. During a late-1930s financial crisis he sold off the cream of his holdings, though impressive pieces, such as the tapestries in Casa Grande's entrance hall, remain. While you take the tour, look up at the hand-carved wooden ceilings Hearst acquired from European estates and monasteries.

In the tour guides' commentary and the large-format film screened in the five-story, Hearst Castle Theater (included with a Tour 1 ticket), Randolph Hearst comes across as an amiable visionary and arts lover, not the mercenary businessman who bullied civic leaders and annihilated anyone who crossed him. The truth is most likely a combination of the two.

TAKING A BREAK

The visitor center has a snack bar, but you're better off stopping to eat in nearby **Cambria** (➤ 120).

✚ 208 B3
✉ Highway 1, San Simeon
☎ 916/444-4445; www.hearstcastle.org
🕓 Daily from 9; evening tours (times vary) Mar–May and Sep–Dec
💵 $25

INSIDER INFO

- You can only visit Hearst Castle on **one of six tours**. All pass the outdoor Neptune Pool, made of marble, and the indoor Roman Pool, lined with blue Venetian glass and glittery gold tiles. For first-time visitors, the castle's staff recommends Tour 1, which takes in the gardens, a guest house and Casa Grande's ground floor. More interesting is Tour 2, which covers Casa Grande's upper floors, passing through the library, the Doge's Suite (a copy of a room in the Doge's Palace in Venice), four guest rooms and Hearst's private suite. Guests are also allowed to explore the pools and gardens again on their own after the tour.

Insider Tip

- **Make tour reservations** at least 48 hours ahead, especially in summer.
- There is a **wheelchair-friendly tour** offered daily.

California's Fairytale Castle

Hearst Castle, California's very own Fairytale Castle, was built by newspaper tycoon William Randolph Hearst for many millions of dollars. By the time of his death in 1951, it had been under construction for 30 years and still wasn't complete. Despite boasting more than 100 rooms, there wasn't enough space to house all the artworks Hearst had collected during his lifetime.

❶ La Casa Grande The main house had expanded to include over one hundred rooms by the time Hearst passed away, including a staggering 38 bedrooms, 31 bathrooms, 14 living rooms, 2 libraries, a dining hall, a kitchen, a theater/cinema and a large reception hall.

❷ Refectory Measuring around 100ft (30m) in length and 23ft (7m) high, this dining hall is adorned with Flemish tapestries and old church pews. The hand carved ceiling from Italy shows depictions of saints.

❸ The Gothic Suite Hearst, a wildly successful publisher, was particularly fond of this suite, which boasts a study and a library.

❹ The Celestial Suite The castle's two magnificent towers are linked together by the Celestial Suite. Both the suite and the towers offer fantastic views out over the glittering Pacific Ocean.

❺ The Theater The walls of this theater and cinema are covered in damask. The lamps are held aloft by gilded Caryatids.

Hearst Castle

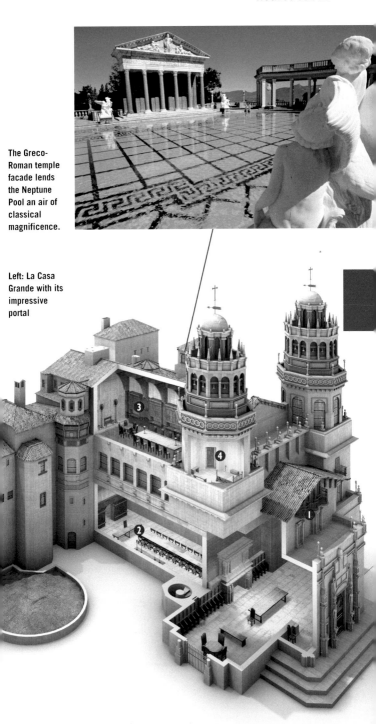

The Greco-Roman temple facade lends the Neptune Pool an air of classical magnificence.

Left: La Casa Grande with its impressive portal

At Your Leisure

The beach at Natural Bridges State Park in Santa Cruz is a magnet for surfers

44 Santa Cruz

Outdoor enthusiasts, New Age types and students all rub shoulders in easy-going Santa Cruz. With a 1911 Looff carousel and the 1924 Giant Dipper, the only wooden roller-coaster on the West Coast, the Beach Boardwalk (Beach Street) retains a retro feel. Nearby is the wharf, good for a sunset stroll. Unlike elsewhere along the northern Central Coast, you can swim during summer at the main beach without freezing to death. To watch surfers in action, stand at Lighthouse Point (West Cliff Drive). The **Mystery Spot** challenges what you think you know about physics. Santa Cruz's best cafés, restaurants and boutiques are in the downtown Pacific Avenue business district.

➕ 208 B4 ✉ Highway 1 and Highway 17, 74mi (119km) south of San Francisco

The Mystery Spot
✉ 465 Mystery Spot Road
☎ 831/423-8897; www.mysteryspot.com
🕐 Mon–Fri 10–6 (last tour 6:05),
Sat, Sun 9–8 (last tour 8:05):05) 💰 $8

45 Cambria

The largest town near Hearst Castle contains shops, galleries, restaurants and lodgings, and beautiful beaches. Walk the paths at **San Simeon State Park** (www.parks.ca.gov/?page_id=590) for close-up views of clear-blue ocean, white-cap waves and swaying patches of kelp; low tide at **Leffingwell's Landing** reveals the sea life that thrives offshore. From just south of Cambria you can detour on Highway 46 into the **wine region** centered around Paso Robles and Templeton. Stop by the Chamber of Commerce (767 Main Street; tel: 805/927-3624; www.cambria chamber.org, Mon–Fri 9–5, Sat, Sun noon–4) for wine touring maps and brochures. At **Eberle Winery** (3810 Highway 46 East; tel: 805/238-9607; www.eberlewinery.com),

> ### 🐾 WILDLIFE SPOTTING
> The **California Sea Otter Game Refuge** extends from Monterey to Cambria. The prime spots for otter viewing are near Hearst Castle at Santa Rosa State Beach, Hearst State Beach and Leffingwell's Landing, off Highway 1.
>
> *Insider Tip*
> Four miles (6km) north of Hearst Castle (just south of Mile Marker 63), **a colony of northern elephant seals** resides near the vista point parking lot.

you can tour the wine caves or have a picnic on the scenic deck. Other wineries of note include Turley, Justin, Wild Horse, Windward, Chumeia and Midnight Cellars.

✚ 208 B3 ✉ Highway 1, 6mi (10km) south of Hearst Castle

46 Harmony

With a name like Harmony, you could expect the two dozen or so residents of this tiny, artsy former dairy town to get along, and that they do. You can watch glassblowers at work, visit shops selling crafts, taste wine and sit in a brick-lined courtyard where flowers sprout from rusting farm implements.

✚ 208 B3
✉ Highway 1, 5mi (8km) south of Cambria

47 Morro Bay

Meander along this fishing village's Embarcadero, and you may feel you have entered another era. Geologically speaking, you have: Morro Rock, the 576ft (175m) town landmark, is one of several dormant volcanic peaks in the area. The estuary here shelters endangered species that include falcons and other birds and fish.

✚ 208 C3 ✉ Highway 1, 20mi (32km) south of Cambria ☎ 805/773-4661; www.parks.ca.gov/?page_id=594

Wildlife thrives on Morro Rock

48 Avila Beach / Pismo Beach

If you're driving south, these will be the first of the Southern California-style beaches that you'll reach, with wide swathes of sand and some surfside diversions. A walk along the beach and Pismo Pier will help you recover from the curves and swerves of Highway 1. (Follow the signs to the Prime Outlets for shopping.)

✚ 208 C2/3
✉ Highway 1, 47mi (75km) south of Cambria

49 Ojai

Frank Capra used Ojai as the setting for Shangri-La in his 1937 film *Lost Horizon*, which should tell you everything you need to know about this captivating haven that's an easy 33-mile (53km) trip from Santa Barbara. The diversions are varied: You can hike the trails through **Los Padres National Forest** or relax at the **Ojai Valley Inn & Spa** (905 Country Club Road; tel: 885/697-8780; www.ojairesort. com). Many Ojai artists exhibit their works at the **Ojai Arts** Center (113 S. Montgomery Street). Large oaks shade **Bart's Books** (302 W. Matilija Street), an outdoor bookstore.

✚ 209 D2 ✉ Highway 150, east from US 101

Where to...
Stay

Prices
Expect to pay per double room, per night (excluding tax)
$ under $100 $$ $100–$175 $$$ over $175

MONTEREY PENINSULA

Red Roof Inn $–$$
Located just a few miles from the major attractions at Monterey, this recently renovated 55-room inn is a good option for budget travelers. Some guest rooms have Jacuzzis, fireplaces and kitchenettes; all have free wireless.

➕ 208 B4 ✉ 2227 N Fremont Street, Monterey, CA 93940 ☎ 831/372-7586 or 800/733-7663; www.redroofinnmonterey.com

Green Gables Inn $$–$$$
Of Pacific Grove's landmark mansions, the Green Gables Inn, an 1888 green-and-white Queen Anne that overlooks the rocky coastline, is one of the most dramatic to behold. Its interior details – original woodwork, moldings, fixtures, arches, stained glass – are equally compelling. Most rooms have bay windows with breathtaking water views. The rear carriage house has larger, more modern rooms, all with private bath (four rooms in the main house share baths). A generous buffet breakfast and afternoon wine and hors d'oeuvres are included.

➕ 208 B4 ✉ 301 Ocean View Boulevard, Pacific Grove, CA 93950 ☎ 831/375-2095 or 800/722-1774; www.greengablesinnpg.com

Monterey Plaza Hotel & Spa $$$
A rooftop luxury spa and other amenities reinforce the reputation of this attractive four-story Cannery Row hotel as Monterey's finest full-service lodging. The bay views are dramatic not only from the spa, but also from the many room balconies and the big outdoor patio, where you can spot sea lions and sea otters in the waters below. On a site once occupied by a cannery, the hotel now draws its design from early California and Mediterranean influences. Rooms are spacious. The Duck Club restaurant serves breakfast and elegant dinner with a view.

➕ 208 B4 ✉ 400 Cannery Row, Monterey, CA 93940 ☎ 831/646-1700 or 800/334-3999; http://montereyplazahotel.com

Old Monterey Inn $$$
This historic Tudor-style home in a quiet residential section of Monterey was restored and transformed into one of the finest B&Bs in California. No detail is left unattended and service is legendary. The rooms are themed – the Library, for instance, contains shelves of books – and stocked with featherbeds and down comforters. You can take breakfast in the dining room, the rose garden or your room, perhaps on your sundeck or in front of the fireplace.

➕ 208 B4 ✉ 500 Martin Street, Monterey, CA 93940 ☎ 831/375-8284 or 800/350-2344; www.oldmontereyinn.com

Pine Inn $$–$$$
The three-story Pine Inn dates from 1889, and was the town's first inn. Today, it offers convenience – right on one of Carmel's main shopping streets, about four blocks from the beach – and a hint of elegance at reasonable prices for the standard rooms. The decor is Victorian, with antiques and

padded wall fabrics. The in-house restaurant, Il Fornaio, is known for its outstanding breads, good Italian food and dining patio.

✚ 208 B4 ✉ Ocean Avenue and Monte Verde, Box 250, Carmel, CA 93921 ☎ 831/624-3851 or 800/228-3851; www.pineinn.com

BIG SUR

Ventana Inn & Spa $$$
Ventana Inn, the quintessential Big Sur retreat, rests serenely atop a wooded ridge overlooking the Pacific Ocean in one of the most spectacular stretches of the California coastline. Rooms are clustered within small buildings. (For maximum romance, ask for a room with a fireplace and ocean view.) The service is efficient and the pools relaxing. Spa treatments include thalassotherapy, pelotherapy and aromatherapy. If you opt for a basic massage or other dry treatment, you can enjoy the experience in your room. Room rates include breakfast and afternoon wine and cheese.

✚ 208 B4
✉ 48123 Highway 1, Big Sur, CA 93920
☎ 831/667-2331 or 800/628-6500;
www.ventanainn.com

CAMBRIA

Pelican Cove Inn $$–$$$
Pelican Cove Inn offers proximity to sea, sand and Hearst Castle. The 26 suites have private balconies or patios facing the water, and custom-designed furniture including king-size beds. Larger rooms with whirlpool tubs, full ocean views and more space are more expensive. All suites have fireplaces and kitchenettes. In addition to the suites, there are 22 rooms in two separate buildings. Full breakfast, afternoon tea and snacks included.

✚ 208 B3 ✉ 6316 Moonstone Beach Drive, Cambria, CA 93428
☎ 805/927-1500 or 800/966-6490;
www.pelicansuites.com

SANTA BARBARA

Four Seasons Biltmore Santa Barbara $$$
Overlooking the beautiful Pacific, surrounded by gardens and lawns, this grand Spanish colonial-style resort has attracted celebrities since the 1920s. Though all rooms are luxurious, the choicest are the airy cottage suites behind the main building, which have fireplaces and patios. With swimming pools, hot tubs, saunas, exercise facilities, tennis courts, two restaurants (one indoor, one outdoor) a bar and a DVD player, you never really have to leave.

✚ 208 C2 ✉ 1260 Channel Drive, Montecito, CA 93108 ☎ 805/969-2261 or 800/819-5053; www.fourseasons.com/santabarbara

Inn by the Harbor $$–$$$
A number of hotels and inns line Santa Barbara's waterfront, but by staying three blocks away from the harbor in this comfortable and good-value motel, you can save a lot of money. The majority of rooms, done in French country decor, have kitchenettes, and there's an outdoor pool and hot tub in the garden.

✚ 208 C2 ✉ 433 W. Montecito Street, Santa Barbara, CA 93101 ☎ 805/963-7851 or 800/626-1986; www.innbytheharbor.com

White Jasmine Inn $$–$$$
Three Victorian and Craftsman houses along prim Bath Street make up this delightful inn, where breakfast is delivered in a picnic basket to your room or may be taken on the outdoor patio. The understated room decor varies but conforms to each house's architectural style – expect a few well-chosen lamps or other accessories rather than knick-knacks. Several rooms and suites have private hot tubs, fireplaces or patios. Spa services are available.

✚ 208 C2 ✉ 1327 Bath Street, Santa Barbara, CA 93101 ☎ 805/966-0589; www.whitejasmineinnsantabarbara.com

Where to...
Eat and Drink

Prices
Expect to pay per person for a meal, excluding drinks and service:
$ under $15 $$ $15–$25 $$$ over $25

MONTEREY PENINSULA

Baja Cantina $
This Carmel Valley Mexican restaurant serves classics, such as spicy burritos and enchiladas along with more California-influenced dishes like delicious bacon-wrapped prawns, enchiladas with mango sauce, and a salad with goat's cheese and sweet apples. Along with the wide-ranging food menu, the tequila and wine lists are also extensive. Vintage car memorabilia dominates the decor, and there's an attractive outdoor patio for dining in fine weather.
➕ 208 B4
✉ 7166 Carmel Valley Road, Carmel
☎ 831/625-2252; www.carmelcantina.com
🕐 Mon–Fri 11:30–10:30, Sat, Sun 10–10

Casanova $$$
Transformed from an old house into a restaurant in the late 1970s, this romantic Carmel culinary destination serves fare from southern France and northern Italy. It's known for conjuring up beautifully presented, creative dishes made from locally sourced produce, including salmon with pomegranate, shallots and kabocha, and osso buco veal served with polenta, carrots, kale and gremolata.
➕ 208 B4
✉ 5th Street between Mission and San Carlos, Carmel ☎ 831/625-0501;
www.casanovarestaurant.com
🕐 Lunch daily 11:30–3;
dinner daily 5–10, Fri, Sat until 10:30

Rio Grill $$–$$$
Rio Grill's creative California cooking combined with authentic Southwestern touches, helped pioneer New American cuisine in Carmel back in the early 1990s. The festive, relaxing surroundings include original artwork on the walls; butcher paper on the tables comes complete with crayons. Pork ribs and chicken are all wood-smoked here, seafood is grilled and produce is fresh and local. There's a full bar and extensive wine list.
➕ 208 B4
✉ Highway 1 and Rio Road, Carmel
☎ 831/625-5436; www.riogrill.com
🕐 Lunch daily 11:30–4, Sun until 3; dinner daily 4–10

Tarpy's Roadhouse $$–$$$
A short drive outside Monterey is Tarpy's, set in a century-old stone-covered ranch house. Sit inside by the fireplace, or in a peaceful flower-filled courtyard. The innovative roadhouse cuisine features sandwiches, salads and pasta at lunch. For dinner, expect duck, braised pork shank, steaks and seafood, cooked on a wood-burning grill.
➕ 208 B4 ✉ 2999 Monterey-Salinas Highway (Highway 68), Monterey
☎ 831/647-1444; www.tarpys.com
🕐 Mon–Thu 11:30–9, Fri–Sat 11:30–10, Sun 11:30–3, 4:30–9

BIG SUR

The Restaurant at Ventana $$$
Located in landmark Ventana Inn, about 28mi (45km) south of

Carmel, Cielo serves beautifully cooked, eclectic California cuisine – highlighted by seafood, game, pastas and vegetarian dishes – accompanied with dramatic views of the ocean and mountains. You can eat indoors, with its picture windows and open-beam, vaulted ceiling, or on the year-round outdoor terrace, which regularly fills up with customers for lunch.

➕ 208 B4
✉ 48123 Highway 1, Big Sur
☎ 831/667-4242; www.ventanainn.com
🕐 Lunch daily 11:30–4; dinner daily 6–9

CAMBRIA

Sea Chest Restaurant and Oyster Bar $$–$$$

The Sea Chest turns out food worthy of the great ocean views from its cliff-top perch. You won't find better seafood this close to Hearst Castle; fresh oysters and locally caught ocean fish are the highlights. Since the restaurant doesn't take reservations, it's a good idea to arrive early – you'll also have a better chance of catching the sunset. Credit cards aren't accepted.

➕ 208 B3
✉ 6216 Moonstone Beach Drive, Cambria
☎ 805/927-4514; www.seachestrestaurant.com
🕐 Dinner Wed–Mon from

SANTA BARBARA

The Harbor Restaurant $$–$$$

Actor Ronald Colman owned the pier's first restaurant, and later James Cagney. But while the star-studded ownership has changed, the incomparable views of the harbor have not. Steaks and local seafood dominate the dinner menu, while the lunch menu includes burgers and sandwiches. The wine list is excellent, and the cocktail menu includes a variety of martinis.

➕ 208 C2
✉ 201 Stearns Wharf, Santa Barbara
☎ 805/963-3311; http://harborsb.com
🕐 Mon–Fri 11–2:30, 5–10, Sat, Sun 10–10

Palace Grill $$–$$$

You'll get spicy Cajun and Creole fare paired with the spirit of New Orleans at the Palace Grill, where every night feels like Mardi Gras. House specialties include jambalaya, crawfish etouffée, New Orleans barbecue shrimp and Creole-Italian pastas. The restaurant is known for its service, plus there's live music (Thu–Sat nights and Fat Tuesday celebrations.

➕ 208 C2
✉ 8 E Cota Street, Santa Barbara
☎ 805/963-5000; www.palacegrill.com
🕐 Daily lunch 11:30–3;
dinner Sun–Thu 5:30–10, Fri–Sat 5:30–11

Palazzio $$

This often crowded Italian trattoria is one of the best bargains in the Santa Barbara area. Portions are huge – a single order of pasta, such as a mound of cappellini with shrimp, can usually be split into two meal-sized portions. It's also fun to eat here: Waiters unexpectedly break into song, and wine self-service is by the honor system.

➕ 208 C2
✉ 1026 State Street, Santa Barbara
☎ 805/564-1985; www.palazzio.com
🕐 Daily lunch 11:30–4;
dinner from 4

Tee-Off $$

The motto at this surf 'n' turf restaurant says it all: "Where the drinks are stiff but the people aren't." Steaks, prime rib and grilled lamb chops share space on the menu with oysters in the half shell, scallops and shrimp scampi. Golf figures in the decor, as you would expect in this sports restaurant, along with TVs for watching games and sports events.

➕ 208 C2
✉ 3627 State Street, Santa Barbara
☎ 805/687-1616; http://teeoffsb.com
🕐 Sun–Thu 5–10, Fri–Sat 5–11
(bar opens daily at 4pm)

The Central Coast

Where to...
Shop

Two affluent resort towns, Carmel and Santa Barbara, dominate the Central Coast shopping scene. You can also find good wines for sale among vineyards in the areas around Monterey and Santa Barbara.

Carmel has a wealth of art galleries, especially along Dolores Street. For works by local artists, check out the **Carmel Art Association** (Dolores Street; tel: 831-624-6176; www.carmelart.org). The town is also known for its trinket and gift shops.

For bargains on brand-name merchandise, head to Pacific Grove and the **American Tin Cannery Outlet Center** (125 Ocean View Boulevard; tel: 831/372-1442; www.americantincannery.com) near Monterey's Cannery Row.

Several dozen stands sell a selection of organic fruits and vegetables alongside baked goods and tasty treats from all over the world every Tuesday from 4pm at the **Old Monterey Farmers Market** on Alvarado Street.

Insider Tip

In Santa Barbara, the prime shopping territory is along **State Street**, where the shops range from elegant to funky. The **Paseo Nuevo** (State and de la Guerra streets; tel: 805/963-7147) is an attractive open-air mall showcasing several department stores and specialty shops.

Nearby is **El Paseo**, an older arcade whose boutiques, art galleries and courtyards lie along Cañon Perdido Street between State and Anacapa streets.

Two blocks west of State Street on Brinkerhoff Avenue is a row of Victorians housing antiques and gift shops.

Where to...
Go Out

In the Monterey area, check weekend editions of the *Monterey Herald* newspaper or visit www.monterey.com for information about activities and events.

In Santa Cruz, try the free newspaper *Good Times*, and in Santa Barbara, *The Independent*, a free weekly.

MUSIC AND THEATER

The **Cabrillo Festival of Contemporary Music** (tel: 831/426-6966; www.cabrillomusic.org) and **Shakespeare Santa Cruz** (http://shakespearesantacruz.org; ticket office: 831/459-2159) are among summer arts events in Santa Cruz.

The Monterey Peninsula also hosts a number of summer arts festivals, including the **Carmel Bach Festival** (tel: 831/624-1521; www.bachfestival.org), the **Monterey International Blues Festival** (tel: 831/601-9609; www.montereyinternationalbluesfestival.com), and the **Monterey Bay TheatreFest** (tel: 831/622-0700; www.pacrep.org).

The famous **Monterey Jazz Festival** (tel: 831/373-3366; www.montereyjazzfestival.org) is held each September.

NIGHTLIFE

In **Santa Cruz**, clubs along Pacific Avenue often feature rock and blues acts.

In **Monterey**, much of the action is in the Cannery Row area.

In **Santa Barbara**, nightlife is centered in the upmarket bars on Lower State Street that present regular live music.

Los Angeles Area

 **Little Treats**

L.A. on Foot and in the Saddle
Believe it or not, but this automobile paradise is accessible for cyclists and pedestrians. Some buses even have bike racks.

The Muscle Men of Venice Beach
Eccentric fitness junkies live out their California Lifestyles at "Muscle Beach", an open-air gym at **Venice Beach** (➤ 147).

Huntington Botanical Gardens
The nephew of a famous railroad tycoon created glorious gardens and a great deal more for his wife in **San Marino** (➤ 150).

Los Angeles Area

Getting Your Bearings

Many aspiring actors come to Los Angeles in search of stardom, and many visitors come to L.A. for the movie star culture, too: For celebrity sightings, studio tours, Hollywood landmarks and the famous streets and neighborhoods that appear in film and on TV.

Hollywood and all its trappings are a big tourist draw, but Los Angeles has much more to offer. Covering five counties (Los Angeles, Orange, Riverside, San Bernadino and Ventura), the metropolitan area contains 16.4 million people, more than every U.S. state except New York, Texas and California itself. The area has miles of wide sandy beaches, reliably great weather, first-rate museums and architecture, shopping for all budgets and tastes, and authentic cuisines from a variety of cultures (this Pacific Rim hub is home to America's largest Hispanic and Asian/Pacific Islander populations).

Freeways bind this diverse and seemingly boundless region. Key routes you might need include the San Diego Freeway (I-405), Hollywood Freeway (US 101 near Hollywood and Downtown, Highway 170 north of Hollywood), Golden State Freeway (I-5 in Los Angeles) and the Santa Ana Freeway (I-5 in East Los Angeles and Orange County) travel more or less north–south through the area. The Foothill Freeway (I-210), Ventura Freeway (Highway 134/US 101 in the San Fernando Valley), Santa Monica Freeway (I-10) and Century Freeway (I-105) are major east–west routes. Sunset, Santa Monica and Wilshire boulevards are key east–west streets.

These thoroughfares keep Los Angeles in seemingly perpetual motion. Nevertheless, the extended metro and bus lines, the cycle lanes on many streets, and the revival of downtown L.A. mean you can discover a great deal without jumping in the car.

Getting Your Bearings

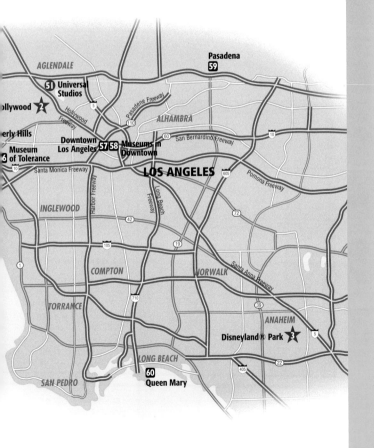

Perfect Days in...

Three Perfect Days

If you're not quite sure where to begin your travels, this itinerary recommends a practical and enjoyable three days exploring the Los Angeles Area, taking in some of the best places to see. For more information see the main entries (➤ 132–152).

Day 1

Morning
Hooray for ☆**Hollywood** (➤ 132), where you'll have your first brush with the stars (well, the ones along the Walk of Fame anyway). Then it's off to the **Griffith Observatory** (➤ 134) for a lofty perspective on a great city.

Afternoon
Have lunch at jolly **Fred 62** diner in Los Feliz (1850 N Vermont Avenue; 323/667-0062; http://fred62.com), then either tour **Warner Bros**. or check out 🔟**Universal Studios** (➤ 144). If you've gone to Warner's, you'll have time in the late afternoon to explore a little of 🔟**Beverly Hills** (➤ 142).

Evening
Drive or walk the **Sunset Strip** (➤ 160). Stop for dinner at Wolfgang Puck's Express at Gelson's Market (8330 W. Santa Monica Blvd.; tel: 323/656-1268) or at his ritzier venture, **Spago Beverly Hills** (➤ 157).

Day 2

Morning
Have breakfast at **Du-par's** or a snack at **Gordon Ramsay** at the London West Hollywood (➤ 154) then continue south on Fairfax Avenue to Wilshire Boulevard and make a left. Check out **La Brea Tar Pits** (➤ 147) and perhaps the **Petersen Automotive Museum** (➤ 147). By late morning make your way to ☆**The Getty Center** (left; ➤ 138).

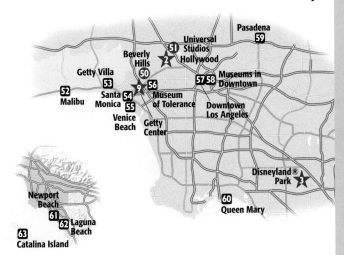

Afternoon

Wander through the Getty's galleries and gardens, interrupting your tour with lunch at the café or restaurant. Work off your meal on a half-hour, guided architectural walk. When you depart the Getty, head south on Sepulveda Boulevard and west on Wilshire Boulevard to **54 Santa Monica** (▶146). Walk the beach and check out Santa Monica Pier.

Evening

Catch a little of the action along the 3rd Street Promenade (▶146). Enjoy Northern Italian fare at the convivial **Locanda del Lago** (231 Arizona Avenue; tel: 310/451-3525; www.lagosantamonica.com), preferably on the patio or try the zippily contemporary Asian selections at the pricier **Chinois on Main** (2709 Main Street; tel: 310/392-9025; www.wolfgangpuck.com).

Day 3

Morning/afternoon

Devote the day to fantasy at **⭐Disneyland® Park** (right; ▶136) or, if you didn't get there before, at **51 Universal Studios** (▶144).

Evening

After the evening traffic has died down, head north to **The Ivy** (113 N. Robertson Boulevard; tel: 310/274-8303; www.theivyrestaurants.com) for dinner and perhaps some last-minute celebrity sighting.

Los Angeles Area

★2 Hollywood

Pity poor Hollywood – but perhaps not for long. Once the quint-essence of glamour, it deteriorated after several movie studios moved to the San Fernando Valley. The town, however, is making a comeback, the most potent symbol of this was the return of the Academy Awards ceremony to Hollywood Boulevard, where the event first took place.

The must-see along Hollywood Boulevard is **Grauman's Chinese Theatre**, and there are a few other points of interest within walking distance. Hollywood showman Sid Grauman erected the Chinese Theatre in 1927. For years the scene of chic Hollywood premieres, the whimsical pagoda-style structure has a frenetic, dragon-festooned exterior.

Grauman's Chinese Theatre with its fire-breathing dragon

Famous Prints

Stars of the past and present have left their prints – hand, foot or otherwise (Jimmy Durante's nose, Lassie's paw) – in the cement courtyard. Legend has it that an actress (Norma Talmadge in some versions, Mary Pickford in others) accidentally stepped in wet cement during construction and that Grauman immediately grasped the promotional possibilities. (According to Grauman's biographer, the impresario came up with the idea on his own.) With another tourist bus pulling up nearly every minute, pandemonium reigns, but in this case it's a plus – every day seems like a major motion-picture event. In the 1940s, the theater hosted the Academy Awards ceremony, but since 2002 the event has been held a few doors east at the Dolby Theatre, part of the Hollywood and Highland entertainment-and-retail complex (that also includes Grauman's).

Though it's not as glamorous as it was in the 1920s, the **Hollywood Roosevelt Hotel** (7000 Hollywood Boulevard; tel: 323/466-7000; www.thehollywoodroosevelt.com), across the street, retains its Spanish-Moorish arches and painted ceramic tiles. An informative mezzanine-level exhibit surveys Hollywood's glory days.

El Capitan Theatre on Hollywood Boulevard

Hollywood Walk of Fame

The Chinese Theatre and Hollywood Roosevelt Hotel are near the western end of the **Hollywood Walk of Fame** (Hollywood Boulevard from Vine Street west to La Brea Avenue; Vine Street from Yucca to Sunset). Along the walk, the names of entertainment figures stand out in brass letters amid a pink terrazzo star surrounded by charcoal-gray terrazzo. One of five logos – a motion-picture camera, radio microphone, TV set, theatrical mask or record – indicates the honoree's profession. Barbra Streisand, Elton John and Jack Nicholson are among those with stars near the Chinese Theatre.

Along Hollywood Boulevard

As you stroll east on Hollywood Boulevard, you'll shortly pass one of the street's most ornate structures, the Spanish Colonial Revival **El Capitan Theatre** (6838 Hollywood Boulevard, tel: 818/845-3110; www.elcapitantheatre.com), a veritable riot of carved terra-cotta patterns and figures. The Disney Company showcases its animation pictures here.

A little east of the El Capitan is the **Egyptian Theatre** (6712 Hollywood Boulevard; tel: 323/461-2020; http://egyptiantheatre.com). Things Egyptian were all the rage following the discovery of King Tut's tomb in the 1920s, and Sid Grauman capitalized on the fad with the theater's design. Rows of palm trees line the long exterior courtyard of this exquisitely restored movie palace.

Across the street and east of the Egyptian is **Musso & Frank Grill** (6667 Hollywood Boulevard; tel: 323/467-7788; www.mussoandfrank.com), which opened in 1919 and evolved into the hangout of screenwriters such as Lillian Hellman, Dashiell Hammett and William Faulkner. Hoist one of the textbook martinis in their honor. The food's nothing special, but the atmosphere's great.

Stars bustled in and out of nightclubs and eateries at the intersection of Hollywood and Vine, and newcomers were dis-covered (or so the planted publicity went) right on the street. Two period theaters, the **Pantages** (6233 Hollywood Boulevard) and the **Avalon** (formerly the Palace, 1735 N. Vine Street) have survived more or less intact.

VITAL STATISTICS

- Billions of people watch the **Academy Awards** ceremony, but a mere 270 people attended the first event, in the Blossom Room of the Hollywood Roosevelt Hotel. The private dinner was held in 1929 to honor the films of 1927 and 1928.

- Fame doesn't come cheap. Getting a star on the **Walk of Fame** costs $25,000, which is usually paid by the entertainment company promoting the honoree's project at the time of the unveiling.

Los Angeles Area

Look out for the circular **Capitol Records Building** (1750 N. Vine Street), erected in the 1950s north of Hollywood and Vine, said to have been designed to resemble a stack of records.

A memorial to James Dean stands in Griffith Park Observatory

Griffith Park and Observatory

East on Hollywood Boulevard and north on Vermont Avenue lies 4,107-acre (1,662ha) **Griffith Park**. A bust of the actor James Dean outside the **Griffith Observatory** (inside the park, follow signs) commemorates several pivotal scenes in his picture *Rebel Without a Cause* that took place at the hillside facility. The planetarium puts on enjoyable shows about the galaxies, but the (free) views of this world – Hollywood in particular – and the building's Mayan-deco exterior design are other reasons to visit. Because you're often above the smog level, you may even see blue sky. Also within Griffith Park are a zoo, the Autry Museum of the American West (tel: 323/667-2000, http://theautry.org), a celebration of the American West and the outdoor Greek Theatre concert venue.

The observatory is one of many places (the Hollywood Freeway's another) with a good vantage point overlooking the famous **HOLLYWOOD** sign. From the 1920s to the 1940s, the letters on the slope of Mt. Lee spelled out "Hollywoodland" to advertise a real-estate development. The letters are 50ft (15m) high.

If you're driving, leave the observatory via West Observatory Drive (if you followed the above directions, you got here via East Observatory Drive). Make a left on Canyon Drive, which eventually becomes Western Avenue and leads you south out of the park.

Hollywood Forever

Continue south to Santa Monica Boulevard and make a right. **Hollywood Forever** (6000 Santa Monica Boulevard; tel: 323/469-1181; www.hollywoodforever.com, daily 8–5) is the current name of the former Hollywood Memorial Park Cemetery, final resting place of directors Cecil B. DeMille and John Huston, actors Rudolph Valentino, Marion Davies and Tyrone Power, the gangster Bugsy

INSIDER INFO

Insider Tip

- For a quick taste of Hollywood's golden age, **park your car in one of the lots near the Chinese Theatre** and check out the immediate area.
- Most of Hollywood's museums are a bit tacky with the exception of the **Hollywood Museum** (1660 N. Highland Avenue; tel: 323/464-7776; www.thehollywoodmuseum.com; $15) in the art-deco Max Factor Building. The artifacts tell the story of movies from the silent era to present.

Siegel and even the notorious Virginia Rappe. Douglas Fairbanks Sr. has a memorial that includes a long, lotus-filled pool. Unlike at Forest Lawn and other burial grounds, visitors are encouraged to seek out star graves – pick up a map at the gift shop (it closes an hour before the cemetery), just inside the entrance.

TAKING A BREAK

Farmers Market (6333 W. 3rd Avenue; tel: 323/933-9211; MTA Bus 217, 218, 16, 17, 316, DASH Fairfax)) began as an open-air market in the 1930s and expanded into the present warren of hot-food and souvenir stalls. Longtime favorites are **Gill's old fashioned Ice Cream**, **Magee's** and **Du-par's**.

One of the most famous signs in the world set high in the hills above Hollywood

🚩 210 B3 🚇 Metro Red Line (Hollywood and Highland)
🚌 MTA Bus 212/213, 217, 222; DASH buses loop north and south of Hollywood Boulevard

Grauman's Chinese Theatre
✉ 6925 Hollywood Boulevard
☎ 323/461-3331; www.tclchinesetheatres.com
💵 Free (to courtyard; interior open only to movie attendees)

Griffith Observatory
✉ 2800 East Observatory Road (south entrance to park is at Los Feliz Boulevard and Vermont; follow signs)
☎ 213/473-0890; www.griffithobservatory.org
🕐 Tue–Fri noon–10, Sat, Sun 10–10
🚌 MTA Bus 180 💵 Free; planetarium shows $7

Los Angeles Area

⭐Disneyland® Park

A sign at the entrance to the famed 🎎 theme park proclaims that you're leaving the world of reality and entering a place where fantasy reigns. And aside from the rampant, if discreet, commercialism and the occasional views of Orange County's smog from the park's loftier points, you have stepped into another world.

Main Street, U.S.A. leads into the Central Plaza, off which are several themed areas, including Fantasyland, Tomorrowland, Frontierland and Critter Country. Tyke-sized amusements enchant young ones at Mickey's Toontown.

The absolute don't-miss attraction is the **Indiana Jones™ Adventure**, which puts you inside re-created scenes from the Indiana Jones movies. You'll face untold "dangers," from boulders to snakes, in this daffy living cartoon that's the highlight of Adventureland. **Matterhorn Bobsleds**, a 1/100th-scale re-creation of a Swiss mountain, is Disneyland Park's oldest roller-coaster and still one of its best. **Space Mountain**, an indoor roller-coaster in Tomorrowland, is deliriously disorienting. Buzz Lightyear Astro Blasters, also in Tomorrowland, let you battle evil in your own star cruiser. The **Splash Mountain** flume ride, found in Critter Country, climaxes with a drenching five-story drop in a floating ride.

Water Attractions
You'll get less wet on a Jungle Cruise, an Adventureland attraction that passes through re-creations of the rivers of

© Disney Enterprises, Inc.

The romantic Sleeping Beauty's Castle at Disneyland Park

© Disney Enterprises, Inc.

four continents. The other two great boat attractions are **Pirates of the Caribbean** in New Orleans Square, while younger children will enjoy **"It's a Small World"**, a boat ride in Fantasyland, which introduces countries around the world and some of the characters created by Disney and Pixar. The **Mad Tea Party** ride and **Mickey's House** are two perennial favorites for younger kids.

Disney California Adventure Park, an adjacent theme park, was completely overhauled for $1 billion after suffering poor visitor numbers. The intervention

Spectacular motor racing at the new Disney California Adventure Park

worked, and the park has been extremely popular ever since reopening in 2012. It's designed in a classic, 1920s Hollywood style that combines a nostalgic ambience with cutting-edge attractions in themed zones like Bug's Land, Grizzly Peak and Paradise Pier.

TAKING A BREAK

Cafés, restaurants and take-out stands abound. Three good choices: **Blue Bayou** (New Orleans Square), **Carnation Café** (Main Street) and **Redd Rockett's Pizza Port** (Tomorrowland).

✚ 210 B3 ✉ 1313 Harbor Boulevard (off I-5), Anaheim
☎ 714/781-4565; http://disneyland.disney.go.com
🕐 Hours vary (open as early as 8am or as late as 10am; closed as early as 6pm or as late as midnight). Call 714/781-7290 for particular dates or log on to https://disneyland.disney.go.com
🚍 MTA Bus 460 (from downtown); Orange County Transit (OCTA) 43
🍴 $–$$$ 🎫 $95 (one park)

INSIDER INFO

- Arrive early and head immediately to one of the popular rides/attractions such as **Indiana Jones™ Adventure** or **Splash Mountain**. Then take a ride on the **Disneyland Railroad**, which will orient you to the rest of the park.
- Disneyland is **more fun during off-peak times**, especially on weekdays just before and after summer, when the weather's still fine but lines are shorter.
- If you've arrived during a busy period, **go on the rides/attractions in the morning or the evening** and hit the shows in the afternoon.
- If you want to visit more than one park during your trip, purchase a **Southern California City Pass** ($330), which includes entry to Universal Studios, Sea World and a 3-day Disneyland Park Hopper Ticket.
- Try to catch at least **one of the live shows**, whose production numbers rival those of many a Broadway presentation. And stick around for the parade (and accompanying fireworks some nights) that closes each day.
- **Don't miss Fantasmic!**, an evening show in which Mickey Mouse battles villains galore. It's a dazzling multimedia extravaganza (lasers, pyrotechnics, flashing lights, lit-up dancing fountains), but you need to snag a good spot two or three hours ahead of time or your sight lines will be blocked.

Insider Tip

Los Angeles Area

⭐9 The Getty Center

With striking modern buildings, sleek galleries and the stunning Santa Monica Mountains setting competing for your attention, you may occasionally have to remind yourself to look at the abundance of art, though the architecture of the Getty Center was intended as a work of art in itself.

Richard Meier designed the beige, rough-hewn travertine buildings, whose overall effect is of a suave, modernist variation on the Acropolis of Athens. Artist Robert Irwin groomed the controversial Central Garden, which Meier is said to have hated for its darker colors and unruly foliage

WHAT'S WHERE
North Pavilion Before 1600
East Pavilion 1600–1800
South Pavilion 1600–1800
West Pavilion 1700–1900
Exhibition Pavilion (between the museum entrance and the West Pavilion): Temporary exhibitions

(notice Meier's more orderly cactus garden and tree arrangements closer to the main buildings). French architect Thierry Despont designed the cases and chose the finishes for the **14 decorative arts galleries** (again with some reported grumbling from Meier). The Getty's few architectural incongruities aside – that garden really does clash with Meier's aesthetic – the Center (plan to visit for at least 2 hours) is truly a sight to behold. A tram whisks you from the parking area to an arrival plaza. Stairs sweep up from here to the **Main Plaza**, off which are five two-story pavilions. Four house the permanent collection; the fifth hosts temporary exhibitions. Paintings are on the upper levels; decorative arts, drawings, manuscripts and photographs on the lower.

Highlights of the Collection

The particular loves of collector and oil magnate J. Paul Getty were **antiquities** (displayed in the Getty Villa in Malibu ➤ 145) and **medieval illuminated manuscripts**. Over the years, curators have filled in the gaps in the museum's largely European holdings, which include paintings, drawings, sculpture, decorative arts and 19th- and 20th-century American and European photographs. Titian, Gainsborough, Rembrandt, Turner, Monet and Cézanne are among the painters represented. **Van Gogh's *Irises*** is the highlight of the Post-Impressionist collection.

Light and color are the two key elements of the Central Garden, which Irwin designed as a fluctuating work of art, varying with the time of day or year. Waterfalls and streams reflect the ever-changing colors.

TAKING A BREAK

The Getty operates a full-service restaurant and two cafés, one with table service, the other self-service.

➕ 210 B3
✉ 1200 Getty Center Drive off I-405, Brentwood
☎ 310/440-7300; www.getty.edu
🕐 Sun, Tue–Fri 10–5:30, Sat 10–9. Closed Mon
🚌 MTA Bus 761
♿ Free; parking $15

Richard Meier imported 16,000 tons of Italian travertine limestone for the Getty

INSIDER INFO

- You can explore the artworks in chronological order or at random. A good strategy is to **watch the 10-minute introductory film** shown in the entrance hall and then proceed to the areas that most interest you. The audio guide available at the entrance is worth the small fee.

- If you're traveling with children, **check out the 🎨 family room**, where displays and hands-on activities, such as a set-up for portraiture, help kids make sense of the artistic process

Insider Tip

The Getty Center

Constructed from 1984 to 1997 following plans by architectural luminary Richard Meier, this dazzling, billion-dollar structure sits like a postmodern temple to the visual arts atop a rise in the Brentwood Hills. The interior spaces were fashioned by Thierry Dupont, a prominent interior designer.

❶ Tram station A tram service shuttles between the parking garage and a station that lies just a short distance downhill from the Getty Center itself.

❷ The museum's facade Around 16,000 tons of Italian travertine limestone were used to fashion the surface of the museum's pale brown, rough-hewn facade. It contrasts with the smooth-cut stone, tinted metal and rounded surfaces that dominate the other buildings.

❸ Lobby The Getty Center's circular, light-flooded lobby looks out over a courtyard that's home to a water feature and the four exhibition pavilions.

❹ The pavilions' collections Paul Getty (1892–1976) made his fortune in the oil business and used it to fuel his passion for collecting European painting, sculpture and crafts. His particular enthusiasm was for pieces dating from the Renaissance to the Post-Impressionist period.

❺ North pavilion This building is home to manuscripts from the 6th to the 16th centuries and masterpieces from the Byzantine, Ottonian, Romanesque, Gothic and Renaissance eras.

❻ East pavilion Contains works of art from 1600–1800, with sculptures and drawings on the first floor and paintings on the story above. Boasts beautiful views of Bel Air and the San Diego Freeway.

❼ South pavilion Head to the first floor for Decorative Arts. Venture to the upper level to see paintings from 1600–1800.

❽ West pavilion This pavilion is dedicated to art after 1800. Includes sculpture, crafts, photography and painting.

❾ Central garden Designed by Robert Irwin, this living work of art is home to hundreds of magnificent azaleas and a tiny waterfall that drops into an elegant pool below.

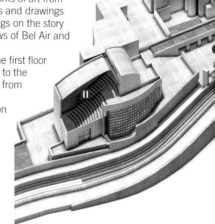

❿ Research Institute Interesting temporary exhibitions are displayed in this building.

⓫ Auditorium Used for film screenings and musical performances. You'll find the program of events in the lobby.

The Getty Center

The play of light and form at the Getty Center

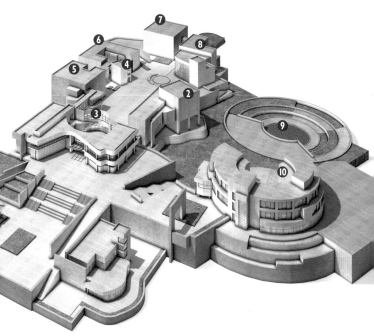

The curved surfaces and white, checkered facades are typical of Richard Meier's architectural style

⑤⓪ Beverly Hills

Few words connote wealth and glamour more succinctly than "Beverly Hills," where movie-star mansions have captured the world's imagination since the days of silent pictures. A visit to Beverly Hills provides you with a chance to take a peak at the lifestyles of the rich and famous, along residential streets and the renowned Rodeo Drive shopping area.

Stars, movie execs and TV titans don't find it charming when fans drop in, but you can often glimpse the facades and gardens of their mansions from Sunset Boulevard, Roxbury and Summit Drive. The most lavish homes are just outside the city limits. In the 1990s, the late Aaron Spelling, the producer of *Beverly Hills 90210*, *Melrose Place* and other such fare, built a 123-room, 56,550ft² (5,253m²) abode – "bigger than the Taj Mahal" gushed one newspaper account – in Holmby Hills. (Proving that all things are – pardon the pun – relative, daughter Tori, a former star of *90210*, reportedly flew the coop because she needed "space.") And media mogul David Geffen spent about $47.5 million on his nearby manse.

The Beverly Hills City Hall was built in 1932

CITY HALL

Beverly Hills style

Insider Tip

To get closer to the good life, dress up and have a drink or breakfast in the Polo Lounge at the **Beverly Hills Hotel** (9641 Sunset Boulevard, tel: 310/887-2777, www.beverlyhillshotel.com). The hotel, which opened in 1912, was swank even before the city was.

Southern California's most chic boutiques do business south of Sunset along **Rodeo Drive**. The street's not quite as exclusive as it was in past days, though the wealthy still shop by appointment and the rents are among the world's highest. Frank Lloyd Wright designed the mini-mall at 332 N. Rodeo Drive, whose ramp zigzags to the upper floors (be careful walking up it if you've just had a cocktail). At Rodeo Drive and

Chic boutiques line Rodeo Drive

Wilshire Boulevard are the chichi Via Rodeo shopping lane – Versace, Jimmy Choo, et al. – and the posh Regent Beverly Wilshire Hotel.

Richard Meier, architect of the Getty Center (➤ 138), designed the stylish digs of the **Paley Center for Media**. You can view tapes of TV shows and listen to radio shows in private booths, or attend screenings in various theaters.

TAKING A BREAK

Perch yourself at a table at **208 Rodeo** (208 N. Rodeo Drive, tel: 310/275-2428; http://208rodeo.com), above Wilshire Boulevard and Rodeo Drive, and enjoy world fusion cuisine.

➕ 210 B3 ✉ Sunset, Santa Monica and Wilshire boulevards, west of Doheny Drive 🚌 MTA Bus 2, 302 (Sunset Boulevard); MTA Bus 4, 16, 17, 28, 316 (Santa Monica Boulevard); MTA Bus 20, 14, 31 (Wilshire Boulevard) and many others

Beverly Hills Conferences & Visitors Bureau
✉ 9400 S. Santa Monica Boulevard
☎ 310/248-1015; www.lovebeverlyhills.com
🕐 Mon–Fri 9–5, Sat, Sun 10–5

The Paley Center for Media
✉ 465 N. Beverly Drive ☎ 310/786-1091; www.paleycenter.org
🕐 Wed–Sun noon–5 🚌 MTA Bus 4, 704 🎟 Free (donation)

INSIDER INFO

- **Parking is free for the first two hours** in lots on and just off Beverly Drive. Look for public-parking signs.
- West of Beverly Hills is even more exclusive **Bel-Air**, home to Jack Nicholson and other superstars.

Los Angeles Area

🔟 Universal Studios

Founded by immigrant Carl Laemmle back in 1913, the legendary 🎬 Universal Studios have since been turned into a theme park. Guests have a unique opportunity to navigate this 415-acre (168ha) movie studio complex of soundstages and sets to see how many well-known movie and TV shows are made.

A statue of the Egyptian god Anubis at the entrance to "Revenge of the Mummy: The Ride" at Universal Studios

Thanks to creative consultation from Steven Spielberg, the experience includes the largest movie-set street expansion in Hollywood history, passing such famous movie sets as Spielberg's *War of the Worlds*, Wisteria Lane from ABC's *Desperate Housewives*, the Bates Motel from *Psycho*, and hundreds of facades in Hollywood's most famous back lot. The **studio trams** were recently equipped with state-of-the-art flat-screen high-definition monitors and digital playback systems and feature commentary from filmmakers and actors. The theme park's attractions take an innovative and highly successful approach to immersing guests into the action, with many of the newer rides emphasizing 3-D effects: Experience *King Kong* 360 3-D or *Shrek* 4-D.

Other highlights include The Simpsons Ride, Transformers, and Revenge of the Mummy: The Ride, a super-fast, super-scary roller-coaster. Cool off on a hot day by climbing aboard Jurassic Park: The Ride, a thrilling water attraction that sees you plunging into a raging river at 45mph (70km/h) and chased by a ravenous T-Rex. After your day, visit **Universal CityWalk Hollywood** located next to Universal Studios, a three-block entertainment, dining and shopping promenade.

TAKING A BREAK

Samba Brazilian Steakhouse (tel: 818/763-0101; www.sambabraziliansteakhouse.com), at Universal CityWalk, is a trendy restaurant with an energetic vibe.

➕ 210 B3 ✉ Universal Center Drive, off Hollywood Freeway (US 101), Universal City ☎ 800/864-8377; www.universalstudioshollywood.com 🕐 Hours vary widely; call ahead or check online 🚇 Metro Red Line (Universal City) 🚌 MTA Bus 150, 155, 224, 240, 750 💲 $99–110

At Your Leisure

52 Malibu

Upscale Malibu is famous for its celebrity palaces and occasional mudslides and firestorms. For all the star wattage, the scene is remarkably subdued, with the shoreline along the Pacific Coast Highway (PCH) the main draw. Surfers head to **Leo Carrillo State Beach** (35000 PCH), whose **Insider Tip** tide pools teem with sea creatures. A stairway leads down the cliffs to secluded **El Matador State Beach** (32215 PCH). Tanned babes and pumped-up Adonises frolic along Zuma Beach (30000 PCH).

Overlooking **Malibu Lagoon State Beach** (23200 PCH at Serra Road), whose namesake waterway shelters many migratory birds, is the Adamson House. Locally produced ceramic tiles decorate the fetching 1929 Spanish Colonial Revival structure.

➕ 210 B3 ✉ Pacific Coast Highway north of Santa Monica and Pacific Palisades
🚌 MTA Bus 534 (along PCH)

53 Getty Villa

The location of the J. Paul Getty Museum in the Malibu hills is stunning, as is the scenic drive up Pacific Coast Highway to get here. The museum was closed for many years, while it underwent a $275 million renovation, and reopened in 2006. Once inside, the museum doesn't disappoint.

In a building modeled after the Roman Villa dei Papiri in Herculaneum in Italy, the museum houses Getty's collection of Greek, Roman and Etruscan antiquities, and contains approximately 44,000 works of art; more than 1,200 are on view. Dozens of the works, however, were returned to Greece and Italy after an embarrassing scandal, in which their governments questioned how the artwork had left their countries. The galleries are arranged thematically, including topics such as gods and goddesses, monsters and minor deities, and the Trojan War. Don't miss the Statue of a Victorious

Superb views along Malibu coast, at the Adamson House in Malibu

Los Angeles Area

Sunset over Santa Monica with the pier and fairground in the background

Youth – also called the **Getty Bronze** – a rare surviving Greek bronze, on display in a climate-controlled room on the second floor. Also on the second floor, are six galleries used for changing exhibits, although still with a focus on antiquities.

The 🔧 **Family Forum** on the first floor has hands-on, tactile activities for kids. Outside, the gardens are not to be missed, particularly the Outer Peristyle, which has lovely pathways, a 220ft (67m) long mirror-like pool, and plants that would have been found in Ancient Rome. There's also a classical theater that's used for plays and concerts.

➕ 210 B3
✉ 17985 Pacific Coast Highway, Malibu
☎ 310/440-7300; www.getty.edu
🕐 Wed–Mon 10–5   🚌 MTA Bus 534   🎫 Free
(advanced timed ticket required); parking $15

54 Santa Monica

Appealing, independent-minded Santa Monica has a slightly bohemian style. Though heavily gentrified, the town attracts yuppies, tourists, the homeless, street artists, beachgoers, teens

Tricycle for hire on Venice Beach; the perfect way to cruise by Muscle Beach

and older people. They all head to the beach and the 3rd Street Promenade, the pedestrianized stretch of 3rd Street between Broadway and Wilshire Boulevard. Continue west on Wilshire and you'll run into Santa Monica State Beach, where the sand is clean, the views are great and there is plenty to entertain you on the 🔧 **Santa Monica Pier**. To the south on Main Street, trendy boutiques and restaurants line the blocks from Hollister Avenue south to Venice.

➕ 210 B3   ✉ West end of I-10
🚌 MTA Bus 4, 6, 534, 33 (and others)

55 Venice Beach

A carnival atmosphere prevails along Ocean Front Walk, the paved promenade that straddles exuberant

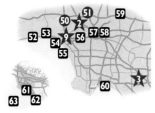

Venice Beach. Stroll Ocean Front south of Rose Avenue and you're liable to encounter trained parrots, skilled and unskilled musicians, and proselytizers for all sorts of religious and social movements. On a sunny day the place to go is Muscle Beach, an outdoor pavilion where guys and gals pump iron and chat up the crowd. Vendors sell sunglasses, clothing, records and more, and you can dine on anything from focaccio to *foie gras.* Figtree's Café (429 Ocean Front Walk) is a good quick stop.

✚ 210 B3 ✉ Ocean Front Walk (main action between Rose Avenue and Venice Boulevard) 🚍 MTA Bus 33 (and others)

56 Museum of Tolerance

This museum at the Simon Wiesenthal Center provides a vivid introduction to bigotry in action. The Holocaust Section, which takes about an hour to tour alone, uses documents, sound recordings and video projections to show visitors the despotism of the National Socialist dictatorship in Europe.

✚ 210 B3 ✉ 9786 W. Pico Boulevard ☎ 310/553-8403; www.museumoftolerance.com 🕐 Sun–Fri 10–5 (3:30 on Fri Nov–Mar); last entry1.5 hours before closing time 🚍 Santa Monica Big Blue Bus 7 💲 $15.50

57 Downtown Los Angeles

Many years in the making, the stunning $274 million home of the Los Angeles Philharmonic, the **Walt Disney Concert Hall** was designed by architect Frank Gehry, with a wavy, ship-like facade that stuns from every angle. On most days, self-guided audio tours are available, though, due to rehearsals and performances, they don't include the auditorium.

Controversy surrounded downtown's other grand edifice of recent vintage, the Roman Catholic **Cathedral of Our Lady of the Angels**, designed by Spanish architect José Rafael Moneo. But his supposed sins – some of the faithful (and a few architecture critics) initially found the ambiance unsettlingly futuristic – seem to have been forgiven, and the austere building is a marvel to visit. Free tours (1pm on weekdays) leave from the Plaza at Temple Street.

MUSEUM ROW

The delightful **Petersen Automotive Museum** displays roadsters, coupés, touring cars, sedans, trucks and motorcycles, many of them in amusing and innovative settings. The historical displays include gas pumps through the ages and show the automobile's influence in city planning and other areas. (6060 Wilshire Boulevard; tel: 323/930-2277; www.petersen.org; daily 10–6; Admission: $15.)

Key holdings at the comprehensive **Los Angeles County Museum of Art** include European, Chinese and contemporary American and European art. A separate pavilion holds the superlative Japanese collection. Sunday is 👪 family day, with various themed projects for kids and their parents. (5905 Wilshire Boulevard; tel: 323/857-6000; www.lacma.org; Mon, Tue, Thu 11–5, Fri 11–8, Sat, Sun 10–7. Admission: $15; free second Tue of month)

Primordial ooze – well, to be more precise, prehistoric asphalt – still bubbles up from 👪 **La Brea Tar Pits**, which you can view for free (until 10 pm) along outdoor pathways. The **George C. Page Museum of La Brea Discoveries** contains dinosaur bones and other fossils recovered from the pits (Hancock Park; 5801 Wilshire Boulevard; tel: 323/857-6300; www.tarpits.org; daily 9:30–5. Admission: $12.)

Insider Tip

Los Angeles Area

Fanciful **Union Station** is one of Los Angeles' great public spaces. With its Spanish-Moorish and late art-deco flourishes, the station radiates subdued whimsy yet also has a cathedral-like feel. Union Station has appeared in iconic movies such as *Blade Runner*, *Sunset Boulevard* and many other films.

Insider Tip The best time to visit Downtown is on weekends, when parking is easy everywhere but near **Olvera Street**, a Mexican-style plaza often aflutter with mariachi music, folklorica dancing and the chatter of patrons at open-air restaurants (daily 10–7). Spanish and Mexican settlers established the pueblo that became Los Angeles in this area in 1781. North of Olvera, L.A.'s workaday **Chinatown** contains gift shops and restaurants, though the area is less of a tourist attraction than its counterparts in other cities.

Walt Disney Concert Hall
🚇 212 C3 ✉ 111 S. Grand Avenue
☎ 323/850-2000 for event information;
www.laphil.com 🚇 Metro Red Line
(Civic Center) 🚌 MTA Bus 2, 14, 37;
DASH Route A (weekdays), D (weekends)

Cathedral of Our Lady of the Angels
🚇 213 D4 ✉ 555 W. Temple Street
☎ 213/680-5200; www.olacathedral.org
🕐 Mon–Fri 6:30–6, Sat 9–6, Sun 7–6 🚇 Metro
Red Line (Civic Center)
🚌 MTA Bus 2, 78, 81 (and others);
DASH Route B (weekdays), D (weekends)

Union Station
🚇 213 F3 ✉ 800 N. Alameda Street
🚇 Metro Red and Gold Lines (Union Station)
🚌 MTA 33, 42; DASH Route B (weekdays),
D (weekends)

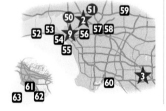

Multiple architectural styles rarely blend as pleasingly as they do in Union Station

Olvera Street/Chinatown
🚇 213 F3 ✉ West of Alameda Street, between
Aliso Street and Cesar E. Chavez Avenue
☎ 213/485-6855; www.olvera-street.com
🚇 Metro Red Line (Union Station)
🚌 MTA Bus 2, 4, 81, 94;
DASH Route B (weekdays), D (weekends)

58 Museums in Downtown

The Museum of Contemporary Art has two Downtown branches. The main **MOCA at California Plaza** location is known for its international collection of post-1940s art. Works by Rauschenberg, Johns, Beuys, Rothko and Serra are among the key holdings. The warehouse-like

MORE THAN A FACADE

Broadway, downtown's main street a century ago, contains several architectural gems, among them the 1893 **Bradbury Building** (304 S. Broadway, at 3rd Street), whose designer was inspired in part by a popular novel by Edward Bellamy (*Looking Backward*, 1888). Natural overhead light floods the lobby (open weekdays 9–6) and its tile floors, marble and exposed wrought-iron staircases. The building has proved popular with movie directors and scenes from *Blade Runner* (1982) were shot here before the structure was restored; the 1994 Jack Nicholson film *Wolf* (1994) shows the refurbished interior.

MOCA at The Geffen Contemporary, renovated by Frank Gehry, often presents huge installations – large sculptures, billboard art and the like.

Museum of Contemporary Art
☎ 213/626-6222; www.moca.org
🕓 Mon, Wed, Fri 11–6, Thu 11–8, Sat 11–3
🎫 $15 (free on Thu after 5. Two-for-one general admission with valid TAP card)

MOCA Grand
✚ 213 C3 ✉ 250 S. Grand Avenue
🚌 DASH Route B (weekdays), D (weekends); or shuttle from Geffen Contemporary)

MOCA Geffen
✚ 213 E2 ✉ 152 N. Central Avenue
🚌 MTA Bus 30, 40, 439;
DASH Route A (weekdays), D (weekends)
Ⓜ Metro Red Line (Civic Center)

59 Pasadena

This San Gabriel Valley town hosts the **Tournament of Roses Parade** each New Year's Day. The entire Old Pasadena district, much of it built in the 1920s and 1930s, is on the National Register of Historic Places. Chain clothing stores, boutiques, restaurants and cafés line Old Pasadena's main drag, Colorado Boulevard, and nearby streets and alleys from Pasadena Avenue east to Arroyo Parkway.

🎬 BEHIND THE SCENES
For an insight into how TV shows and movies are made, head to **Warner Bros.** (tel: 877/492-8687) or **Paramount** (323/956-1777) where the two-hour tour pass includes working sets, technical departments and the back lots.

The three-story **Gamble House**, the handiwork of Charles and Henry Greene, is a superb example of early 20th-century Craftsman architecture. The brothers incorporated many natural woods into a meticulous design that is pragmatic yet exudes a *joie de vivre* and a subtle appreciation of nature. The stained-glass entry doors, which depict coastal live oaks, are among the highlights.

"Visit the Getty for the architecture and the **Norton Simon Museum** for the art." This tip from LA's cultural cognoscenti acknowledges the discriminating taste of the financier Norton Simon, who assembled one of America's finest private collections of European art from the Renaissance to the early 20th century. Pivotal works by Ingres, Courbet, Corot, Rubens, Goya, Rembrandt, Renoir, Manet,

The Museum of Contemporary Art outside the MOCA on Grand Avenue in L.A.

Los Angeles Area

Renaissance-style City Hall in Pasadena

Degas, Picasso and Kandinsky attest to Simon's preference: quality over quantity.

The slate floors and columns, designed by architect Frank Gehry for the **South Asian Galleries**, create a stunningly contemporary yet reverent, temple-like setting for the mostly religious-oriented artworks. Impressionist Claude Monet's beloved garden in Giverny, France, inspired the sculpture garden.

You may have a hard time deciding whether to spend your time indoors or outdoors at the **Huntington Library, Art Collections and Botanical Gardens**, southeast of Pasadena in the town of San Marino. Significant holdings include a rare copy of the Gutenberg Bible on vellum, the Ellesmere manuscript of Geoffrey Chaucer's *Canterbury Tales*, Thomas Gainsborough's *The Blue Boy* and Sir Thomas Lawrence's *Pinkie*.

The Japanese, rose and desert gardens are three standouts of the 120-acre (48ha) botanical gardens. On most days, reservations are required for English tea in the Rose Garden Tea Room.

➕ 210 B3
✉ Northeast of downtown Los Angeles, off the 110 freeway
🚇 Metro Gold Line (various stations)
🚌 MTA Bus 180, 181

Gamble House

✉ 4 Westmoreland Place, off Orange Grove Boulevard (west side, north of Walnut Street)
☎ 626/793-3334; www.gamblehouse.org
🕐 Tue 11:30–1:30, Thu–Sun noon–3
🚌 MTA 180 💲 $15

Norton Simon Museum

✉ 411 W. Colorado Boulevard
☎ 626/449-6840; www.nortonsimon.org
🕐 Fri, Sat 11–8, Sun 11–5, Mon, Wed, Thu noon–5 🚌 MTA Bus 180, 181 💲 $12

Huntington Library, Art Collections & Botanical Gardens

✉ 1151 Oxford Road, off San Marino Avenue (south of I-210) ☎ 626/405-2100 (info); www.huntington.org; 626/683-8131 (tea room)
🕐 Wed–Mon 10–5
🚌 MTA Bus 79 (from downtown L.A.; exit at San Marino Avenue and walk about 0.25mi/0.4 km)
💲 $23 (free first Thu of the month with advance tickets), $25 (weekends)

60 *Queen Mary*

The era of plush luxury liners peaked with the construction of the art-deco-style *Queen Mary*, built in the mid-1930s. The ship's speed was renowned – she set a world record by sailing from Europe to New York in four days – but opulence was her true calling card. The ship transported troops during World War II – the pool was turned into barracks. The Behind-the-scenes Tour takes you to the ballroom and some private staterooms. You can dine on board. Long Beach's other draw, the **Aquarium of the Pacific**, sits just across Rainbow Harbor from the grand ship.

➕ 210 B3 ✉ 1126 Queens Highway (follow signs at southern end of I-710), Long Beach

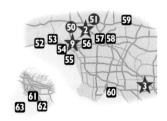

☎ 877/342-0738; www.queenmary.com
🕙 Daily from 10, closing times vary from
tour to tour 🚇 Metro Blue Line (Transit
Mall station; transfer to free Passport
Shuttle C: "Aquarium/Queen Mary") 💵 $44.95
(combined ticket Aquarium/Queen Mary)

🔢 Newport Beach

With mansions, yachts, fancy cars
and plush hotels, Newport Beach
is one of California's ritziest communities, but it manages to retain
the homey beachside flavor that has
drawn vacationers for more than a
century. Wide, white-sand beaches
stretch from the Santa Ana River
south several miles to the tip of
Balboa Peninsula, which separates
Newport Bay from the ocean.

Newport Boulevard heads south
and then east into **Balboa Peninsula**
from the Coast Highway (the Pacific
Coast Highway's name in most of
Orange County). Park when you see
signs for the Newport Pier, which
like Balboa Pier, 2mi (3km) farther
along, stretches several hundred
yards into the ocean and makes for
a pleasant stroll. Near each you
can rent bicycles or in-line skates,
an ideal way to see the peninsula.

Two short blocks across east
of the harbor pier stands the
Balboa Pavilion, a large
Edwardian building that   *Insider Tip*
houses a restaurant with a superb
view of the harbor.

Nearby are the 🎠 **Balboa Fun
Zone** amusement park and booths
where you can buy tickets to
45- or 90-minute Newport   *Insider Tip*
Harbor cruises, which sail
past palatial homes (some owned
by celebrities) and other sights
unseen by landlubbers. Another
fun excursion is the five-minute
ferry ride to **Balboa Island**. Catch
the ferry two blocks west of the
pavilion at Palm Street. The island
has some nice shops and cafés
along Marine Avenue.

✚ 210 B2 ✉ Fashion Island, 401 Newport
Center Drive ☎ 949/719-6100; www.visit
newportbeach.com 🚌 OCTA Bus 1, 55, 57, 79

🔢 Laguna Beach

The foliage that adorns Newport
Beach along the Coast Highway
becomes even greener and lusher
as the road snakes southward to
Laguna Beach. Park in one of the
public lots off Broadway and head
to Main Beach (Coast Highway and
Broadway), a protected sandy cove
fronted by a grassy lawn with shade
trees and picnic tables. After spend-
ing time at the beach, you can stroll
Forest and Ocean avenues, which
contain boutiques, art galleries,
restaurants and cafés. Stop into the
visitor bureau at 381 Forest Avenue
to pick up brochures with self-
guided tours of Laguna's historic
bungalows and cottages and to
find out what's happening in town
during your stay. Laguna Beach's
deservedly celebrated **Festival of
Arts** (650 Laguna Canyon Road;
tel: 949/494-1145) takes place
each July and August.

North of Main Beach, close
enough to walk, is **Heisler Park**
(Cliff Drive, off Coast Highway),
whose bluff-top trail yields stunning
ocean views. Sharing those vistas
is **Las Brisas** (361 Cliff Drive; tel:
949/497-5434), a Mexican seafood
restaurant open for breakfast, lunch
and dinner. At the north end of
Heisler Park lies Diver's Cove, a
great place to snorkel.

Among the less crowded beaches
are Crescent Bay (to the north of
downtown, off Coast Highway) and

*A secluded palm-fringed cove at Laguna
Beach – perfect for bathing*

Los Angeles Area

Victoria Beach (to the south). Seals and other wildlife congregate on Seal Rock, in the waters of Crescent Bay. Just north of town at **Crystal Cove State Park**, which encompasses 3.5mi (5.5km) of coastline, you can hike, swim, surf, fish and more.

➕ 210 B2 ✉ Coast Highway at Highway 133 (Broadway) ☎ 949/497-9229 or 800/877-1115 (tourist information); www.lagunabeachinfo. com 🚌 OCTA Bus 1 (connects with Laguna Beach Transit)

63 Catalina Island

Pristine natural settings can be hard to come by in overbuilt Southern California, but Catalina Island (officially Santa Catalina Island), most of which is owned by a nature conservancy, is a marvelous exception. On a clear day you can see the island from the mainland – Catalina's 22mi (35km) offshore.

Resort activities center around the town of Avalon. You could spend an enjoyable day just hanging out in town or at nearby Descanso Beach or Lover's Cove, but natural and man-made pleasures await elsewhere.

If you're making a day trip, maximize your time by taking a guided sightseeing tour on land,

sea or both. **Santa Catalina Island Company** conducts some of its outings aboard a sub-marine-like "semisubmersible" that's the next best thing to snorkeling for seeing the abundant marine life – anything from moray eels to colorful fish (tel: 800/626-1496). If you're up for something more strenuous than touring, you can go snorkeling or horseback riding or play golf, tennis or other sports.

Insider Tip

Popular sights include the island's landmark, the **Casino,** said to be the world's largest circular ballroom. Within the Casino is an art deco-style movie palace, the Avalon Theatre, adorned inside and out with stunning murals on aquatic and American West themes. The main artists also decorated the Chinese Theatre in Hollywood.

To get to the island from San Pedro, Long Beach or Dana Point, take the **Catalina Express ferry** (tel: 800/481-3470) or the **Catalina Flyer** (tel: 949/673-5245 or 800/830-7744) from Newport Beach's Balboa Pavilion (▶ 151). If you get seasick, take the appropriate medication before boarding the boats.

➕ 210 A1 ✉ Visitors Bureau: 1 Green Pleasure Pier, Avalon ☎ 310/510-1520 (tourist information); www.catalinachamber.com

Catalina Island: A beautiful view of Avalon Bay and the Casino

Where to...
Stay

Prices
Expect to pay per double room, per night (excluding tax)
$ under $100 $$ $100–$175 $$$ over $175

The Ambrose $$$
The creators of this boutique hotel drew on sources such as feng shui principles and Asian art to produce an instant hit in Santa Monica. With its soothing colors, Italian bed linens, Aveda bath products and high-tech internet hookups, there's plenty to like. You may not need all the amenities – room service is available 24 hours – but a Pilates trainer is on call – but their presence typifies the attention to detail.
⊞ 210 B3
✉ 1255 20th Street, Santa Monica, CA 90404
☎ 310/315-1555 or 855/426-2767;
www.ambrosehotel.com

The Beverly Hills Hotel $$$
Opened in 1912, predating the exclusive city of Beverly Hills itself, this classic hotel has hosted the likes of Marilyn Monroe and Charlie Chaplin, and Elizabeth Taylor honeymooned with six of her husbands in the bungalows. The famed Polo Lounge is the film industry's original power-dining spot. The hotel is a shimmering pink beauty, set in a ritzy residential area. The luxuriously appointed rooms have marble bathrooms and stereos; the bungalows have cozy fireplaces.
⊞ 210 B3 ✉ 9641 Sunset Boulevard, Beverly Hills, CA 90210 ☎ 310/276-2251 or 800/283-8885; www.beverlyhillshotel.com

Beverly Laurel Motor Hotel $–$$
Close to the Miracle Mile, mid-Wilshire district of Los Angeles – not far from Beverly Hills – this 52-room motel has a small outdoor pool, rooms that are well-maintained, Air-conditioning, cable and microwaves. Some rooms also have kitchenettes. Having Swingers, a hip LA diner, in the motel is another bonus.
⊞ 210 B3 ✉ 8018 Beverly Boulevard, Los Angeles, CA 90048 ☎ 323/651-2441; http://beverly-laurel.hotel-rn.com

Carlyle Inn $$$
If you're looking for good value accommodations close to all the sights and Beverly Hills, try this 32-room, four-story, European-style hotel, one of the reliable Best Western hotel chain. Amenities include high-speed internet access, refrigerators, coffee makers, ironing boards and irons, and safes. A hot tub and fitness room are located on the sundeck and available to all guests. Rates include a big buffet breakfast.
⊞ 210 B3 ✉ 1119 S. Robertson Boulevard, West Los Angeles, CA 90035 ☎ 310/275-4445 or 800/322-7595; www.carlyle-inn.com

Disneyland® Resort $$$
The three hotels in the Disney complex represent a universe unto themselves: they are conveniently located, the rooms are perfectly fine – comfortable and well-appointed – and guests enjoy privileges, chief among them re-entry to the two theme parks. There are plenty of distractions, from pools to video arcades to shops, and the many restaurants serve everything from burgers to haute cuisine. Disney's Grand Californian is the nicest (and priciest) of the properties, but the

Los Angeles Area

Disneyland Hotel and Disney's Paradise Pier Hotel are well-appointed and more than suitable for most visitors.

✚ 210 B3
✉ Disneyland Hotel:
1150 Magic Way, Anaheim, CA 92802;
✉ Disney's Grand Californian:
1600 S. Disneyland Drive, Anaheim, CA 92802;
✉ Disney's Paradise Pier Hotel:
1717 S. Disneyland Drive, Anaheim, CA 92802
☎ 714/956-6425 (all three hotels);
http://disneyland.disney.go.com/hotels

The Georgian Hotel $$$

This historic hotel with its turquoise and gold art-deco exterior will catch your eye on Santa Monica's Ocean Avenue. The architecture is right out of the 1930s, but the rooms are nicely up to date, and most have ocean views. Spend the late afternoon relaxing in the sunshine on the hotel's amiable rattan chair-lined veranda with a drink in hand, just as Clark Gable and Carole Lombard once did. Service is friendly.

✚ 210 B3 ✉ 1415 Ocean Avenue, Santa Monica, CA 90401 ☎ 310/395-9945 or 800/538-8147; www.georgianhotel.com

Hotel Villa Portofino $$–$$$

This Italian-style hotel fits in well with the overall Mediterranean feel of Avalon, Santa Catalina Island's main town. Located along Avalon's main street, the hotel is convenient to the harbor, beach, restaurants and shops. Rooms have cable TV, and many have good views of the water; some even come with cozy fireplaces and refrigerators. You can also lounge on a private guest sundeck. The hotel also has an excellent restaurant, Ristorante Villa Portofino, which serves Italian food.

✚ 210 B2 ✉ 111 Crescent Avenue, Santa Catalina Island, CA 90704 ☎ 310/510-0555 or 888/510-0555; www.hotelvillaportofino.com

Inn at Laguna Beach $$$

This three-story hotel has wonderful views from its dramatic position atop a cliff overlooking the Pacific Ocean, with flower-filled grounds. The hotel offers easy access to both beach and the town. Many of the 70 rooms have ocean views. The rooms are comfortable and have a wealth of room amenities: refrigerators, CD players, bathrobes, hair dryers, irons and ironing boards, complimentary newspaper and Continental breakfast are all included. There's also a heated swimming pool and a hot tub on a sunny terrace.

✚ 210 B2 ✉ 211 N. Pacific Coast Highway, Laguna Beach, CA 92651 ☎ 949/497-9722 or 800/544-4479; www.innatlagunabeach.com

London West Hollywood $$$

This premier hotel, near Sunset Strip, is a luxurious respite for travelers. The 200 suites feature open floor plans and modern decor; other amenities include a rooftop pool and, indoor and outdoor, workout facilities. British celebrity chef Gordon Ramsay, of TV's *Hell's Kitchen* and *Kitchen Nightmares* fame, is the creative mind behind the cuisine, both poolside snacks and restaurant dining. His "London Breakfast Table" is included in the rate.

✚ 210 B3 ✉ 1020 N. San Vicente Boulevard, West Hollywood, CA, 90069
☎ 310/854-1111 or 866/282-4560;
www.thelondonwesthollywood.com

Sunset Plaza Hotel $$$

Though several of L.A.'s priciest hotels are on the Sunset Strip, you don't have to pay top dollar to stay there. This comfortable Best Western property combines reasonable rates with a raft of amenities in the clean, attractively decorated rooms – refrigerators, phones with voice mail, cable TV, high-speed DSL and complimentary newspapers among them. Many rooms have kitchens.

✚ 210 B3 ✉ 8400 Sunset Boulevard, West Hollywood, CA 90069
☎ 323/654-0750;
www.sunsetplazahotel.com

Where to...
Eat and Drink

Prices
Expect to pay per person for a meal, excluding drinks and service:
$ under $15 $$ $15–$25 $$$ over $25

230 Forest Avenue $$–$$$
The regular-changing collection of artworks on the walls of this bistro is in keeping with the artsy tradition of Laguna Beach. The California cuisine has flair, with intriguing dishes such as sugar-cane tenderloin, short-rib ravioli, and chopped seafood salad, while the portions won't leave you hungry. Martinis are the focus at the bar, though they also have a good beer and wine list. The restaurant gets loud, but diners can retreat to the front patio, which is more romantic, on warm evenings.
🞤 210 B2
✉ 230 Forest Avenue, Laguna Beach
☎ 949/494-2545; www.230forestavenue.com
🕔 Lunch daily from 11; dinner from 5

Celistino Ristorante & Bar $$$
This Pasadena restaurant exudes a welcoming, laidback feel, despite the crisp white tablecloths and bowtie-clad waiters. The atmosphere is loud and bustling, and the excellent kitchen serves up a wide variety of remarkably good homemade pastas and meat dishes, such as veal shank with saffron risotto and roast rabbit with black olive sauce. The distinguished wine list features Italian wines from Sicily, Sardinia and Umbria. Outdoor seating is available for warm evenings.
🞤 210 B3
✉ 141 S. Lake Avenue, Pasadena
☎ 626/795-4006; http://celestinopasadena.com
🕔 Lunch Mon–Fri 11:30–2:30; dinner Mon–Sat 5–11, Sun 5–10:30

Chaya Venice $$$
This energetic restaurant in Venice Beach displays Japanese and French influences, with a 14-seat sushi bar, lofty ceilings, an Asian-inspired mural, an expansive wine and imported sake list, while the main focus is seafood. Be warned that the restaurant gets very loud and crowded. Beverly Hills and downtown LA also have popular Chaya restaurants.
🞤 210 B3 ✉ 110 Navy Street, Venice
☎ 310/396-1179; www.thechaya.com
🕔 Lunch Mon–Fri 11:30–2:30; dinner Mon–Thu 6–10:30, Fri–Sat 6–11, Sun 6–10

Cut $$$
Wolfgang Puck's new Beverly Hills venture is this expensive, sleek steakhouse in the Beverly Wilshire Hotel. The restaurant, designed by Getty Center architect, Richard Meier, features white walls, oak wood floors and large windows. The menu offers Puck's creative spin on steaks, sauces and an array of sides, along with an international wine list and impeccable service – your waiter will painstakingly review your choices with you.
🞤 210 B3
✉ 9500 Wilshire Boulevard, Beverly Hills
☎ 310/276-8500; www.wolfgangpuck.com/restaurants/fine-dining/3789
🕔 Mon–Thu 6–10, Fri 6–11, Sat 5:30–11

El Cholo Cafe $$
You can find cheaper, and probably more authentic, Mexican food in L.A., but El Cholo, the city's oldest Mexican restaurant, is a landmark

Los Angeles Area

and a festive place to chow down on Tex-Mex favorites washed down with dynamite margaritas. You can make your own tacos with beef, chicken, beans and salsas. From May through October only, order El Cholo's famous homemade green corn tamales. There's a newer branch in Santa Monica (1025 Wilshire Boulevard; tel: 310/899-1106).

🟥 210 B3
✉ 1121 S. Western Avenue, Los Angeles
☎ 323/734-2773; www.elcholo.com
🕐 Sun, Mon 11–9, Tue–Thu 11–10, Fri– Sat 11–11

James' Beach $$

Located between the Venice Canals and the beach, this stylish restaurant serves American fare in a Craftsman building. Dine inside – closer to the bar scene – or on the outdoor patio. The health-conscious can order the "swimsuit special" – grilled chicken, brown rice and steamed vegetables – everyone else can opt for more interesting steaks, seafood or vegetarian dishes. The restaurant is also famous for its guest appearances on TV and in the movie *I Love You, Man.*

🟥 210 B3
✉ 60 N. Venice Boulevard, Venice
☎ 310/823-6396; www.jamesbeach.com
🕐 Mon, Tue 6pm–1:30am, Wed–Fri 11:30am–1:30am, Sat, Sun 11am–1:30am

Jar $$$

This retro-style chophouse focuses on beef with a touch of Asian flair. The surroundings are simple, with wood-paneled walls and brown booths and chairs; the menu is dominated by steak – ribeye skirt, filet – alongside braised pork shank and Jar's tasty signature pot roast. The creative cocktail list includes the Starburst (orange-infused vodka, peach tree, orange juice and cranberry juice) and the Koh Samui (vodka, lychee juice and muddled lychees).

🟥 210 B3
✉ 8225 Beverly Boulevard, West Hollywood
☎ 323/655-6566; www.thejar.com
🕐 Tue–Sun from 5:30pm

Lucques $$$

Chef Suzanne Goin serves French-inspired fare in a relaxed setting of exposed brick and wood beam ceilings in West Hollywood. Goin focuses on seasonal ingredients and allows them to speak for themselves. Spiced lamb tagine and Alaskan black cod may share space with unusual desserts, such as butterscotch tart with pecans and banana ice cream, or peanut butter sherbet. There is also a bar menu, and dining on the garden patio.

🟥 210 B3 ✉ 8474 Melrose Avenue, West Hollywood ☎ 323/655-6277; www.lucques.com
🕐 Lunch Tue–Sat noon–2:30; dinner Mon–Thu 6–10, Fri, Sat 6–10:30, Sun 5–9:30

Matsuhisa $$$

This upscale Japanese restaurant is a hit with L.A. residents who are willing to pay mightily for a memorable meal that often makes more standard Japanese dishes seem lame. Named for star chef Nobu Matsuhisa, the restaurant turns out supremely fresh, imaginative and often dazzling seafood creations that range from sushi to sea scallops with black truffles and caviar.

🟥 210 B3
✉ 129 N. La Cienega Boulevard, West Hollywood ☎ 310/659-9639;
http://nobumatsuhisa.com 🕐 Lunch Mon–Fri 11:45–2:15; dinner daily 5:45–10:15

Ocean & Vine $$–$$$

As you'd expect from the name, this wonderful New American restaurant, housed in the Loews Santa Monica Beach Hotel, offers lovely ocean views to accompany its sizzling steaks and fresh seafood. Produce is sourced fresh from the local farmers' market, and the breakfast menu includes standard favorites along with juice "martinis," – your choice of juices shaken together.

✚ 210 B3 ✉ 1700 Ocean Avenue, Santa Monica
☎ 310/576-3180; www.loewshotels.com/
santa-monica ⏱ Daily 11–10

Patina $$$

Patina, relocated in late 2003 to a
space in the Walt Disney Concert
Hall (▶160), is one of the city's
most beloved restaurants. Chef-
owner Joachim Splichal still
produces food that people adore;
creative California-French cuisine
that includes German and Austrian
touches. Try one of the five-course
tasting menus, which may feature
all-vegetarian dishes or all-shellfish
variations. There is a caviar service
and gourmet cheeses, too.

✚ 212 C3
✉ 141 S. Grand Avenue, Los Angeles
☎ 213/972-3331; www.patinarestaurant.com
⏱ Tue–Sat 5pm–9pm, Sun 4pm–8pm
(last seating 30 minutes after the show ends
on performance days)

Philippe the Original $

You might find yourself sitting next
to a business executive, a cop, an
actor or a street person at the long
communal tables in this old-time
downtown restaurant, where everyone comes for the French dip
sandwiches: roast beef, lamb, pork
or turkey on a French roll, dipped
in natural juices, which the founder
invented in 1908. Philippe isn't
much for aesthetics, with sawdust
on the floor and lines of customers
waiting to order at the counter. But
prices are rock bottom – coffee is
all of 45 cents – and it's a classic
L.A. experience, which should not
be missed.

✚ 213 F4
✉ 1001 N. Alameda Street, Los Angeles
☎ 213/628-3781; www.philippes.com
⏱ Daily 6am–10pm

République $$–$$$

Renowned San Diego chef Walter
Manske and his Filipino-born wife
Margarita have opened large
numbers of bakeries in Manila and
restaurants in California over the
years. République is a combination
of their two passions: it acts as a
bakery and café by day and turns
into a French bistro at night.

✚ 210 B3 ✉ 624 S. La Brea, Los Angeles
☎ 310/362-6115; http://republiquela.com
⏱ Lunch daily 8–4; dinner Sun–Wed 5:30–10,
Thu–Sat 5:30–11

Rockwell Table & Stage $$

Contemporary American cuisine
with influences from French, Italian
and Spanish cooking is served up
between the mighty pillars at this
new events venue. Guests journey
from far and wide to this joint in
the hip Los Feliz district to feast on
Ahi tuna or goats cheese and truffle
ravioli, enjoy a drink or two at the
elegant cocktail bar, and listen to
the selection of top-class musical
performances on offer.

✚ 210 B3
✉ 1714 N. Vermont Aveenue, Hollywood
☎ 323/669-1550; www.rockwell-la.com
⏱ Lunch Mon–Fri 11:30–3, Sat, Sun 10–3;
dinner daily from 3

Spago Beverly Hills $$$

This spin-off from the original Spago
Hollywood (now closed) is the most
glamorous of Wolfgang Puck's fleet
of prestigious restaurants. You may
well spot the odd movie star or
studio head here – possibly as
they're being led to that prized open-
air patio table ahead of you. Expect
to wait some time for your table,
even with a reservation, and prepare
for a high-decibel, high-energy experience. But the California cuisine,
which sports Asian, Mediterranean
and Austrian accents – the chef's
original veal Wienerschnitzel is one
winner – seldom disappoints.
There is an excellent wine list to
accompany your meal and the
more informal bar menu includes
Puck's trademark designer pizzas.

✚ 201 E1 ✉ 176 N. Cañon Drive, Beverly Hills
☎ 310/385-0880; www.wolfgangpuck.com/
restaurants/fine-dining/3635
⏱ Lunch Tue–Sat noon–2:30; dinner Mon–Fri
6–10, Sat 5:30–10:30, Sun 5:30–10

Los Angeles Area

Where to…
Shop

The range of merchandise in Los Angeles is staggering, whether you're looking for ultra-chic or retro fashions, antiques, Hollywood memorabilia, Mexican imports or surfer gear.

The best-known shopping area is **Beverly Hills**, particularly **Rodeo Drive** between Santa Monica and Wilshire boulevards, where you'll find pricy jewelry and clothing stores: Armani, Christian Dior, Harry Winston, Tiffany & Co., Van Cleef & Arpels, Valentino, Hugo Boss, Bijan, Dolce & Gabbana, Prada, Chanel, Gucci, Hermès, Jimmy Choo and Versace. Brighton Way, just off Rodeo, has a Cartier boutique and other noted retailers.

For all-purpose shopping, head to the outdoor **Westfield Century City Mall** (10250 Santa Monica Boulevard, Los Angeles; tel: 310/277-3898, http://westfield. com), home to some 100 stores, including Macy's, Bloomingdales and many designer boutiques.

Several big department stores are found along the 9500–9900 blocks of Wilshire Boulevard, including Barneys New York, Neiman-Marcus and Saks Fifth Avenue.

One of the funkiest shopping streets is **Melrose Avenue**, between Fairfax and La Brea, where clothing stores carry both retro and new fashions.

The Fred Segal Center (8118 Melrose Avenue; tel: 323/651-4129) sells high-end designer clothing at Ron Herman and other boutiques.

Wasteland (7428 Melrose Avenue; tel: 323/653-3028) sells secondhand clothing for men and women. On the west end of Melrose, Melrose Place, made famous by a TV show of the same name, is lined with high-end antiques shops.

Three hot areas for clubwear, retro fashions and quirky boutiques are **North La Brea Avenue** and **Robertson Boulevard** in West Hollywood, and **Sunset Boulevard** in Los Feliz.

Farther west, on Sunset Strip, Sunset Plaza offers a mix of cafés and high-end shops. L.A.'s best bookstore, **Book Soup** (8818 Sunset Boulevard; tel: 310/659-3110), is open till 10pm and has a newsstand, carrying both domestic and foreign publications.

Hollywood Boulevard is still a good place for movie memorabilia and souvenirs. **Frederick's of Hollywood** (6751 Hollywood Boulevard; tel: 323/957-5953) is legendary for lingerie.

The Citadel Factory Stores (5675 E. Telegraph Road; tel: 323/888-1724; www.citadeloutlets. com) are located in a landmark building off I-5 and carry discount brand-name clothing.

The venerable **Farmers Market** (6333 W. 3rd Street) has stores and a food court. The adjacent Grove offers shops, restaurants, movie theaters and a "dancing" fountain.

Olvera Street, in the city's historic El Pueblo downtown, is the place to find Mexican-style trinkets and souvenirs. The colorful **Grand Central Market** (317 S. Broadway), also downtown, is filled with exotic produce stands and food booths.

🚇 **Universal CityWalk** near Universal Studios has offbeat stores, many geared toward kids, and a lively, offbeat ambiance.

In Santa Monica, the **3rd Street Promenade** is lined with boutiques, restaurants and movie theaters. At 3rd Street and Broadway is **Santa Monica Place** with shops and a new dining deck with sunset views.

Where to...
Go Out

For entertainment and live music listings, check the free tabloid *L.A. Weekly* (www.laweekly.com), the weekend Calendar section of the *Los Angeles Times* (www.latimes.com), or the useful *Los Angeles magazine* (www.lamag.com).

For information on music and theater performances call the Music Center of Los Angeles County (tel: 213/972-7211; www.musiccenter.org), which gives 24-hour recorded information about all the current productions at the Dorothy Chandler Pavilion, the Ahmanson Theater and the Mark Taper Forum, among others.

The wonderful Los Angeles Philharmonic performs at the Walt Disney Concert Hall.

HOTEL BARS

With great weather for much of the year, poolside hotel bars are popular in Los Angeles. In Santa Monica, stop by the sexy **Cameo Bar** at the Viceroy (1819 Ocean Avenue; tel: 310/260-7500), lounge at the sleek **Skybar** at the Mondrian (8440 Sunset Boulevard; tel: 323/848-6025), or head to the **Roof Bar** at the Standard Downtown (550 S. Flower Street; tel: 213/892-8080).

The Penthouse (1111 2nd Street; tel: 310/394-5454) in Santa Monica's Huntley Hotel is on the 18th floor, so you can enjoy views of the ocean with your cocktail.

Also in Santa Monica, the beach-front **Veranda Bar** at Casa del Mar (1910 Ocean Way; tel: 310/581-5533) offers a relaxing yet elegant setting for a drink, with gentle piano or louder live music and comfortable wicker chairs.

BARS & LIVE MUSIC

The **Hotel Café** (1623 ½ N. Cahuenga Boulevard, no phone; www.hotelcafe.com) is a cozy spot to hear live music; they have a full bar along with panini sandwiches, espresso drinks and other snacks.

The **Comedy Store** (8433 Sunset Boulevard; tel: 323/650-6268; www.thecomedystore.com) has spawned a number of star stand-up comics. **The Groundlings** (7307 Melrose Avenue; tel: 323/934-4747) improvisation troupe has hilarious – and popular – shows, five nights per week.

Popular bars in Santa Monica and Venice include **Father's Office** (1018 Montana Avenue; tel: 310/736-2224), a gastropub known for its burgers and 30-plus beers on tap.

The **Bodega Wine Bar** (814 Broadway; tel: 310/394-3504) focuses on grape vintages and tasty accompanying snacks.

James Beach (P146) is another congenial place to eat. Santa Monica's Main Street also has a number of busy and ambient bars in the space of a few blocks.

A popular gay bar in Venice is **Roosterfish** (1302 Abbot Kinney Boulevard; tel: 310/392-2123), a laidback spot with a jukebox, pool table and video games.

West Hollywood's gigantic bar **The Abbey** (692 N. Robertson Boulevard; tel: 310/289-8410) was voted best gay bar in the world by Logo, MTV's gay and lesbian network. In addition, numerous gay and lesbian clubs are located along Santa Monica Boulevard in West Hollywood.

NIGHTCLUBS

Hollywood and West Hollywood are the centers of nightlife in L.A. Nightclubs usually close by 2am, when it's no longer legal to serve liquor. Remember that this week's

Los Angeles Area

hot, trendy club is next week's fading memory.

One of the enduring areas for action is West Hollywood's famed Sunset Strip, where you'll find **Whisky A-Go-Go** (8901 Sunset Boulevard; tel: 310/652-4202; www.whiskyagogo.com), the **Viper Room** (8852 Sunset Boulevard; tel: 310/358-1881; www.viperroom. com), the **Rainbow Bar** (9015 Sunset Boulevard; tel: 310/278-4232; www.rainbowbarandgrill.com) and the **House of Blues** (8430 Sunset Boulevard; tel: 323/848-5100; www. houseofblues.com), which all present big-name acts from rock, blues and jazz, depending on the venue.

Los Feliz and Silver Lake are two trendy areas for bars and clubs. Several popular gay and lesbian clubs are located along the vibrant **Santa Monica Boulevard** in West Hollywood.

MOVIE THEATERS

Classic movie theaters are attractions in and of themselves in Hollywood. Watching a flick at **Grauman's Chinese Theatre** (6801 Hollywood Boulevard; tel: 323/461-3331, www. tclchinesetheatres.co) or **El Capitan** (6838 Hollywood Boulevard; tel: 818/8453110, http://elcapitan theatre.com) adds a touch of class and cachet to the experience.

At **ArcLight Hollywood** (6360 W. Sunset Boulevard; tel: 323/464-1478) you can reserve seats – and they're roomier than seats in regular movie theaters. You also enjoy an alcoholic drink before, after, or during the film – a relatively new concept for American movie theaters.

The **Nuart Theatre** (11272 Santa Monica Boulevard; tel: 310/473-8530) shows foreign and independent films.

The Laemmle movie theater chain (tel: 310/478-1041) also shows independent films at locations throughout Los Angeles. Visit www.

laemmle.com for locations, schedules and showtimes.

THEATER & CONCERT MUSIC

Tickets by telephone, with a service charge, are available through **Ticketmaster** (tel: 800/745-3000).

Concerts and operas are held at the Walt Disney Concert Hall (111 S. Grand Avenue; tel: 323/850-2000) and the **Dorothy Chandler Pavilion** (135 N. Grand Avenue; tel: 213/972-7211; www.music center.org) in the Los Angeles Music Center.

The season for the famous **Hollywood Bowl** (2301 N. Highland Avenue; tel: 323/850-2000; www. hollywoodbowl.com), which presents open-air concerts by the LA Philharmonic Orchestra, is June to mid-September.

Griffith Park's **Greek Theatre** (2700 N. Vermont Avenue; tel: 323/665-5857) is an outdoor amphitheater that seats 5,801 and hosts musical acts ranging from pop to classical to rock.

Major venues for stage include two theaters at the Los Angeles Music Center on Grand Avenue: the **Ahmanson Theater** and the **Mark Taper Forum**. The **Pantages** (6233 Hollywood Boulevard; tel: 323/468-1770; www.hollywood pantages.com) and the **Wiltern Theater** (3790 Wilshire Boulevard, Beverly Hills; tel: 213/388-1400) are both splendid art-deco theaters that present Broadway-style musicals and other productions.

The **Geffen Playhouse** (10886 Le Conte Avenue; tel: 310/208-5454; http://geffenplayhouse.com), under the auspices of nearby U.C.L.A, stages everything from musicals to satires.

The **John Anson Ford Amphitheater** (2580 Cahuenga Boulevard East, Hollywood; tel: 323/461-3673; http:// ford-theatres.org) is a pleasant place to watch a production under the stars in summer.

San Diego & Southern California

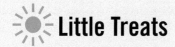 **Little Treats**

Surfing USA
The waves on **Windansea Beach** (▶ 174) should be left to experienced surfers. You'll find tamer tides elsewhere.

A Whale of a Time!
Head to **Point Loma** (▶ 170) on San Diego's Pacific Coast to be in with a chance of spotting gray whales from the shore.

Famous Scenes
The red sandstone rocks at **Red Rock Canyon State Park** (▶ 181) have provided the backdrop for numerous Hollywood Westerns.

Getting Your Bearings

Southern California encompasses the state's two largest cities, Los Angeles and San Diego, but away from the coast much of the region is arid desert, where the color brown comes in more shades than you might imagine possible. The quest for water has in many ways defined Southern California, though with plentiful sources having been tapped in Northern California and points east, many people here take the continued flow of water for granted.

Such was not the case in the mid-1800s, when a band of 100 gold-seekers got lost and stumbled across a long, low valley. The giant lake it once held had long since dried up. The group suffered a torturous month of heat and dehydration. The one who didn't survive inspired the region's name: Death Valley. Death Valley presents perhaps the desert's harshest face, but this land that at first glance appears so barren illustrates the resilience of living things: About 900 plant varieties and several rare wildlife species flourish here. In the Coachella Valley, which contains Palm Springs and other resort communities and is part of a different desert zone, the numbers are even higher.

As you head west to the coast, sagebrush and other low-lying desert shrubs give way to greenery and pinyon pines. You sense the moisture in the air and fog occasionally rolls in. Though San Diego has its hot days, ocean breezes often cool the air. Pleasant weather and dry skies have made San Diego a vacation mecca for outdoorsy types and families headed for the many theme parks. But this is a cultural oasis as well, with a slew of museums and an active performing arts scene.

The main north–south highway through Southern California is I-5, which connects Los Angeles and San Diego and ends at the US border with Mexico. I-15 heads north and east from San Diego through the desert and beyond to Las Vegas, Nevada. I-10 heads east from Los Angeles into the Palm Springs area and then on to Arizona. Except in parts of San Diego and downtown Palm Springs, a car is pretty much essential.

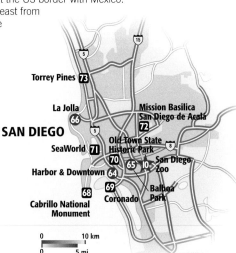

Getting Your Bearings

Bishop
Big Pine

Kings Canyon
78 National Park
Independence

Olancha

78
Sequoia
National Park

⭐ Death Valley
National Park

395

178
Ridgecrest

14

ersfield

58
Four Corners
Mojave
58 Barstow

Baker

15

77
Mojave
Desert

40
Ludlow

Lancaster
395
Victorville

5 Santa
Clarita Palmdale
14

Hesperia

15

Twentynine Palms

Glendale Ontario San Bernardino
62

101 LOS ANGELES Riverside Palm 67
Springs
62

Long 10
Beach Santa 74
1 Ana 15
Temecula

86

San Clemente 5
Oceanside

San Diego Zoo
Safari Park

Legoland® 74 75
California 15

78

76
Anza-Borrego
Desert State Park

86

SAN DIEGO El Cayon 8

0   50 km
Chula Vista

0   30 mi
Tijuana

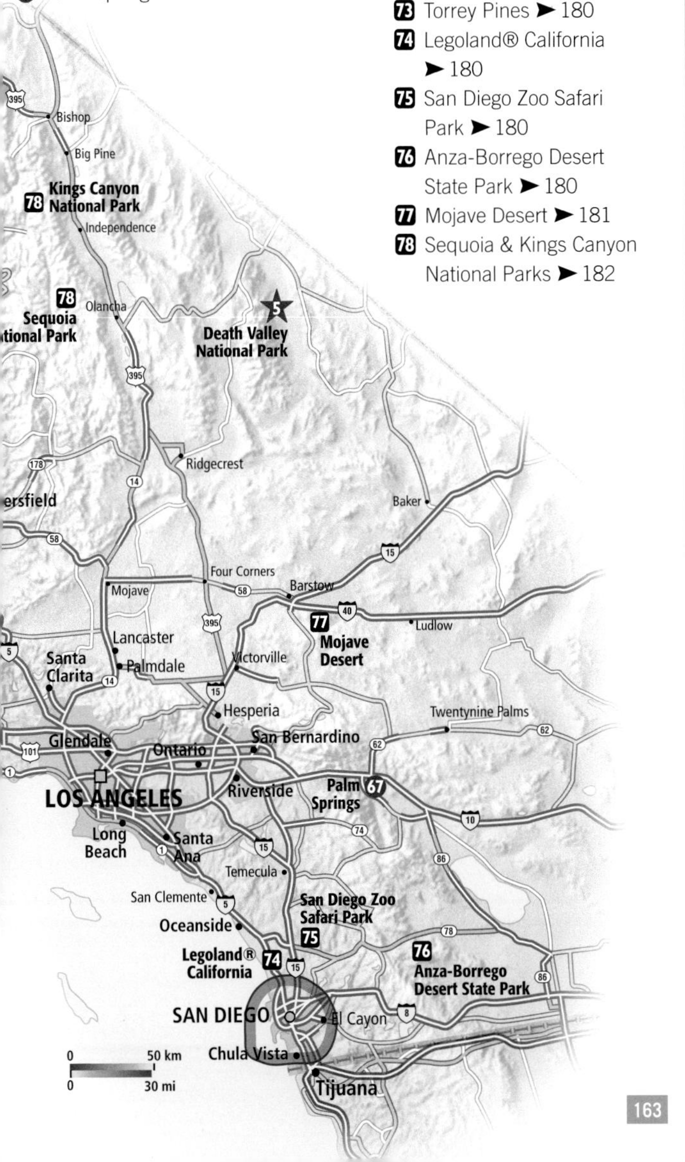

San Diego & Southern California

Four Perfect Days

If you're not quite sure where to begin your travels, this itinerary recommends a practical and enjoyable four days exploring Southern California, taking in some of the best places to see. For more information see the main entries (➤ 166–182).

Day 1

Morning
You will need at least two days in San Diego to see all the main sights. Start by arriving early at ⭐**San Diego Zoo** (right, ➤ 169).

Afternoon
Slip up to **66 La Jolla** (➤ 173)for a late lunch, then explore the area around La Jolla Cove. As the afternoon winds down, head south along Coast Boulevard, La Jolla Boulevard and then Mission Boulevard to **Pacific Beach**. Walk out on the Crystal Pier, fun anytime and a magical place at sunset.

Evening
Have dinner at **George's at the Cove** (➤ 185), where the sparkling cuisine complements the gorgeous ocean views. After dinner stroll the **Gaslamp Quarter** in San Diego's **64 Harbor & Old Town** (➤ 170), stopping at a nightclub to hear some jazz or blues.

Day 2

Morning
Wake yourself up for a two-hour harbor cruise, then walk south along the Embarcadero for a peek at **Seaport Village**.

Afternoon
Have lunch in the Gaslamp Quarter, then take the San Diego Trolley to **70 Old Town State Historic Park** (➤ 178).

Evening
If the weather's fine and you're feeling romantic, take a gondola ride in Mission Bay (book in advance to ensure a slot) and have dinner at **100 Wines** (➤ 186).

Four Perfect Days

Day 3

Morning
67 Palm Springs (► 175) can be explored easily in a day, although you may want to spend more time here. Start your day by boarding the **Palm Springs Aerial Tramway** for breathtaking views of the Coachella Valley. Back near sea level, view the natural history and art exhibits at the **Palm Springs Art Museum**.

Afternoon
Have lunch at **Las Casuelas Terraza** (222 S. Palm Canyon Drive; tel: 760/325-2794; www.lascasuelas.com), known for its Mexican specialties. Afterward, stroll a bit of Palm Canyon Drive. If it's not too hot, visit the **Indian Canyons** and walk one of the shorter loop trails within Palm Canyon.

Evening
A snack will get you through the **Fabulous Palm Springs Follies** (show starts at 7pm; www.psfollies.com), after which you can have a late dinner at **Le Vallauris** (385 W. Tahquitz Canyon Way; tel: 760/325-5059; www.levallauris.com).

Day 4

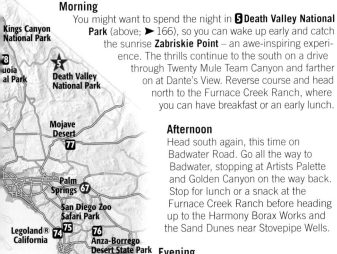

Morning
You might want to spend the night in **5 Death Valley National Park** (above; ► 166), so you can wake up early and catch the sunrise **Zabriskie Point** – an awe-inspiring experience. The thrills continue to the south on a drive through Twenty Mule Team Canyon and farther on at Dante's View. Reverse course and head north to the Furnace Creek Ranch, where you can have breakfast or an early lunch.

Afternoon
Head south again, this time on Badwater Road. Go all the way to Badwater, stopping at Artists Palette and Golden Canyon on the way back. Stop for lunch or a snack at the Furnace Creek Ranch before heading up to the Harmony Borax Works and the Sand Dunes near Stovepipe Wells.

Evening
Have dinner at the **Furnace Creek Inn** (► 184) or the steakhouse at the **Furnace Creek Ranch** (► 184).

Map labels: Kings Canyon National Park; uoia al Park **8**; **5** Death Valley National Park; Mojave Desert **77**; Palm Springs **67**; San Diego Zoo Safari Park; Legoland ® California **74** **75**; **76** Anza-Borrego Desert State Park

⭐5 Death Valley National Park

The western slopes of the barren Panamint Mountains often glow a soothing red in the early morning sun. Within an hour, red gives way to warmish browns. But as the day unfolds in Death Valley, the colors quickly mutate into brighter, more severe hues, a fitting visual metaphor for the treacherous beauty of what on many days is the hottest place on earth.

Furnace Creek, the valley's hub, contains a resort and some no-nonsense lodgings, a gas station, a grocery store and a few restaurants. Exhibits at the National Park Service visitor center describe the region's geology and wildlife; and park rangers can give you details and maps about short and long hiking possibilities. Read and heed the warnings about dealing with the heat and other conditions in Death Valley.

Sunrise at Zabriskie Point

Death Valley National Park

A road at the southern end of Furnace Creek leads south from Highway 190 to three points of interest: **Golden Canyon**, where a short hike will introduce you to the area's terrain; the multihued rocks of **Artists Palette**; and the salt flats of **Badwater**, at 282ft (86m) below sea level the lowest point in the Western Hemisphere. The loop road to Artists Palette is one-way heading north, so most people visit this sight on the way back from Badwater.

Surrounded by Panoramas

A bit farther south (and east) of Furnace Creek, Highway 190 passes serenely desolate **Zabriskie Point**. Most of the land here is sandy-colored, though to the north are some reddish-brown hills – the point at which they meet looks like a swirl of coffee and chocolate ice cream. About a mile (1.5km) farther is **Twenty Mule Team Canyon**, seen

on an exciting unpaved loop so narrow in places that you can touch the canyon walls. Past this a few miles, Highway 190 forks left and **Dante's View** Road forks right, rising for 13.3mi (21km) to more than 5,000ft (1,525m) at Dante's View, which yields a panorama of nearly the entire valley, of mountains rising from the salt beds.

North of Furnace Creek

To the north of Furnace Creek off Highway 190 are the remains of the **Harmony Borax Works**, where 19th-century miners and processors of borax spent their grueling days. A little farther north, past the road to Scotty's Castle (below), even the slightest wind alters the shape of a long stretch of sand dunes. A gravel road leads from the highway to a parking lot from which you can hike into the dunes.

The gravel road continues north past the lot to the road to **Scotty's Castle** (tel: 760/786-2392); make a left if you've come this way. The castle, 53mi (85km) north of Furnace Creek, can only be seen on guided

INSIDER INFO

- Drink plenty of water (up to 1 gallon/4 liters per day is recommended) to **avoid dehydration**.
- Fuel up before you head into the valley – **stations are few and far between**.
- Restaurant food and groceries are expensive, so if you're on a budget, **stock a cooler in Ridgecrest (➤ 181)** or elsewhere. *Insider Tip*
- West of the dunes on Highway 190 is **Stovepipe Wells**, a small town with basic services.
- Not much goes on in **Death Valley Junction**, southeast of Furnace Creek where highways 190 and 127 meet, but the small town's **Amargosa Opera House** (tel: 760/852-4441) draws crowds for engaging performances of "dance mime in a program of musical theater".

tours (currently closed until at least 2019 due to flood damage). The Spanish-style house is named for Walter E. Scott (also known as Death Valley Scotty), the genial con man and raconteur who swindled and charmed Albert Johnson, the Chicago millionaire who actually built the structure itself. Its fanciful appointments include medieval-inspired wrought-iron chandeliers, carved redwood beams and glazed ceramic tiles. Before or after your trip to the castle, take the detour to nearby **Ubehebe Crater** (follow the signs), the impressive result of a volcanic eruption a thousand years ago.

✚ 209 F3
✉ Highway 190 (east and north from US 395 on Highway 178 and Panamint Valley Road; east on Highway 190)
☎ 760/786-3200; www.nps.gov/deva
💵 $25/per car & week (annual pass for all NP $80)

The eastern entrance to Death Valley National Park

⭐10 San Diego Zoo

One of the world's best, 🏨 San Diego Zoo features a staggering array of exotic animals, and large-scale environments for hippos, polar bears, primates, denizens of the Asian rainforest and some highly colorful birds. Animal shows take place throughout the day – the schedule of shows is on the map provided when you enter the zoo.

Zebras and other animals from around the world delight old and young visitors alike at San Diego Zoo

The San Diego Zoo straddles a canyon, so you may have to cover steep terrain to see all the exhibits. Moving walkways assist you on the steepest climbs – back uphill from the pandas, for instance.

The 35-minute **Guided Bus Tour** (included in the day ticket) allows you to get a good overview of the park. You can't get off the regular bus, but several pauses along the way are long enough that you may not feel the need to return to some exhibits, saving you the walk and freeing up time to see other areas. Your ticket is also good for a ride on the Express Bus, which you can get off and reboard as you please. Sit on the right-hand side on both buses and you won't have to peer over the other passengers as much as you would on the left. The **Skyfari** aerial tram (also part of the day ticket) crosses the canyon between the zoo entrance and the Polar Bear Plunge.

Insider Tip

TAKING A BREAK

The best of the zoo's many cafés and restaurants is **Albert's** (seafood, steaks, pastas, chicken, salads), but also good are the **Front Street Café** (serving Mexican and American cuisine) and **Sydney's Grill** (salads, burgers and sandwiches).

➕ 210 B2 ✉ Off Park Boulevard, Balboa Park
☎ 619/231-1155; www.sandiegozoo.org
🕐 Late Jun to early Sep daily 9am–8pm; shorter hours in spring and winter
🚌 Bus 7, 215 🎫 $52

KIDS' DELIGHT

Create art projects, enjoy performances, and explore interactive exhibits at the 🏨 **New Children's Museum** (200 W. Island Avenue, tel: 619/233-8792; open: Mon–Thu, Sat 10–4, Fri 9:30–4, Sun noon–4. Bus: 3, 4, 7, 15, 30; Trolley: Convention Center West; $12).

San Diego & Southern California

� out 64 Harbor & Downtown

California's sunny, second-largest city has long played a role in the state's history. Spanish friars established the first of their California missions in San Diego. Most people come for the near-perfect climate and attractions but you may find yourself wanting to learn more about this city's rich heritage.

Several points of interest lie along the **Embarcadero,** south from Ash Street on N. Harbor Drive and then southeast on Harbor Drive to the San Diego Convention Center.

The **Maritime Museum of San Diego** maintains the *Star of India*, a restored 1863 bark, on board which you'll get a vivid sense of life at sea. Moored to the north is the *Berkeley*, an 1898 steam-powered ferry with deluxe appointments – don't miss that stained glass. Nearby is the USS *Midway*, home to the **San Diego Aircraft Carrier Museum**, which has engaging exhibits about naval aviation. You can tour the mess hall, crew berths, bomb-making area, and more. One- and two-hour **harbor cruises** sail from piers

Insider Tip south of the museum. The longer trips, which take in more of the harbor and swing by Point Loma, are best. Ferries to Coronado also depart from here.

An atmospheric impression of San Diego Harbor

Seaport Village and Petco Park
A touristy collection of shops, restaurants and other diversions, **Seaport Village** has a winning design and fine harbor views going for it. With an infusion of corporate

money in recent years, the area has had
a facelift, and is now a charming place to
walk around; it is also used as an outdoor
concert venue that attracts top-notch artists
and musicians.

Petco Park, home to the local baseball
team, the San Diego Padres, opened in
2004 as part of a revitalization of the
downtown area. The large ballpark also
serves as a concert venue.

The Gaslamp Quarter

The reclamation of San Diego's 19th-century
Gaslamp Quarter is one of urban America's
great success stories. Cast-iron and other buildings, many
of which had been slated for demolition, were converted
into stores, restaurants and nightclubs. The district, whose Insider
Tip
liveliest streets are 4th and 5th avenues between Market
Street and Harbor Drive, is more fun by night (▶ 188), but
there are a few historic sights to visit by day. You can learn
about these at the **William Heath Davis House** (410 Island
Avenue, at 4th Avenue; tel: 619/233-4692). Hours vary, so
call ahead.

TAKING A BREAK

The bar at the **US Grant Hotel** (326 Broadway; www.usgrant.
net) is a swank, old-timey place for a cocktail.

✚ 202 B2

Maritime Museum of San Diego
✉ 1492 N. Harbor Drive, at Ash Street
☎ 619/234-9153; www.sdmaritime.org 🕐 Daily 9–9; until 8 in autumn
🚌 Bus 280, 290 923; Trolley (Santa Fe Depot) 💰 $16

San Diego Aircraft Carrier Museum
✉ 910 N. Harbor Drive, at Navy Pier ☎ 619/544-9600; www.midway.org
🕐 Daily 10–5 🚌 Bus 992; Trolley (Santa Fe Depot) 💰 $20

Harbor Cruises
Hornblower Cruises ✉ Navy Pier, 970 North Harbor Drive
☎ 619/686-8700 or 619/686-8715; www.hornblower.com 💰 From $25
Flagship Cruises ✉ Broadway Pier, 990 North Harbor Drive
☎ 619/234-4111; www.flagshipsd.com
🚌 Bus 992; Trolley (Santa Fe Depot) 💰 From $25

Seaport Village
✉ 849 W. Harbor Drive from Pacific Highway to Market Place
☎ 619/235-4014; www.seaportvillage.com
🚌 Bus 7; Trolley (Seaport Village)

Gaslamp Quarter
✉ 4th, 5th and 6th avenues between Broadway and Harbor Drive;
www.gaslampquarter.org 🚌 Bus 3, 5, 120; Trolley (5th Avenue)

⑥⑤ Balboa Park

With approximately 1,200 acres (485ha), Balboa Park ranks as one of the nation's largest urban parks (greenswards), but attractions here are intellectual as well as natural. Take a wander along El Prado, a wide promenade lined on both sides with museums and other cultural institutions.

Nearly all the Spanish-Moorish structures along El Prado were built for international fairs in 1915 and 1935–36. Chandeliers hang in the arched walkways that connect many of the buildings. The exterior decorative touches, such as the scallop-shaped entry arch to the San Diego Museum of Art and the accompanying heraldry, medallions and scrollwork, are extraordinary. Pick up maps and events calendars at the 🏛 **Balboa Park Visitor Center**. The park's standout museums include the **Mingei International Museum** (folk-art displays), the **San Diego Air and Space Museum** and the **Reuben H. Fleet Space Theater and Science Center** (home to an Imax Dome Theater and some clever interactive exhibits). The **San Diego Automotive Museum** has captivating specimens, from Model Ts and early prototypes to Corvettes and recent sport cars.

> **DON'T FORGET YOUR PASSPORT**
> The **Passport to Balboa Park** gains you entry to 14 Balboa Park museums at a huge discount. Pick up passports at the visitor center or at the participating museums.

Three facilities share the Casa de Balboa. The **San Diego History Center** and the **Museum of Photographic Arts**. Less erudite, but well worth a stop, is the **San Diego Model Railroad Museum**. The **San Diego Museum of Art** often hosts traveling exhibits; its key holdings include Renaissance and Spanish baroque paintings and California art. The nearby **Timken Museum of Art** is known for its Russian icons. **Centro Cultural de la Raza**, on Park Boulevard south of El Prado, presents works by Mexican, Latino and Chicano artists. Reputable but missable if you're pressed for time are the **San Diego Museum of Man**, which specializes in the anthropology of the American Southwest and Latin America, and the **San Diego Natural History Museum. The San Diego Hall of Champions – Sports Museum** honors local sporting heroes.

TAKING A BREAK

Seaport Cookie Co. (813 West Harbor Drive; tel: 619/231-8787) offers 10 varieties, baked on the premises of a former lighthouse.

➕ 210 B2 ✉ Balboa Park, Park Boulevard (12th Avenue), off Highway 163 or I-5
🕐 Park: 24 hours. Museums: hours vary (a few closed Mon and/or Tue)
🚌 Bus 1, 3,7B, 2, 120 🅿 Park: free

Balboa Park Visitor Center (House of Hospitality)
✉ 1549 El Prado ☎ 619/239-0512; www.balboapark.org 🕐 Daily 9:30–4:30

⑥⑥ La Jolla

The origins of the name of La Jolla, some saying it derives from the Spanish word for jewel, others the one for hole, are disputed. But few would dispute that this town, where tall palms tower over fancy Spanish-Mediterranean and modernist homes, is one of San Diego's gems.

Hoodoo rock formations at La Jolla Beach

A good walking tour might begin with the **La Jolla Caves** (1325 Coast Boulevard; tel: 858/459-0746). Here you enter a bungalow, pay the fee and head down 145 steps to the caves (the climb back up is steep). A platform at the base of the steps has water and shoreline views – the waves break near it at high tide, a thrilling sight.

From La Jolla Caves continue west then south past rocks inhabited by pelicans and other species. Wander out among the tide pools during low tide and you'll see crabs, snails and other creatures amid the rocks and multihued seaweed.

Exploring the Coast

You can explore more of the coast south past Ellen Scripps Browning Park, the grassy area that abuts La Jolla Cove. Or head inland a block to the **Museum of Contemporary Art, San Diego**. The postmodern building is more noteworthy than the art collection, though a significant number of post-World War II California artists are represented. The expanded **MCASD** Downtown adds 16,000ft² (1,500m²) of exhibition space to the museum.

La Jolla is also home to great shopping, particularly along Prospect Street, a few blocks north of the museum, and Girard Avenue. There are dozens of antiques stores,

Insider Tip

THE BEACHES

On a sunny day, with leisure sailors taking to the waters and picnickers cavorting on shore, the 4,235-acre (1,714ha) 🚺 **Mission Bay Park** (Mission Bay Drive, off I-8) becomes a fun place indeed. Rollercoasters zoom and carousel horses twirl at nearby **Belmont Park** (3146 Mission Boulevard, at West Mission Bay Drive; tel: 858/228-9283), which abuts wide and sandy **Mission Beach**. Immediately north lies **Pacific Beach**, where the **Crystal Pier** (Garnet Avenue, west of Mission Boulevard) juts so far into the ocean that you'll get a fascinating rear perspective on surfers as they battle the waves (Bus: 8/9, 27, 30).

Insider Tip

San Diego & Southern California

galleries, jewelry stores, boutiques and a range of specialty shops, along with a few big-name chain stores.

Heading north from Prospect, follow signs off Torrey Pines Road to La Jolla Shores Drive and turn west on Avenida de la Playa. This will lead you to flat, sandy, palm-lined **La Jolla Shores Beach**, yet another of those Southern California strands that look like a movie set.

Windansea Beach is a well-known spot for surfers, but the concentrated surf breaks can be challenging for novices.

Insider Tip La Jolla Shores is recommended for beginners.

For a **self-guided 90-minute walking tour** of La Jolla, which highlights historical buildings and nature sites, contact the La Jolla Historical Society (7846 Eads Avenue; tel: 858/459-5335).

TAKING A BREAK

The **Brockton Villa Restaurant** (1235 Coast Boulevard; tel: 858/454-7393), great for lunch or weekend brunch, perches above these rocks and sheltered La Jolla Cove. Alternatively, stop for a genteel cocktail in the ocean-view lobby bar of **La Valencia Hotel** (1132 Prospect Street;), built in 1926. **Insider Tip** From here or the nearby **George's at the Cove** (➤ 185), which serves up tasty food, you might see a pod of dolphins swimming just beyond the cove.

➕ 210 B2 ✉ From downtown San Diego, take I-5 north, Ardath Road west and Torrey Pines Road (south to Coast Boulevard, north to La Jolla Shores) 🚌 Bus 30

La Jolla Visitor Information Center
✉ 1162 Prospect Street ☎ 85/454-5718; www.lajollabythesea.com
🕐 Tue–Sun 10–5

Museum of Contemporary Art (MCASD), San Diego
✉ 700 Prospect Street (La Jolla); 1001 Kettner Boulevard (San Diego)
☎ 858/454-3541; www.mcasd.org 🕐 Thu–Tue 11–5; till 7 on 3rd Thu of month
💵 $10 (valid for 7 days at both locations)

Seagulls on the cliffs at Windansea Beach

67 Palm Springs

When it's cloudy in San Diego or Los Angeles, or anytime Southern Californians feel the need to unwind, their thoughts often turn to Palm Springs. "Perfect climate, wonderful scenery, pure mountain air," declared an 1887 newspaper advertisement for what was briefly known as Palm Valley. The mountain and desert air may not be as pristine as they were in days past, but, except during the very hot summers, the climate is agreeable and the scenery varied.

The Aerial Tramway cable car in the San Jacinto Mountains

The city of Palm Springs is the hub of the **Coachella Valley** and lies at its western edge. About 500,000 people live in the valley year-round, and around 100,000 extra inhabitants move in during the winter. Most of the ultra rich reside (often in gated communities) in **Rancho Mirage**, **Palm Desert** and **La Quinta**, all on Highway 111 east of Palm Springs. Other valley towns include the resort area of **Desert Hot Springs** and the relatively laid-back **Cathedral City** and **Indio**. The southern entrance to Joshua Tree National Park (► 177) lies 25mi (40km) east of Indio which is 22mi (35km) east of Palm Springs.

An Elite Getaway

The pace in Palm Springs began to pick up in the 1920s and 1930s, when it became a favorite getaway of Hollywood's elite. Actors, directors and producers relaxed at La Quinta Hotel (now La Quinta Resort & Club) and El Mirador Hotel and played tennis at the Racquet Club. Radio stars such as Jack Benny broadcast their shows from their vacation paradise.

According to local surveys, shopping is the top tourist activity in Palm Springs. Three key shopping districts are **Palm Canyon Drive** in Palm Springs, El Paseo street in Palm Desert (The Gardens complex, at **73–585 El Paseo**, is a

San Diego & Southern California

good place to start) and the **Desert Hills Premium Outlets** (48–400 Seminole Drive, off I-10; tel: 951/849-6641; www. premiumoutlets.com) in Cabazon.

Golfing, sitting by the pool and taking a spa treatment are other popular diversions. **Tahquitz Creek Palm Springs Golf Resort** (1885 Golf Club Drive; tel: 760/328-1005; www. tahquitzgolfresort.com) is a major public course. Two good spas are the moderately priced **Spa Resort Casino** (401 East Armado Road; tel: 888/999-1995; www.sparesortcasino. com) and the more upscale **Spa La Quinta** (La Quinta Resort & Club, 49–499 Eisenhower Drive, La Quinta; tel: 760/564-4111; www.laquintaresort.com).

Joshua Tree (*Yucca brevifolia*) in the Joshua Tree National Park

Highlights

With its rotating tram cars, the **Palm Springs Aerial Tramway** provides a thrilling ascent up 10,804ft-high (3,293m) Mt. San Jacinto. At certain points along the ride from the Valley Station (elevation 2,643ft/805m) to the Mountain Station (8,501ft/2,591m), the tram dangles in mid air between solid slabs of grayish granite several hundred feet high. The terrain changes from desert to arctic/alpine – from cacti and yuccas to pines and firs of the type found in Alaska – and the temperature drops about 40°F (22°C). You can hike or picnic.

Insider Tip

The **Palm Springs Art Museum** on Museum Drive provides a fine introduction to the desert's cultural and natural history. On the ground level are rooms with Native American art, furniture made by the Western film actor George Montgomery and exhibits about the desert's flora and fauna. The top level contains a post-World War II American art.

Cacti, agave and other desert plants inhabit the marvelously overgrown **Moorten Botanical Garden** on S. Palm Canyon Drive and tall palm trees line Palm Canyon, the lushest of the **Indian Canyons** (Indian Canyon Drive, 3mi (5km) south of E. Palm Canyon Drive; tel: 760/323-6018 or www.indian-canyons.com for guided tour times). As you hike through the canyon, you may spot rock art and Indian food preparation areas. The most easily identified of the latter are the smooth indentations in rocks where acorns were mashed to make flour.

The 1,200-acre (485ha) **Living Desert Zoo & Gardens** on Portola Avenue, north of Highway 111, contains exotic species from around the world.

Joshua Tree National Park straddles two distinct desert regions. The more interesting terrain – lunar-like boulders towering over cacti, Joshua trees and other succulents – is in the high desert to the north.

TAKING A BREAK

In Palm Springs try the **Hair of the Dog English Pub** (238 N. Palm Canyon Drive; tel: 760/323-9890). In Palm Desert the **Café des Beaux Arts** (73–640 El Paseo; tel: 760/346-0669).

Palm Springs
➕ 210 C2 ✉ Highway 111, off I-10 (110mi/177km from Los Angeles)
ℹ Palm Springs Visitors Center: 2901 N. Palm Canyon Drive; 760/778-8418; www.visitpalmsprings.com

Palm Springs Aerial Tramway
✉ Tramway Road off N. Palm Canyon Drive (at San Rafael Road)
☎ 760/325-1449 or 888/515-8726; www.pstramway.com
🕐 Mon–Thu 10–8 (last car down: 9:45), Fri, Sat, Sun from 8am
🚌 SunBus 24 (2-mile/3km walk uphill to Valley Station) 💲$25.95

Palm Springs Art Museum
✉ 101 Museum Drive ☎ 760/322-4800; www.psmuseum.org
🕐 Tue–Wed, Fri–Sun 10–5, Thu noon–8 💲$12.50 (free Thu 4–8)

Moorten Botanical Garden
✉ 1701 S. Palm Canyon Drive ☎ 760/327-6555; http://moortenbotincalgarden.com 🕐 Daily 10–4; closed Wed 💲$5

Living Desert Zoo & Gardens
✉ 47–900 Portola Avenue, north of Highway 111
☎ 760/346-5694; www.livingdesert.org 🕐 Jun–Sep daily 8–1.30 (last admission 1pm); Oct–May 9–5 (last admission 4pm) 💲$19.95

Joshua Tree National Park
✉ Main entrance: Utah Trail, off Highway 62, Twentynine Palms ☎ 760/367-5500; www.nps.gov/jotr 💲$20/per car & week (annual pass for all NP $80)

INSIDER INFO

- If you're without a car, call **Yellow Cab of the desert** (tel: 760/340-8294) or SunBus (tel: 800/347-8628; www.sunline.org).
- On Thursday night, S. Palm Canyon Drive becomes a **pedestrians-only open-air market**, with street musicians and food and craft vendors.

Insider Tip

At Your Leisure

The Cabrillo National Monument

68 Cabrillo National Monument

The explorer Juan Rodriguez Cabrillo dropped anchor in 1542 not far from the monument that bears his name. "A very good enclosed port" was his description of San Diego Bay. Exhibits at the visitor center here will clue you into the history, but on a clear day you'll need no assistance appreciating the views of the Pacific Ocean, San Diego, the Cuyamaca Mountains and even Mexico. You can also watch the migration of the gray whales in winter.

🔲 210 B2 ✉ 1800 Cabrillo Memorial Drive (southern end of Catalina Boulevard) ☎ 619/557-5450; www.nps.gov/cabr ⏰ Daily 9–5 🚌 Bus 84 💲 $10/per car (annual pass for all NP $80)

69 Coronado

For a low-key excursion, take a 15-minute ferry to Coronado. The sights to see include Victorian-era mansions along the waterfront, the stores and small parks along Orange Avenue, the 19th-century Hotel del Coronado and Silver Strand State Beach. You can rent a bicycle at the ferry landing (the terrain's mostly level).

🔲 210 B2 ☎ 619/437-8788; www.coronado visitorcenter.com 🚌 Bus 901, 904

70 Old Town State Historic Park

Even many San Diegans find their city's history a tad dry, but the 19th-century highlights come to life in colorful **Old Town State Historic Park**. Restored or replicated buildings line dirt streets set around the original town plaza. You get an inkling of the past, but the feel is refreshingly un-museumlike.

The free *Old California Gazette* souvenir newspaper contains a map. A good starting point is the **Robinson-Rose House**, where a diorama and early photos depict Old Town in the 1800s. From here head south (to your right as you exit the front door) to the re-created **San Diego House** and what was the **Commercial House** restaurant (listed on the Gazette map as the U.S. House). East of this is **Racine & Laramie**, San Diego's first cigar store, which has been painstakingly re-created to recall the 1870s. It is still in business.

Don't miss the no-nonsense **Mason Street School**, a one-room wooden structure built in 1865 and tucked behind the **Brick Courthouse**. It's furnished for a late-1800s schoolday, complete with a punishment chart prescribing various numbers of lashes, depending on the infraction. And speaking of torture, those leery even of today's techniques may find the exhibits in the nearby **McKinstry Dentist Office** too harrowing to view.

North of the dentist's office stands the sturdy **Casa de Estudillo** – notice the broad ceiling beams tied together with cowhide. Furnished to illustrate the lifestyle of an important ranching family around the mid-19th century, the casa is the largest original adobe in Old Town. Across Calhoun Street is **Seeley Stables**, which contains an excellent collection of stagecoaches, some of them behind the main building.

Heading down Calhoun past the Casa de Bandini, you'll shortly run into the even more festive **Bazaar del Mundo**. Bright yellows, reds and oranges are among the clues that this outdoor mini-mall celebrates the city's Mexican heritage.

From Old Town head north on Taylor Street and east up Presidio Drive to the **Presidio** (great views of downtown and beyond), where the **Junipero Serra Museum**, a repository of San Diego artifacts, sits on the site of the original Mission San Diego.

🚩 210 B2 ✉ Old Town San Diego State Historic Park, bordered by Taylor, Juan, Twiggs and Congress streets (main parking lot off Twiggs) ☎ 619/220-5422; www.parks.ca.gov/?page_id=663 🚌 Bus 8/9, 10, 28, 30, 35, 44, 8, 105, 150 🎟 Free

71 🐋 SeaWorld

Did you know that sperm whales can hold their breath for up to an hour or more? And that killer whales can reach incredible speeds? You'll learn facts like that and more at San Diego's SeaWorld, which has been sharing the wonders of marine life with visitors since 1964. SeaWorld's highlights include dolphin shows, killer whale shows, shark, penguin and polar-bear exhibits, and the Journey to Atlantis thrill ride. The park serves up a reasonably good mix of education and entertainment, the latter including the thrilling Shipwreck Rapids water ride. On summer evenings, they also have fireworks shows.

🚩 210 B2 ✉ SeaWorld Drive, off I-5 (follow signs), Mission Bay ☎ 619/226-3901; https://seaworldparks.com/en/seaworld-sandiego ⏱ Hours vary, but generally 10–dusk (late hours in summer) 🚌 Bus 9 🎟 From $73

72 Mission Basilica San Diego de Alcalá

Franciscan padres founded Mission Basilica San Diego de Alcalá in 1769 near Old Town, but relocated it to its present site in 1774. Native Americans promptly burned down the first church, an 1803 earthquake leveled its successor, and the third building deteriorated until restoration began during the 20th century. Notable features are the 46ft-high (14m) *campanario* (bell

Visitors come face to face with the killer whales (orcas) at the aquarium

San Diego & Southern California

tower), gardens (roses, bougainvillea and indigenous succulents) and the long, narrow church – because taller trees for use as beams weren't available.

✚ 210 B2 ✉ 10818 San Diego Mission Road ☎ 619/281-8449; www.missionsandiego.com 🕐 Daily 9–4:45 🚌 Bus 13, 18 🚊 Trolley: Mission San Diego 💲 Donation

73 Torrey Pines

If you continue north from La Jolla, you'll eventually run into **Torrey Pines State Beach and Reserve** (N. Torrey Pines Road, south of Carmel Valley Road; tel: 858/755-2063; www.torreypine.org), where you can investigate the migrating shore-birds or just relax on the beach. Off Torrey Pines farther north lies the **Birch Aquarium at Scripps**, which has knockout ocean views and equally breathtaking sea-life and oceanographic exhibits.

Torrey Pines is also home to one of the most scenic public golf courses in the state. Even if you don't play, you can eat lunch while taking in the superb mountain and sea views.

✚ 210 B2 ✉ From downtown San Diego, take I-5 north, Ardath Road west and Torrey Pines Road (south to Coast Boulevard, north to La Jolla Shores) 🚌 Bus 30 💲 Parking fee from $10

Birch Aquarium at Scripps
✉ 2300 Expedition Way, La Jolla
☎ 858/534-3474; aquarium.ucsd.edu
🕐 Daily 9–5 💲 $18.50

74 Legoland® California

This theme park based on the colorful snap-together toys contains rides, games, interactive attractions and other diversions for the 2-to-10 set. Everything's scaled small, and judging by the squeals of delight, this suits the target audience just right.

✚ 210 B2 ✉ 1 Legoland Drive, east on Cannon Road from I-5, Carlsbad
☎ 877/534-6526; www.legoland.com/california

Cholla cacti growing in Anza-Borrego

🕐 Daily 10–5 (later in summer; call for times). Closed Tue–Wed in low season 🚌 County Bus 444 (from Coaster train), 445, 446 💲 $84

75 San Diego Zoo Safari Park

Most of the nearly 1,000 acres (405ha) of this facility associated with the San Diego Zoo are given over to large-scale environments viewed on a 50-minute "safari" railway tour. You'll see rhinos, giraffes and lesser-known creatures living more or less as they would in the wild. Back near the entrance, you can step close to giraffes and other animals in the Heart of Africa, and there's a walk-through aviary. California condors, desert bighorn sheep, burrowing owls and other North American animals inhabit the Condor Ridge exhibit.

✚ 210 B2 ✉ 15500 San Pasqual Valley Road, Escondido, Highway 78 (take Via Rancho Parkway exit east from I-15) ☎ 760/747-8702; www.sdzsafaripark.org 🕐 Daily from 9; closing times vary 🚌 Bus 307 (Mon–Sat only) 💲 $50

76 Anza-Borrego Desert State Park

Off-road vehicle enthusiasts and hikers love the vast desert that lies on the backcountry route between San Diego and Palm Springs. Except during the spring wildflower season, six weeks between late February and April (blooming time varies from year to year), hardly anyone comes here. You need a four-wheel drive to visit some sights, but you can easily hike through **Borrego Palm**

The desolate beauty of the Trona Pinnacles in the Mojave Desert

Canyon, a rare oasis amid this dry and dusty expanse. Stop by the visitor center for trail maps and tips. If you're not up for a hike, pick up the brochure for the informative, self-guiding **Erosion Road** auto tour. ✚ 210 C2 ✉ Visitor center: 200 Palm Canyon Drive, off County Road S22, Borrego Springs ☎ 760/767-4205; www.parks.ca.gov/?page_id=638 🅿 Free

🗺 Mojave Desert
The Mojave Desert wraps around the southern portion of Death Valley National Park. The town of **Ridgecrest**, on the desert's western side at US 395 and Highway 178, serves as a park gateway. Fuel up and buy groceries in one of the other stores – provisions are more expensive and in shorter supply in Death Valley.

Much of the Ridgecrest area lay under water eons ago, a point made clear by the **Trona Pinnacles** (RM 143, off Highway 178, 22mi (35km) east of Ridgecrest); the road off Highway 178 is dirt (some gravel), but you can nearly always make it in a car. The pinnacles appear in sci-fi films (most notably *Star Trek V*) as outer-space landscapes, but there is a similarity between these peaks and lake-bottom formations, which once they were. Likewise at parched **Fossil Falls** (Highway 395, 20mi (32km) north of the junction of Highway 14 and US 395), a former river gorge, now completely

dry, that seems in eerie, perpetual longing for the waters that once roared through it.

The **Maturango Museum** also serves as a visitors center. It's home to some impressive exhibits about the area's long-extinct animal inhabitants and the history of human settlement in the region. Museum guides lead fascinating weekend tours in spring and fall to **Little Petroglyph Canyon**. Book way in advance (U.S. citizens only) to see the rock drawings, some of which are thousands of years old.

South of Ridgecrest, off US 395, lies amusing Randsburg, a still-active mining town with old shacks. The fun and easily walkable downtown strip, a few blocks of Butte Avenue, contains saloons, restaurants and stores selling crafts and collectibles. Burma Road, which loops above town, provides a fine perspective on it all. Head west on the Red Rock–Randsburg Road and you'll wind up at the southern tip of **Red Rock Canyon State Park** (Abbott Road, off Highway 14; tel: 661/946-6092), used as a backdrop for the movie *Jurassic Park*. Much of the eastern Mojave lies within **Mojave National Preserve**. Rangers at the Kelso Depot Visitor Center dispense maps and advice about the preserve's dunes. ✚ 211 D4

Giant sequoias in winter at the beautiful Sequoia National Park

Maturango Museum
✉ 100 E. Las Flores Avenue,
off N. China Lake Boulevard
☎ 760/375-6900; www.maturango.org
🕐 Daily 10–5 💵 $5

Kelso Depot Visitor Center
✉ Kelbaker Road, 22mi/35km north of US 40
☎ 760/252-6108; www.nps.gov/moja
🕐 Daily 9–5

78 Sequoia & Kings Canyon National Parks

Less-trafficked than Yosemite yet equally beautiful, these two tree-studded parks are often visited together. At Grant Grove Visitor Center, you can learn about **Kings Canyon National Park** attractions. The highlight is the scenic drive (closed in winter) along Highway 180 through the Cedar Grove area. The trip (90 minutes each way) follows the twists and turns of the south fork of the Kings River, through lush and then drier terrain before deadending. Three miles

(5km) east of Grant Grove Village on Highway 180 is the parking area for the short hike to **Roaring River Falls**, and farther on a 1-mile (1.6km) trail winds to scenic **Zumwalt Meadow**.

The Generals Highway leads south from Kings Canyon into **Sequoia National Park**, whose Lodgepole Visitor Center contains exhibits about both parks. Rangers sell tickets to the nearby not-to-be-missed **Crystal Cave**, a spectacular marble cavern with several huge "rooms" that are viewable only between mid-May and late September on guided tours.

The rangers can also direct you to the trails, meadows and sequoia groves of the Giant Forest area and to **Moro Rock**, a granite formation that shoots 6,725ft (2,050m) from the Giant Forest floor.

➕ 209 E3/4 ✉ Kings Canyon NP, Highway 180; Sequoia NP, Highway 198 and the Generals Highway ☎ 559/565-3341 (both parks); www.nps.gov/seki 💵 Both parks: $30/ per car & week (annual pass for all NP $80)

Where to...
Stay

Prices
Expect to pay per double room, per night (excluding tax)
$ under $100 $$ $100–$175 $$$ over $175

SAN DIEGO

Blue Sea Beach Hotel $$
If you like to walk directly onto the beach or boardwalk from your room, you can't ask for a better location than this motor lodge on Pacific Beach. The often crowded beach and boardwalk on your doorstep doesn't promote quiet during the day. Half the rooms have kitchenettes.

➕ 210 B2 ✉ 707 Pacific Beach Drive, San Diego, CA 92109 ☎ 858/488-4700 or 800/258-3732; www.blueseabeachhotel.com

Hotel del Coronado $$$
The West Coast's largest beach resort is also one of its most historic hotels. Dating from 1888, the "Del" has hosted U.S. presidents and British royalty. Choose from rooms in the original building – a marvel of ornate gingerbread with cupolas, verandas, a turret, shingled red roofs and white wood – or in two more recent additions. Rooms in the former are often small and lack air-conditioning, but expansive public areas help compensate.

➕ 210 B2 ✉ 1500 Orange Avenue, Coronado, CA 92118 ☎ 619/435-6611 or 800/468-3533; www.hoteldel.com

Hotel Indigo San Diego Gaslamp Quarter $$$
San Diego's first LEED-certified (independent eco-friendly building rating) hotel opened in 2009 in the East Village, near the Gaslamp Quarter. Green is certainly the theme of the hotel, with photomurals of plants in the lobby, a "living" roof and discounted parking rates for drivers of hybrid vehicles. The hotel restaurant uses fresh herbs grown in the eco-roof garden. Pets are also welcome, free of charge. Head up to the Phi Terrace Bar, on the ninth floor, for a drink with a city view.

➕ 210 B2 ✉ 509 9th Avenue, San Diego, CA 92101 ☎ 619/727-4000 or 877/846-3446; www.hotelinsd.com

La Jolla Inn $$–$$$
Lodgings in La Jolla tend to be pricy, but this 23-room inn offers good value for the locale, which is close to the beach and La Jolla Cove. Rooms with balconies enjoy marvelous ocean views. Otherwise, you can use the inn's rooftop patio, a good place to enjoy Continental breakfast while admiring the Pacific.

➕ 210 B2 ✉ 1110 Prospect Street, La Jolla, CA 92037 ☎ 858/454-0133 or 888/855-7829; www.lajollainn.com

Paradise Point Resort & Spa $$$
This resort, on a 44-acre (18ha) island in Mission Bay Park, is geared toward active travelers. Start at one of five swimming pools, soak in an outdoor hot tub, proceed to the resort's sandy beaches, then rent a canoe or paddleboat to take out on the bay. On land, you'll find gardens, tennis courts and an 18-hole putting course. Accommodations are in cottage-style rooms and suites, which all have private patios and an airy, tropical feel.

➕ 210 B2 ✉ 1404 W. Vacation Road, San Diego, CA 92109 ☎ 858/274-4630 or 800/344-2626; www.paradisepoint.com

San Diego & Southern California

Sofia Hotel $$–$$$

This boutique hotel in downtown San Diego is part of the National Trust Historic Hotels of America for the preservation of its Gothic Revival-style architecture. A recent renovation, however, means that the hotel has a clean, modern look, and its 211 guest rooms offer a variety of amenities, including flat-screen TVs, high-speed internet and business-friendly amenities. The hotel is across the street from Horton Plaza and Petco Park is a short walk away.

🚼 210 B2 ✉ 150 W. Broadway, San Diego, CA 92101 ☎ 619/234-9200 or 800/826-0009; http://thesofiahotel.com

PALM SPRINGS

Casa Cody Country Inn $$

Founded in the 1920s, this historic inn has the scenic San Jacinto mountains as a backdrop. Many of the 28 rooms have fireplaces, private patios and kitchens; all have free wireless. A two-night stay is required on weekends; a Continental breakfast is included.

🚼 210 C2 ✉ 175 S Cahuilla Road, Palm Springs, CA 92262 ☎ 760/320-9346; www.casacody.com

The Chateau at Lake La Quinta Inn $$$

It might seem odd in the desert to find a château built in 18th-century French style – on the edge of a man-made lake, no less – but this luxurious bed-and-breakfast delivers grand style in a cozy setting. The rooms are themed with taste and subtle flair. The service is impeccable, the breakfasts divine.

🚼 210 C2 ✉ 78–120 Caleo Bay, La Quinta, CA 92253 ☎ 760/564-7332 or 888/226-4546; www.thechateaulakelaquinta.com

The Willows $$$

A stone pathway winds its way through the large front yard right up to this two-story villa dating from 1927. Most of the eight tasteful, antique-filled rooms offer views out across the town. The price of your stay includes an exceptional home-made gourmet breakfast. Guests can also make use of the relaxing pool outside.

🚼 210 C2 ✉ 312 West Tahquitz Canyon Way, Palm Canyon ☎ 760/320-0771; www.thewillowspalmsprings.com

The Westin Mission Hills Golf Resort & Spa $$$

Guests never have to leave the 360 acres (145ha) of pampered bliss. During your stay you can take advantage of the extensive amenities: two popular golf courses (book your tee times prior to your stay), a spa and wellness center, three pools, seven lit tennis courts, and a 👪 kids' club. The Spanish-Moorish buildings house 472 spacious guest rooms, which have private patios and the Heavenly Bed (a fabulously comfortable bed trademarked by the Westin). There are also 30 grand suites. Several restaurants offer a variety of cuisines and atmospheres to suit your mood.

🚼 210 C2 ✉ 71–333 Dinah Shore Drive, Rancho Mirage, CA 92270 ☎ 760/328-5955 or 888/627-7086; www.westinmissionhills.com

DEATH VALLEY

Furnace Creek Inn and Ranch Resort $$–$$$

A felicitous mix of history, rusticity and casual elegance lends the Furnace Creek Inn, Death Valley's luxury lodging, much of its appeal. Soft colors, swaying palms, gardens, a spring-fed pool and an attentive staff keep the mood here upbeat despite often blisteringly hot weather. All the rooms have a contemporary, stylish look. The nearby Ranch offers less expensive motel-style lodging.

🚼 209 F3 ✉ Highway 190, Death Valley National Park, CA 92328 ☎ 760/786-2361 or 800/236-7916; www.furnacecreekresort.com ⏲ (Closed mid-May–Oct)

Where to…
Eat and Drink

Prices
Expect to pay per person for a meal, excluding drinks and service:
$ under $15 $$ $15–$25 $$$ over $25

SAN DIEGO & AREA

Candelas $$$
Upscale Mexican fare is served up at this Gaslamp restaurant, which has a clubby vibe. Don't skip the appetizers – soups, such as black bean cream soup stewed with dark Mexican beer, and poblano chile cream soup served with half of a lobster tail. Main courses include creatively prepared seafood and steak dishes. The adjacent lounge is open nightly, with live music Thursday through Saturday.
🚇 210 B2 ✉ 416 Third Avenue, San Diego
☎ 619/702-4455; www.candelas-sd.com
🕐 Dinner daily 5–11; Bar: 5pm–1:40am

Casa Guadalajara $–$$
Located in Old Town San Diego, this Mexican spot run by the Bazaar del Mundo shops serves Tex-Mex fare and great margaritas, plus breakfast on weekends. It's a bit touristy (note the roaming *mariachi* band), but it's lively, fun and always crowded. Decorated with bright, festive colors, the restaurant also has outdoor dining in a lovely courtyard. Reservations are advised, especially on weekends.
🚇 210 B2 ✉ 4105 Taylor Street, San Diego
☎ 619/295-5111; www.casaguadalajara.com
🕐 Mon–Thu 11–10, Fri 11–11, Sat, Sun 8am–10pm

Chez Loma $$$
Coronado's Chez Loma, set in a historic 1889 Victorian home, has been serving food for more than three decades. The Continental-cuisine menu changes seasonally, with creative preparations of seafood, lamb, duck and pastas, as well as superb desserts. The tone is intimate, but not overly formal; there's live music on Friday and Saturday nights, a small bar and the wine list is excellent.
🚇 202 B1 ✉ 1132 Loma Avenue, Coronado
☎ 619/435-0661; www.chezloma.com
🕐 Dinner Sun–Wed 5–8:30, Thu until 9; brunch Fri–Sun 9:30–2

The Fish Market $$
Near the Del Mar Fairgrounds and Race Track, this informal seafood spot serves excellent fish at reasonable prices. Offerings include an oyster bar, chowders, smoked fish, sashimi and sushi, seafood cocktail, steamed shellfish, chicken and steak. The flagship location is at 750 North Harbor Drive.
🚇 210 B2 ✉ 640 Via De La Valle, Solana Beach
☎ 858/755-2277; www.thefishmarket.com
🕐 Sun–Thu 11–9:30, Fri–Sat 11–10

George's at the Cove $$–$$$
George's is in effect two restaurants, with two different kitchens. The first floor has a fine indoor dining room with views of La Jolla Cove; reservations are required at weekends. The rooftop terrace is less formal and half of the tables are reserved for walk-ins, but expect a wait on warm weekend evenings. Both kitchens produce sparkling cutting-edge California cuisine.
🚇 210 B2 ✉ 1250 Prospect Street, La Jolla
☎ 858/454-4244; www.georgesatthecove.com
🕐 Sun–Thu 11–10, Fri, Sat 11–11

San Diego & Southern California

Nine-Ten $$$

Locals and tourists alike come here for La Jolla's ocean views, elegant surroundings and superb California cuisine. Soups, seafood and artisan cheeses are the culinary draw, as is the first-rate wine list. Consider the five-course "Mercy of the Chef" tasting menu, which puts you in the chef's capable hands. Request a terrace table for ocean vistas.

➕ 210 B2 ✉ 910 Prospect Street, La Jolla ☎ 858/964-5400; www.nine-ten.com ⏰ Mon–Thu 6:30am–9:30pm, Fri, Sat until 10, Sun 7:30am–9:30pm

100 Wines $$

This popular restaurant in Hillcrest serves a mix of American, French and Spanish cuisine. As the name suggests, they also sell lots of good wines. Guests share tables, making for an unconventional but convivial atmosphere.

➕ 210 B2 B1027 University Avenue, San Diego ☎ 619/491-0100; www.cohnrestaurants.com/100wines ⏰ Tue–Fri 5pm–10pm, Sat until 11, Sun until 9; Sunday brunch 10–2

PALM SPRINGS

Billy Reed's $$

Serving locals and tourists since 1975, Billy Reed's is located on the main drag in Palm Springs, with a Victorian decor that almost belies the diner/coffee shop fare. Breakfast and lunch menus are available all day; dinner portions of dishes, such pot roast, are generous. The cocktail lounge has a DJ and dancing on weekends.

➕ 210 C2 ✉ 1800 N. Palm Canyon Drive, Palm Springs ☎ 760/325-1946; www.billyreedspalmsprings.com ⏰ Daily 8am–9pm

Shame on the Moon $$–$$$

There's harmony in the elegantly muted decor, the attentive but un-hurried service, carefully prepared food and remarkably moderate prices in this stylish Rancho Mirage dinner house. Don't overlook the appetizers, soups and homemade desserts; sautéed calf's liver is the chef's signature entrée. Ask for a table on the heated outdoor patio – it would be a shame to miss a moonlit night here.

➕ 210 C2 ✉ 69–950 Frank Sinatra Drive, Rancho Mirage ☎ 760/324-5515; www.shameonthemoon.com ⏰ Daily from 5pm

Le Vallauris $$$

Le Vallauris has a longstanding reputation for its French cuisine, which ranges from traditional to more creative California-influenced preparations of lamb, veal, beef and fish. Come here to enjoy a romantic, fairly formal dinner, or for a relaxing drink in the piano lounge. Things are more casual at lunch and at the Sunday brunch, especially on the pretty garden patio. Frank Sinatra and President Ford dined here, among other celebrities.

➕ 210 C2 ✉ 385 W. Tahquitz Canyon Way, Palm Springs ☎ 760/325-5059; www.levallauris.com ⏰ Lunch daily 11:30–2:30; dinner 5–10:30

DEATH VALLEY

Furnace Creek Inn Dining Room $$$

By far the most formal restaurant in Death Valley, the Furnace Creek Inn Dining Room brings a nouvelle touch to this old-time desert oasis. Miners and desert rats of yore might be appalled, not to mention puzzled, to see such items as seared salmon or organic vegetable pad Thai on the menu, when a good rattlesnake stew might do. But such seasonal dishes will soon help you forget how out-of-place fresh seafood and vegetables seem in this remote but attractive setting.

➕ 209 F3 ✉ Highway 190, Death Valley National Park ☎ 760/786-3385; www.furnacecreekresort.com ⏰ Mid-Oct to mid-May open from morning until evening, reservations recommended

Where to…
Shop

Southern California offers an array of potential purchases from antiques to desert-grown dates. San Diego and Palm Springs are the two top shopping areas.

SAN DIEGO

Scattered around San Diego are boutiques, shopping centers and specialty shops. Several malls are located in the general area of Mission Valley and Hotel Circle. **Fashion Valley** (7007 Friars Road; tel: 619/688-9113) and **Westfield Mission Valley Shopping Mall** (1640 Camino del Rio North; tel: 619/296-6375, http://westfield.com/mission valley) are two of the largest.

The city's most interesting shopping center, convenient to downtown hotels, is **Westfield Horton Plaza** (bounded by Broadway, G Street, 1st and 4th avenues; tel: 619/239-8180, http://westfield.com/hortonplaza), a multilevel complex of department stores, shops, restaurants and theaters.

For antiques and art galleries, head for the **Gaslamp Quarter** (bounded by 4th and 6th avenues and Harbor Drive and Broadway).

On the waterfront, **Seaport Village** (Harbor Drive at Kettner Boulevard; tel: 619/235-4014; www.seaportvillage.com) is an open-air mall built to resemble an old fishing village.

The hip **Hillcrest** section north of downtown has a good selection of music and bookstores, as well as shops oriented toward gays and lesbians.

In **Old Town**, the plaza-like **Bazaar del Mundo** (Juan and Taylor streets; tel: 619/296-3161; www.bazaardelmundo.com) is the **Insider Tip** place to hunt for inexpensive Mexican folk art, crafts, pottery and textiles.

In **Coronado**, you can comb the boutiques along Orange Avenue for upscale clothing.

The **Ferry Landing Marketplace** (www.coronadoferrylandingshops.com) has more than two dozen stores. La Jolla is home to ritzy boutiques, especially around Prospect.

PALM SPRINGS AREA

In the Palm Springs area, the top shopping venue is **Palm Desert.** El Paseo, an avenue of fountains and Mediterranean-style courtyards, is lined with boutiques, galleries, department stores and restaurants.

When it's too hot to shop outdoors, or when some stores close for the summer, head for **Westfield Palm Desert Town Center** (http://westfield.com/palmdesert), part of Westfield shopping mall chain, a mall with 150 or so stores, restaurants and movie theaters.

In Palm Springs itself, the prime shopping street is **Palm Canyon Drive**, where the Palm Springs Promenade offers a collection of boutiques and larger stores. **North Palm Canyon Drive** is a good place for antiques and collectibles.

For dates (the edible kind) head southeast to the towns of **Thermal** and **Indio**. There you can buy dates or a date shake – a whipped concoction of ice cream, milk and dates) at **Oasis Date Gardens** (59–111 Grapefruit Boulevard; tel: 760/399-5665; www.oasisdate.com) or **Shields Date Garden** (80–225 Highway 111, Indio; tel: 760/347-0996; www.shieldsdategarden.com).

A few miles northwest of Palm Springs, in **Cabazon**, you'll find 130 factory clothing discount outlets at **Desert Hills Premium Outlets** (48–400 Seminole Drive; tel: 951/849-6641; www.premiumoutlets.com/deserthills).

Where to...
Go Out

Southern California offers a mix of nightlife, the arts and outdoor activities, centered primarily in the San Diego and Palm Springs areas.

In San Diego, check listings in the *San Diego* magazine (www.sandiegomagazine.com) or *The Reader*, (www.sandiegoreader.com), a free weekly.

In Palm Springs, *Palm Springs Life* magazine (www.palmspringslife.com) has listings, as does the Friday edition of the *Palm Desert Sun* newspaper (www.mydesert.com).

Call 619/497-5000 for recorded information sponsored by the San Diego Performing Arts League; this is also the number for Arts Tix for discount, same-day tickets (Broadway Circle, Horton Plaza).

THEATER

San Diego

Get half-price, same-day tickets at **Arts Tix** (Broadway Circle, Horton Plaza; tel: 619/497-5000). *Insider Tip*

Balboa Park's **Old Globe Theater** (tel: 619/234-5623; www.theoldglobe.org) is one of the state's oldest professional theater groups. They stage summertime Shakespeare plays.

Shows have been held for kids at the **Marie Hitchcock Puppet Theatre** (tel: 619/544-9203; www.balboaparkpuppets.com) in Balboa park ever since the 1940s.

The La Jolla Playhouse (May to November only), **Horton Grand Theatre**, Coronado Playhouse and the **Old Town Theatre** (www.cygnettheatre.com) are other top venues.

MUSIC & NIGHTLIFE

San Diego

The **Gaslamp Quarter**, especially along 4th and 5th avenues, has the city's greatest concentration of bars and nightclubs. The areas around Pacific, Mission and Ocean beaches also harbor lively nightspots. Options range from dance clubs to those offering rock, jazz and blues. The **Hillcrest section**, especially University Avenue, Park Boulevard and 5th Avenue, is the focus of gay and lesbian nightlife. **La Jolla** is known for its singles bars. Some of the San Diego area's top hotels have piano bars. The **San Diego Opera** (tel: 619/533-7000; www.sdopera.com) season runs from January to May in the downtown Civic Theatre.

Palm Springs

The hot-ticket theater event in Palm Springs is the **Fabulous Palm Springs Follies** (Plaza Theater, 128 S. Palm Canyon Drive; tel: 760/327-0225; www.psfollies.com; Nov–May), a vaudeville-style revue starring singers and dancers over age 50.

More traditional performances take place at the **McCallum Theatre** (73–000 Fred Waring Drive, Palm Desert; tel: 760/340-2787; www.mccallumtheatre.com) and the **Annenberg Theater** (101 Museum Drive, Palm Springs; tel: 760/325-4490; www.psmuseum.org).

SPORT

Palm Springs is famous for its **golf courses**, many open to the public. Other activities include hiking, horseback riding and bicycling; you can also fish in nearby lakes.

San Diego has a wealth of good **swimming beaches**; the largest and most popular include Coronado, Mission, Ocean, Pacific and Silver Strand beaches. Smaller, more secluded beaches, include La Jolla Cove, La Jolla Shores and Torrey Pines State beaches.

Tours

Tours

1

COAST HIGHWAY 1 & POINT REYES NATIONAL SEASHORE

Drive

> **DISTANCE** 57mi/91km (one way)   **TIME** 6–8 hours
> **START POINT** Golden Gate Bridge (US 101 off Doyle Drive) 🚗 206 B1
> **END POINT** Point Reyes Lighthouse 🚗 206 B2

The theme for this tour is stunning vistas – San Francisco, the Golden Gate, towering redwoods, rolling ranchland and a wind-sculpted stretch of the Pacific Coast. On a map it may not look as if you are covering much terrain, but it will take you the better part of an exhilarating day to make this drive. Get an early start, and bring your camera.

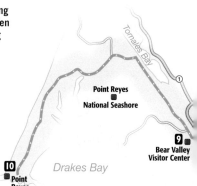

Coast Highway 1 & Point Reyes National Seashore

1 – 2

Head north on US 101 across the **Golden Gate Bridge** (▶58). Stop at the **vista point** at the northern end for a look at San Francisco's skyline.

PLANNING NOTE

The roads to Muir Woods and Stinson Beach can be crowded on sunny weekends, and the last stop, Point Reyes Lighthouse, is closed Tuesday and Wednesday.

2 – 3

Follow US 101 north to the Mill Valley/Stinson Beach exit. You will exit to the right, pass under US 101, veer around to the right past some small shopping areas, then make a left on Highway 1. Continue west on Highway 1, make a right on Panoramic Highway and after a mile (1.6km) turn left on Muir Woods Road, following the signs to **Muir Woods National Monument** (▶66). Take one of the shorter hikes through its old-growth redwoods.

3 – 4

Continue west on Muir Woods Road until it runs into Highway 1, make a right and drive north about 7mi (11km) to **Stinson Beach**. Park the car in the beach's lot (just west of the small downtown) and take a short stroll.

4 – 5

As you continue north out of Stinson, you'll pass the **Bolinas Lagoon**, where even on a slow day you're likely to see white cranes, ducks, pelicans and sea lions without leaving your car.

5 – 6

It's a time-honored tradition of some **Bolinas** residents to destroy signs to their town to keep out tourists,

A long, steep flight of steps leads down to Point Reyes Lighthouse

Seal Rocks in the Golden Gate National Recreation Area

though most folks are actually friendly. Make the first left after the lagoon and another quick left after a short distance onto Olema–Bolinas Road. Make another left at the stop sign at Horseshoe Hill Road (though you'll still be on Olema–Bolinas Road). This leads into Bolinas's small commercial strip, where you'll find the Bolinas Coast Café, Smiley's Schooner Saloon and a few galleries.

6–7
Reverse course north out of town on Olema–Bolinas Road. At Mesa Road make a left, then another left on Overlook Drive and a right on Elm Road (all this covers less than 2mi/3km). Here you'll see the parking area for **Duxbury Reef**, where sea creatures galore live among the tide pools.

7–8
Head back out of Mesa to Olema–Bolinas Road and make a left. Continue north on Horseshoe Hill Road, which shortly thereafter runs into Highway 1. Make a left,

and continue north to **Olema**. If you didn't have lunch in Bolinas, stop for a bite at the **Olema Farm House** (10005 Highway 1; tel: 415/663-1264). The barbecued oysters here are sublime.

8–9
A few blocks to the north, make a left on Bear Valley Road, which leads to the Bear Valley Visitor Center of the **Point Reyes National Seashore** (▶ 66).

9–10
Keep track of the time. It takes nearly an hour to drive north and west along Sir Francis Drake Boulevard to **Point Reyes Lighthouse**. You need to arrive at least a half-hour – preferably an hour – before closing (5pm). The setting's worth the trip, though, even if you don't make it down to the lighthouse. Alternatively, take the easier but still scenic route of Sir Francis Drake Boulevard heading east out of the seashore. It eventually runs into US 101, which you can take south back to San Francisco.

Insider Tip

2 SANTA BARBARA & THE SAN MARCOS PASS

Drive

DISTANCE 51mi/82km (one way) **TIME** 3–5 hours
START POINT Mission Santa Barbara ⊞ 208 C2
END POINT Solvang ⊞ 208 C2

You'll come to appreciate Santa Barbara County's varied splendors on this excursion, which begins in the city of Santa Barbara's colorful foothills and winds past its waterfront. The terrain alters abruptly along an old stagecoach pass – green giving way to nearly barren brown – then mellows as you head into the Santa Ynez Valley vineyard region. The last transformation may confound you the most: the Danish-style village called Solvang.

You could easily drive the route in two hours, leaving plenty of time for gazing at the view, stopping for lunch and tasting a little wine. For the first nine stages of the tour – those in Santa Barbara – the city's "Scenic Drive" signs, which have white letters on a dark-blue background, will provide additional guidance.

❶–❷ Follow the Scenic Drive signs east from Mission Santa Barbara (➤ 109) on Alameda Padre Serra. Bougainvillea and other colorful plants brighten the street as it edges along the foothills. Catch the view of downtown and the waterfront at a small vista point just past the Brooks Institute's Jefferson campus (near Dover Road).

❷–❸ At Salinas Street, Alameda Padre Serra runs into a traffic circle. Follow it three-quarters of the way around to the continuation of Alameda Padre Serra. Shortly after

Mission Santa Barbara in the colorful foothills

this, the street name becomes Alston Road; continue east on it.

❸–❹ Follow Alston to Olive Mill Road and make a right. Several blocks south make another right on Coast Village Road. Galleries, chic shops and outdoor cafés line **Montecito's** petite commercial zone.

❹–❺ Stroll Coast Village Road or continue west to Hot Springs Road, where you'll make a left and follow the road as it passes under US 101 and loops around the southern edge of the **Andree Clark Bird Refuge** (➤ 109).

❺–❻ You are now on Cabrillo Boulevard as it passes west along the palm-lined waterfront past **Stearns Wharf** (➤ 1098) and the **Santa Barbara Yacht Harbor** (➤ 110).

Tours

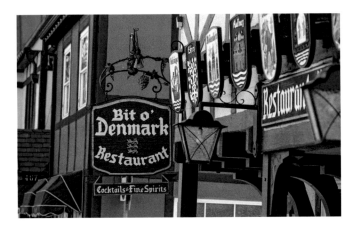

Solvang is an architectural non-sequitur in a region where Spanish Colonial design dominates in the colorful foothills

6–7

By the time you see thin, green **Shoreline Park**, you're atop a cliff and now on Shoreline Drive. Slip into the parking area to take in the sweeping ocean view.

7–8

Shoreline Drive runs into Meigs Road (make a right), shortly after which you'll make a left on Cliff Drive. This leads into the exclusive **Hope Ranch** housing development.

8–9

Along the way, Cliff Drive becomes Marina Drive, which becomes Roble Drive before running into Las Palmas Drive (now heading north). Just keep following the Scenic Drive signs to State Street (right after you pass over US 101), by which time you're on La Cumbre Road. Here's where you depart from the Scenic Drive.

9–10

Make a left on State and shortly thereafter a right on Highway 154 – the sign reads "San Marcos Pass/ Lake Cachuma." Vibrant greenery quickly gives way to stark browns and the muted tones of coyote bush, sage and coastal live oaks as you head through the **San Marcos Pass**.

10–11

Highway 154 winds resolutely up the Santa Ynez Mountains before plunging nearly straight down toward **Lake Cachuma**, which shortly comes into view after you reach the mountain peak. You can interrupt the steep decline by stopping at the vista point a bit past Stagecoach Pass Road.

🕚–🕛

Stay on Highway 154 for a few miles past the intersection with Highway 246. Head south (left) on Grand Avenue, the main street of **Los Olivos**, where you can have smoothies or sandwiches at **Panino** (2900 Grand Avenue; tel: 805/688-9304) or a gourmet meal at **Los Olivos Café** (2879 Grand Avenue; tel: 805/688-7265). At the **Los Olivos Tasting Room & Wine Shop** (2905 Grand Avenue; tel: 805/688-7406), you can sample local vintages and pick up maps to nearby wineries with tasting rooms.

🕛–🕐

Continue south on Grand Avenue a few blocks to Alamo Pintado Road, which rolls past farms and ranches – miniature horses graze at the **Quicksilver Ranch** (1555 Alamo Pintado Road; tel: 805/686-4002, Mon–Sat 10–3, admission free). Past the ranch, Alamo Pintado runs into Highway 246 (Mission Drive). Make a right turn.

🕐–🕑

Just after you pass **Mission Santa Inés**, the Spanish Mission architecture incongruously gives way to old-style Danish, the dominant motif of cheery **Solvang**. Park at meters or in the plentiful public lots. Two key streets for browsing and munching (Solvang is well known for its Danish pastries and pancakes) are Copenhagen Drive and Alisal Road.

Insider Tip

🕑–🕒

To return to Santa Barbara, follow Mission Drive (Highway 246) west. At US 101 head south. (Mission La Purísima Concepcíon, ► 20, is 20mi (32km) west of Highway 246 and US 101.) Take your time, the ocean views are sublime and there are plenty of places to stop and enjoy the sunset.

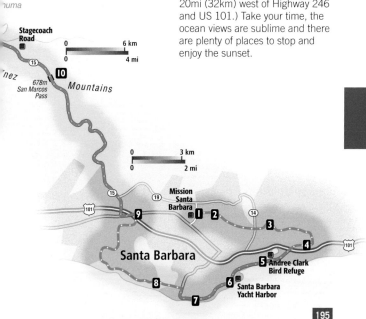

Tours

3 MULHOLLAND DRIVE
Drive

DISTANCE 77mi/124km (one way)   **TIME** 3–5 hours
START POINT North Highland Avenue and Hollywood Boulevard ✚201 E1
END POINT Santa Monica ✚201 E1

Mulholland Drive, named for William Mulholland, who stole – er, developed – Los Angeles's water supply, snakes 55mi (88km) along the ridge of the Santa Monica Mountains from Hollywood to the Pacific Ocean. The spectacular route yields 360-degree views of the best (rugged canyons, movie-star mansions, cacti and sometimes even coyotes) and worst (traffic-clogged freeways) Los Angeles has to offer. But mostly the best, and for long stretches you'll have the road pretty much to yourself.

A few of the directions may seem peculiar, but this drive really is worth tackling. Here's the quick version: Mulholland Drive west until it becomes dirt. Detour north on the paved roads – Encino Hills and Hayvenhurst to the Ventura Freeway heading west. At Topanga Canyon Boulevard head south back to Mulholland Drive. Turn west (right) on Mulholland Drive. When you see signs for Mulholland Highway, continue southwest on that to Malibu.

❶–❷

Finding the very beginning of Mulholland Drive is your first challenge. Head north past Hollywood Boulevard on **Highland Avenue**. Near the Hollywood Freeway (US 101) there's a merge onto **Cahuenga Boulevard West** (signed "Cahuenga Blvd. West/Barham Blvd"), which slithers along the west side of the freeway to Mulholland Drive, where you make a left.

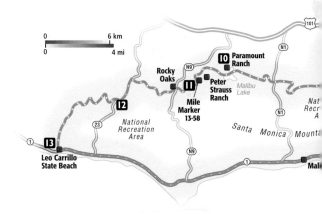

(If you end up on Cahuenga Boulevard East, which is east of the freeway, don't fret. Make a right at Lakeridge Road, in the 2700 block of Cahuenga, just before it looks as if you're getting onto the freeway. Then take an immediate left on Lakeridge Place, which winds around left to a bridge that crosses over US 101. A sign points the short way to Mulholland Drive.)

Views of Hollywood Hills from Runyon Canyon Park, Mulholland Drive in Hollywood

2–3

Mulholland begins its twisting ways immediately, but your first respite – and photo opportunity – comes in less than a mile at the **Hollywood Bowl Overlook.** Signs tell a bit of William Mulholland's story, but here and at future stops the view's the thing.

3–4

This is the busiest stretch of Mulholland, with stars and regular folk rushing to and fro. Pull over when possible and let traffic pass, and don't drive too fast or you may miss the small overlooks, some of them official and others just dirt pullouts. Just past 7701 Mulholland is the **Universal City Overlook** and farther on, and certainly worth a stop, the Fryman Canyon Overlook. Still farther on there's a pullout just past Bowmont Drive and yet another across from **13810 Mulholland**. All have sterling views.

4–5

About 2mi (3km) west of the 405 (the San Diego Freeway), Mulholland

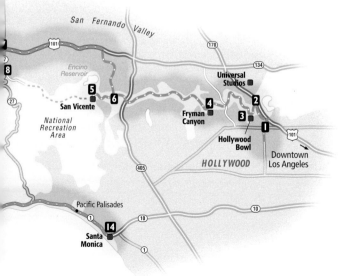

Tours

Drive becomes a dirt road for 7mi (11km). (You can drive a short way to a Cold War relic, the former San Vicente Nike Missile Site, but eventually a gate will stop you.) After taking in the **incredible vista of the San Fernando Valley** from where the dirt road begins, continue down the paved road.

🖐–🗙
You may think you're still on Mulholland, but you're actually on **Encino Hills Drive**, part of a detour into the suburban San Fernando Valley that will bring you back to Mulholland. When you get to **Hayvenhurst Avenue**, make a left.

🗙–🗗
Follow Hayvenhurst north to Ventura Boulevard. Turn west onto Ventura Boulevard and shortly after north onto Balboa Boulevard. Join US 101, now called the **Ventura Freeway**, and get on the freeway for 5mi (8km). At Topanga Canyon Boulevard (Highway 27), turn south.

🗗–🗘
After continuing for less than a mile (1.5km) south on Topanga, you'll come to **Mulholland Drive**. Make a right turn here.

🗘–🗙
In less than a mile (1.5km) you come to the intersection of several roads. Topanga continues south, Mulholland Drive heads northwest, and Mulholland Highway heads southwest. Take **Mulholland Highway**.

🗙–🔟
Mulholland Highway winds west through increasingly desolate terrain, looking so 19th-century American West that Paramount Pictures shot many a Western out here. The studio even built a fake town that you can explore. To do so, make a right turn on Cornell Road and follow the signs a short

TAKING A BREAK
If you're hungry, make a left at Cross Creek Road and, as celebrities often do, stop by the **Marmalade Café** (tel: 310/317-4242) or one of the other eateries in the Malibu Country Mart.

distance to the **Paramount Ranch**, now run by the National Park Service. When the wind blows a few leaves and makes an unpainted, rusty-hinged door creak, you'll half expect Henry Fonda or John Wayne to challenge you to a draw.

🔟–⓫
Backtrack on Cornell Road to Mulholland Highway and make a right. You'll eventually pass the Peter Strauss Ranch and Rocky Oaks, both of which have superb hiking trails and picnic areas. Browns and muted greens become more the norm in this area, which was formed by a volcanic eruption approximately 13 to 16 million years ago.

⓫–⓬
Just past **Mile Marker 13.58** is a super overlook with a view back toward the Strauss Ranch and man-made Malibu Lake. As you continue toward the coast you'll notice the air becoming cooler and moister, a sign that you're entering **Malibu** (➤ 135) (signed "Malibu").

⓬–⓭
Mulholland Highway intersects the **Pacific Coast Highway** (PCH) at **Leo Carrillo State Beach** (➤ 145), where you can watch the surfers riding the waves.

⓭–⓮
Head south on PCH through Malibu's main commercial district. Continue south through **Pacific Palisades** to **Santa Monica** (➤ 146), where you can catch I-10 heading back toward Los Angeles.

Insider Tip

Practicalities

Practicalities

WHAT YOU NEED

		UK	USA	Canada	Australia	Ireland	Netherlands
● Required	Visitors to the US have to complete						
○ Suggested	the ESTA (Electronic System of						
▲ Not required	Travel Authorization) online						
△ Not applicable	(https://esta.cbp.dhs.gov) before traveling.						
Passport/National Identity Card		●	▲	▲	●	●	●
Visa (regulations can change – check before booking)		▲	▲	▲	▲	▲	▲
Onward or Return Ticket		●	▲	▲	●	●	●
Health Inoculations (tetanus and polio)		▲	▲	▲	▲	▲	▲
Health Documentation (▶ 204, Health)		▲	▲	▲	▲	▲	▲
Travel Insurance		○	○	○	○	○	○
Driving Licence (national) for car hire		●	●	●	●	●	●
Car Insurance Certificate		△	●	●	△	△	△
Car Registration Document		△	●	●	△	△	△

WHEN TO GO

Los Angeles

High season   Low season

JAN	FEB	MAR	APR	MAY	JUN	JUL	AUG	SEP	OCT	NOV	DEC
19°C	19°C	19°C	20°C	21°C	22°C	24°C	25°C	25°C	24°C	21°C	19°C
66°F	66°F	66°F	68°F	70°F	72°F	75°F	77°F	77°F	75°F	70°F	66°F

☀ Sun   ⛅ Sunshine and showers

Temperatures are the **average daily maximum** for each month. **Average daily minimum** temperatures are approximately 14 to 18°F (8 to 10°C) lower. The weather varies from region to region in California.
Late spring and early fall are **generally pleasant** throughout the state, and even in winter it's nice in Palm Springs, Los Angeles and other Southern California locales. During summer, temperatures can range from 60 to 90°F (16 to 32°C) in the coastal regions to well over 100°F (37°C) inland in the deserts, Central Valley and the Gold Country. In San Francisco, Monterey and other coastal cities **fog** often rolls in during the summer, making them quite cool. The **rainy season** in California is usually from November through April.

GETTING ADVANCE INFORMATION

Websites
- The official California Website (with links to San Francisco, L.A., San Diego and other sites): www.visitcalifornia.com
- California State Parks: www.parks.ca.gov
- National Park Service: www.nps.gov
- www.magazinusa.com
- http://gocalifornia.about.com

GETTING THERE

By Air California has two main **airports**, San Francisco International (SFO) and Los Angeles (LAX), both served by most major international carriers that fly to the United States and by the major and some smaller U.S. domestic carriers.

There are **direct flights** to Los Angeles and San Francisco from London's Gatwick and Heathrow airports and from Dublin, Montreal, Toronto and Vancouver. **Nonstop flights** to California originate from Auckland, Sydney and Melbourne, usually to Los Angeles, with connections from there to San Francisco. Flights from Germany often route through Frankfurt, but might instead stop at some other European airport (e.g. Heathrow from Berlin). All airport taxes (which are nominal) are included in the price of your ticket.

By Car Interstates 10, 15, 40 and 80 are the main routes into the state from the east; I-5 and US 101 are the principal routes from the north. Except when signs instruct otherwise, you can turn right on a red light after stopping. At intersections with three- or four-way stop signs, the first to arrive is the first to go. Children under age six who weigh less than 60 pounds (27kg) must sit in an approved child-restraint seat. All passengers must wear seatbelts.

By Rail and Bus Alternative options for travelers from Canada or elsewhere in the United States are Amtrak trains (tel: 800/872-7245; www.amtrak.com), which stop in San Diego, Los Angeles, Santa Barbara, Emeryville (shuttle bus to San Francisco provided), Sacramento and many other towns, and the long-distance buses of **Greyhound Lines** (tel: 800/231-2222; www.greyhound.com).

TIME

California is on **Pacific Standard Time** (PST), eight hours behind **Greenwich Mean Time** (GMT −8). Daylight Savings Time (GMT −7) operates from mid-March (when clocks are advanced one hour) through early November.

CURRENCY & FOREIGN EXCHANGE

Currency The basic unit of currency in the United States is the dollar ($). One dollar is 100 cents. **Notes** (bills) come in denominations of $1, $5, $10, $20, $50 and $100. All bills are green and the same size. **Coins** are 1 cent (penny), 5 cents (nickel), 10 cents (dime), 25 cents (quarter), 50 cents and one dollar, though the latter two are not as common. An unlimited amount of U.S. currency can be imported or exported, though amounts over $10,000 have to be declared.

U.S. dollar **traveler's checks** are the best way to carry money and they are accepted by most businesses, as are credit cards (Visa and MasterCard, and, to a lesser extent, Amex and Diners Club).

Exchange The best place to exchange non-U.S. currency is at a bank. Automated teller cards can be used to withdraw money from your account in U.S. currency. Your bank will provide you with details of where your cards will be accepted in California.

CALIFORNIA TOURISM: www.visitcalifornia.com

In the U.S.
555 Capitol Mall, Suite 1100
Sacramento, CA 95814
☎ ++1-916/444-4429

Practicalities

WHEN YOU ARE THERE

NATIONAL HOLIDAYS

January 1: **New Year's Day**; Third Monday in January: **Martin Luther King Day**; Third Monday in February: **Presidents' Day**; March/April: **Easter**; Last Monday in May: **Memorial Day**; July 4: **Independence Day**; First Monday in September: **Labor Day**; Second Monday in October: **Columbus Day**; November 11: **Veterans' Day**; Fourth Thursday in November: **Thanksgiving**; December 25: **Christmas Day**

Boxing Day (Dec 26) is not a public holiday in the US. Some shops open on National Holidays.

ELECTRICITY

 The power supply is 110/120 volts AC (60 cycles). Most sockets take two-pronged or three-pronged plugs. Visitors from Europe, or anywhere that uses 220/240 volt power, will need to bring a converter and a plug adaptor.

OPENING HOURS

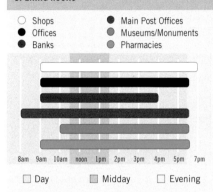

- ○ Shops
- ● Offices
- ● Banks
- ● Main Post Offices
- ● Museums/Monuments
- ● Pharmacies

8am 9am 10am noon 1pm 2pm 3pm 4pm 5pm 7pm

- ☐ Day
- ■ Midday
- ☐ Evening

Stores Most open between 9 and 6 or 7, some until 9pm. Some stores close on Sunday.
Banks Most open between 9 or 10 and 3 or 4; some open until 6pm. Most close on Saturday. Closed on Sunday.
Post Offices Open from 8 or 8:30 until 5 or 6 on week-days; many open until 1pm on Saturday.
Museums Most open by 10 and close at 5 or 6. Late opening Thursday or Friday.

TIPS/GRATUITIES

Tipping is expected and is widespread. Car guards in the street are tipped to watch your car and it's usual to tip petrol station attendants.

Restaurants	15–20%
Bar service	15%
Tour guides	discretion
Taxis	15%
Chambermaids	$1 per day
Porters	$1 per bag

SMOKING

Smoking is prohibited in enclosed workplaces, restaurants, bars, public transportation and cabs. In addition, you can't smoke in a moving vehicle if a minor is present, or within 20ft (6.1m) of an entrance to a public building.

TIME DIFFERENCES

California (PST)	Phoenix, AZ (MST)	New York (EST)	London (GMT)	Sydney (AEST)
12 noon	1pm	3pm	8pm	5am

Practicalities

STAYING IN TOUCH

Post offices You can find listings of U.S. Postal Service facilities in the U.S. Government section of the White Pages of the local telephone directory. Mail boxes can be found on street corners, often near trash cans.

Public Telephones: With the advent of cell phones, pay phones are very hard to find, but most are are coin operated. From public phones dial 0 for the operator and give the name of the country, city and number you are calling. You will need at least $5.50 in quarters for an overseas call. Some phones take prepaid phone cards, available at drugstores and newsstands, and some take credit cards. Dial 1 plus the area code for numbers within the U.S. and Canada. Dial 411 to find U.S. and Canadian numbers.

International Dialing Codes
Dial 011 followed by
UK: 44
Ireland: 353
Australia: 61

Cell phone providers and services: In California these are AT&T, Verizon, Sprint, T-Mobile and Metro PCS. Contact your service provider before traveling to California to find out about charges. Note that you must use a hands-free device to talk on the phone while driving, and it is illegal to text while driving. Cell phones can also be rented for the duration of your stay in the USA (e.g. at international airports).

WiFi and Internet: Internet access is widely available in California. Most hotels have business centers or computers available to guests (some charge and some do not), and most also offer free WiFi in guest rooms. Starbucks cafes now offer free, unlimited WiFi; other cafes may charge a fee. The FedEx Kinko's chain offers internet access and business services.

PERSONAL SAFETY

Crime is not a problem in most tourist-frequented areas, but it is still wise to take precautions, especially in urban areas:
- Carry only the cash you need; leave other cash and valuables in the hotel safe.
- When driving keep all car doors locked.
- Only travel in registered/ licensed taxis.
- If someone threatens you and asks for money, give it to them without hesitation.
- Keep an eye on your belongings at all times in public places.
- Avoid walking alone in remote or lonely places, particularly after dark.
- Incidents of violence against travelers in California are rare. However, it's wise to be prudent. Ask at visitor centers about neighborhoods you should avoid.
- Report theft or mugging to the police to provide a reference for insurance claims.

Police assistance:
☎ 911 from any phone.

EMERGENCY NUMBERS	
POLICE	111 or 911
FIRE	111
AMBULANCE	111

Practicalities

HEALTH

 Insurance Medical insurance cover of at least $1 million is strongly recommended; medical fees in the United States are unregulated. If you are involved in an accident in California, you will be cared for by medical services and charged later.

 Dental Services Your medical insurance cover should include dental treatment, which is readily available but expensive. Many dentists will accept credit cards, but most prefer cash or traveler's checks. To find a dentist, look under "Dentists" in the Yellow Pages telephone directory.

 Weather The sun shines brightly for long periods during the summer. Throughout the state, use a high-factor sunscreen, cover up and drink plenty of fluids.

 Drugs Pharmacies dispensing prescription and over-the-counter treatments are plentiful throughout the state. If you need regular medication, take your own drugs and prescription.

 Safe Water Drinking unboiled tap water is safe. Bottled mineral water is cheap and readily available.

CONCESSIONS

Students/children Holders of an International Student Identity Card (ISIC) are entitled to discounts on many attractions. Children under three are generally allowed into attractions free; children's tickets are usually available up to age 12. Teenagers often have to pay the full adult rate.

Senior Citizens Discounts on many services and attractions, and reductions on hotel room rates during the low season, are available to seniors. Qualifying age varies from 55 to 65. You need to request a discount up front and may be asked to show proof of age and identity.

TRAVELLING WITH A DISABILITY

Public facilities must, by California and U.S. federal law, be accessible to people with disabilities. The only exceptions tend to be older buildings. Most public buses have elevators and wheelchair spaces, and subway and other rail stations provide wheelchair access.

LOST PROPERTY

If you are a victim of theft, contact the police and get a copy of the paperwork for your insurance company.
Airports
SFO ☎ 650/821-7014
LAX ☎ 310/417-0440

Trains
Amtrak ☎ 800/872-7245

👫 CHILDREN

Baby-changing facilities are provided in many restrooms in restaurants and all public facilities. Special attractions for children are marked out in this book with the logo shown above.

RESTROOMS

The cleanest and safest lavatories are in large hotels, chain bookstores and department stores.

EMBASSIES & HIGH COMMISSIONS

UK	Ireland	Canada	Australia	New Zealand
☎ 310/481-0031	☎ 415/392-4214	☎ 415/834-3180	☎ 310/229-4800	☎ 310/566-6555
☎ 415/617-1300			☎ 415/536-1970	

Road Atlas

For chapters: See inside front cover

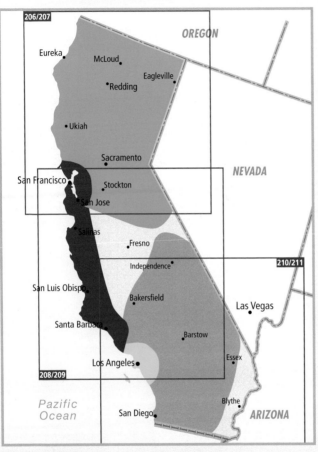

206/207

OREGON

Eureka
McLoud
Eagleville
Redding
Ukiah
Sacramento

NEVADA

San Francisco
Stockton
San Jose
Salinas
Fresno
Independence

210/211

San Luis Obispo
Bakersfield
Las Vegas
Santa Barbara
Barstow
Essex
Los Angeles

208/209

Pazific
Ocean
San Diego
Blythe
ARIZONA

Key to Road Atlas

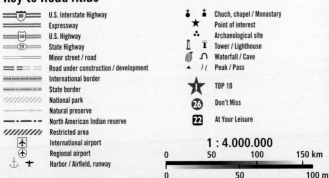

U.S. Interstate Highway	Chuch, chapel / Monastary
Expressway	Point of interest
U.S. Highway	Archaeological site
State Highway	Tower / Lighthouse
Minor street / road	Waterfall / Cave
Road under construction / development	Peak / Pass
International border	
State border	TOP 10
National park	
Natural preserve	Don't Miss
North American Indian reserve	
Restricted area	At Your Leisure
International airport	
Regional airport	
Harbor / Airfield, runway	

1 : 4.000.000

0   50   100   150 km

0   50   100 m

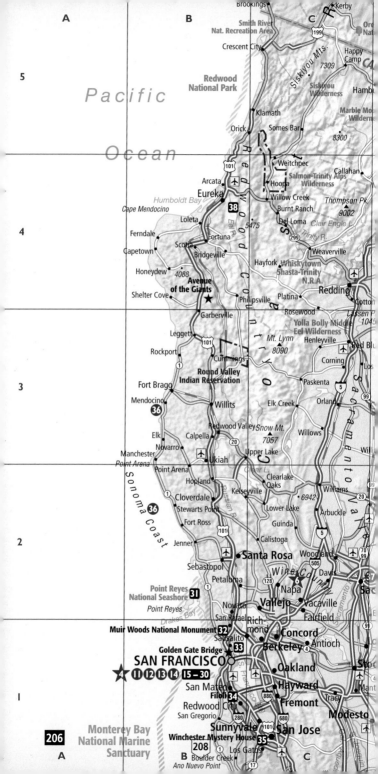

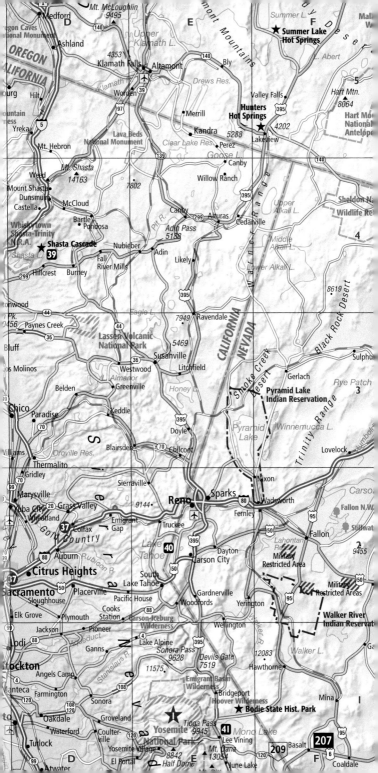

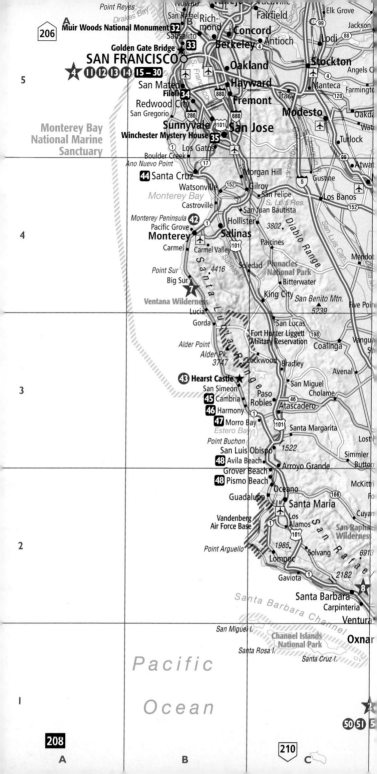

A

Point Reyes

Novato

Muir Woods National Monument **32**

Sausalito

Golden Gate Bridge **33**

SAN FRANCISCO

Richmond

Concord

Fairfield

Elk Grove

Jackson

Berkeley

Oakland

Hayward

Fremont

99

Lodi

Antioch

88

Stockton

Angels C

4

11 12 13 14 15–30

San Mateo

Filoli **34**

Redwood City

San Gregorio

280

Sunnyvale

101

Winchester Mystery House **35**

Los Gatos

Monterey Bay National Marine Sanctuary

Boulder Creek

Ano Nuevo Point

17

Santa Cruz **44**

Watsonville

Monterey Bay

Castroville

Monterey Peninsula **42**

Pacific Grove

1

Monterey

Carmel

Carmel Valley

Point Sur

Santa Lucia Range

4416

Big Sur

Manteca

Farmingt

120

Modesto

4

Oakda

Wat

Turlock

Morgan Hill

Gilroy

152

San Felipe

San Juan Bautista

Hollister

3802

Salinas

101

Paicines

Soledad

Diablo Range

Gustine

5

Los Banos

152

Atwa

99

Mendot

Pinnacles National Park

King City

Bitterwater

San Benito Mtn.

5239

Ventana Wilderness

Lucia

Gorda

Alder Point

Alder Pk.

3747

Lockwood

Bradley

San Lucas

Fort Hunter Liggett Military Reservation

198

Coalinga

Vangu Sa

Five Poin

Hearst Castle **43**

San Simeon

Cambria **45**

Harmony **46**

Morro Bay **47**

Estero Bay

Point Buchon

San Luis Obispo

Avila Beach **48**

Grover Beach

Pismo Beach **48**

Guadalupe

Vandenberg Air Force Base

Point Arguello

Paso Robles

San Miguel

Cholame

Atascadero

101

Santa Margarita

1522

Arroyo Grande

Oceano

166

Santa Maria

1

Los Alamos

101

1985

Lompoc

Solvang

2182

Gaviota

Avenal

Lost

Simmler

Button

McKittri

Cuyan

San Rafael Wilderness

6913

8

Santa Barbara

Carpinteria

Ventura

Oxnar

Santa Barbara Channel

San Miguel I.

Santa Rosa I.

Pacific

Ocean

Channel Islands National Park

Santa Cruz I.

50 51

5

4

3

2

I

210

A **B** **C**

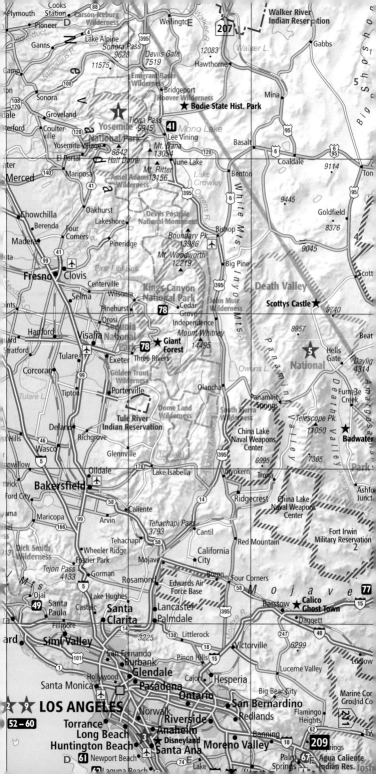

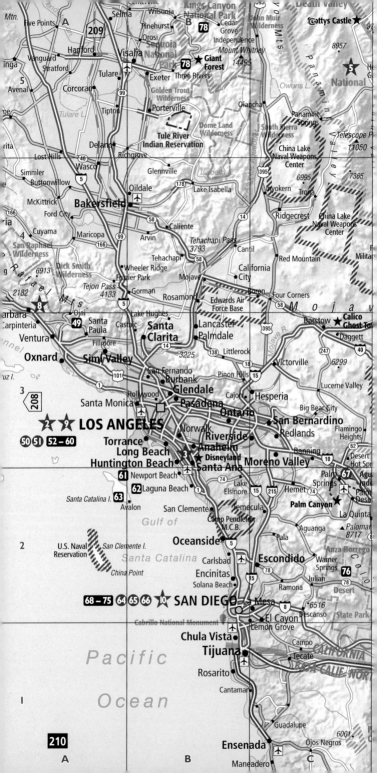

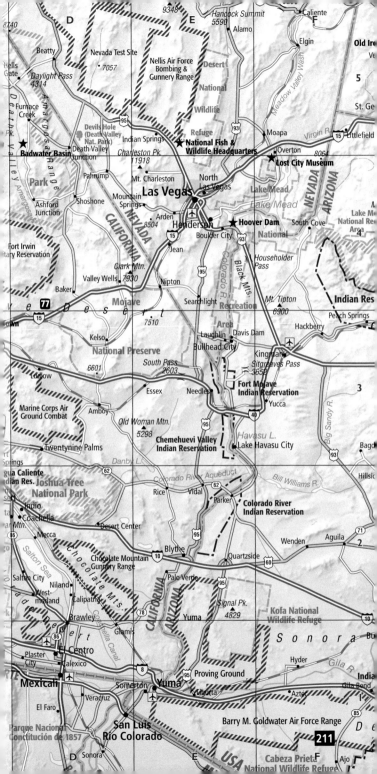

Los Angeles

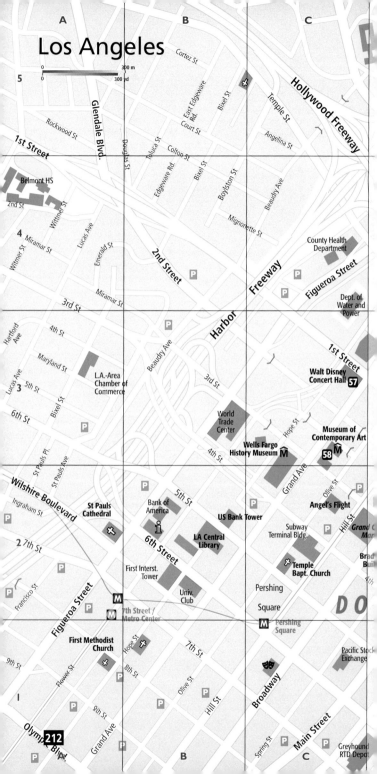

A **B** **C**

5

300 m
300 yd

Cortez St

East Edgeware
Court St

Bixel St

Temple St

Angelina St

Hollywood Freeway

Rockwood St

1st Street

Glendale Blvd.

Douglas St

Toluca St

Colton St

Edgeware Rd.

Bixel St

Boylston St

Beaudry Ave

Belmont HS

2nd St

Wittmer St

Lucas Ave

Emerald St

Mignonette St

4 Miramar St

Witmer St

Miramar St

Lucas Ave

2nd Street

Freeway

County Health
Department

Figueroa Street

3rd St

Dept. of
Water and
Power

Hartford Ave

4th St

Maryland St

Beaudry Ave

Harbor

3rd St

Walt Disney
Concert Hall **57**

1st Street

Lucas Ave

3 5th St

L.A.-Area
Chamber of
Commerce

Bixel St

World
Trade
Center

Hope St

Museum of
Contemporary Art

6th St

4th St

Wells Fargo
History Museum Ⓜ

58 Ⓜ

St Pauls Pl.

St Pauls Ave

Grand Ave

Olive St

Wilshire Boulevard

5th St

Angel's Flight

Hill St

Ingraham St

St Pauls
Cathedral

Bank of
America

US Bank Tower

Subway
Terminal Bldg.

Grand C
Mar

2 7th St

6th Street

LA Central
Library

Temple
Bapt. Church

Brad
Buil

Francisco St

First Interst.
Tower

Univ.
Club

Pershing

Square

D O

Ⓜ
7th Street /
Metro Center

Ⓜ Pershing
Square

First Methodist
Church

Figueroa Street

Hope St

7th St

Pacific Stock
Exchange

9th St

Flower St

8th St

Olive St

Broadway

Main Street

9th St

Grand Ave

Hill St

Spring St

Greyhound
RTD Depot

Olympi **212** Blv

A **B** **C**

1

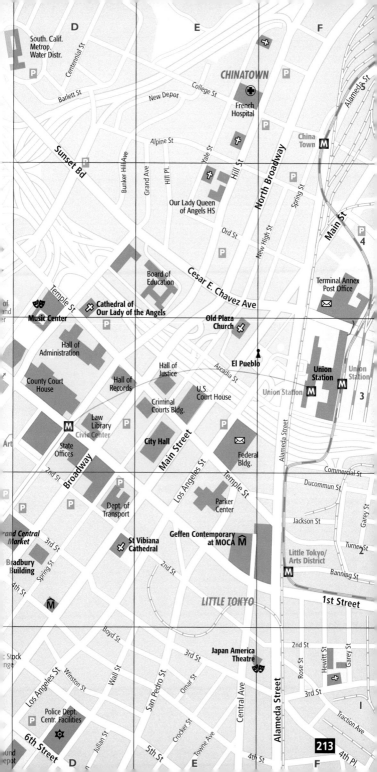

Index

Index

Index

Index / Picture Credits

Picture Credits

Credits

1st Edition 2017

Worldwide Distribution: Marco Polo Travel Publishing Ltd
Pinewood, Chineham Business Park
Crockford Lane, Chineham
Basingstoke, Hampshire RG24 8AL, United Kingdom.
© MAIRDUMONT GmbH & Co. KG, Ostfildern

Authors: Daniel Mangin, Clark Norton, Julie Jares, Axel Pinck
Translation and revised editing: Jon Andrews, jonandrews.co.uk
Program supervisor: Birgit Borowski
Chief editor: Rainer Eisenschmid

Cartography: © MAIRDUMONT GmbH & Co. KG, Ostfildern
3D-illustrations: jangled nerves, Stuttgart

Printed in China

Despite all of our authors' thorough research, errors can creep in. The publishers do not accept any liability for this. Whether you want to praise us, alert us to errors or give us a personal tip – please don't hesitate to email or post to:

MARCO POLO Travel Publishing Ltd
Pinewood, Chineham Business Park
Crockford Lane, Chineham
Basingstoke, Hampshire RG24 8AL
United Kingdom
Email: sales@marcopolouk.com

FSC
www.fsc.org
MIX
Paper from
responsible sources
FSC® C124385

10 REASONS
TO COME BACK AGAIN

1. When California gets hold of you, it never lets go – you'll always be left **wanting more**!

2. Visit in winter next time to experience **New Year's Eve** in San Francisco.

3. There are many miles still left to drive on the windingly alluring **State Road 49**.

4. If you don't come back you'll miss the latest culinary trends in **Californian cuisine**!

5. The Sunshine State's huge variety of wonderful **wines** won't drink themselves…

6. There's a great deal to discover on **Catalina Island**, either on horseback or by bus.

7. Who could ever get tired of the technological wizardry at **Universal Studios**?

8. The tranquility of the **deserts** can be addictive. California's the best place to get your fix.

9. **Los Angeles** is changing at breakneck speed – come and witness its exciting development!

10. One trip is never enough to truly appreciate the coasts, volcanoes and giant sequoias in the **north**.